Death of Christendoms, Birth of the Church

PABLO RICHARD

Death of Christendoms, Birth of the Church

Historical Analysis and Theological Interpretation
of the Church in Latin America

*Translated from the French and Spanish by
Phillip Berryman*

Maryknoll, New York 10545

The Catholic Foreign Mission Society of America (Maryknoll) recruits and trains people for overseas missionary service. Through Orbis Books Maryknoll aims to foster the international dialogue that is essential to mission. The books published, however, reflect the opinions of their authors and are not meant to represent the official position of the society.

First published in French, *Mort des Chrétientés et Naissance de l'Église,* Centre Lebret, Paris, 1978, © Pablo Richard. The English translation incorporates alterations and updatings by the author, in Spanish.

English translation © 1987 Orbis Books, Maryknoll, NY 10545
Manufactured in the United States of America
All rights reserved

Manuscript Editor: William E. Jerman

Library of Congress Cataloging-in-Publication Data

Richard, Pablo.
  Death of christendoms, birth of the church.

  Translation of: Mort des chrétiénts et naissance de l'Église. 1979.
  "Incorporates alterations and updatings by the author in the Portuguese version published . . . 1984"—T.p. verso.
  Bibliography: p.
  1. Catholic Church—Latin America—History.
2. Liberation theology. 3. Latin America—Church history.
I. Title.
BX1426.2.R5313   1987   282'.8   87-14825
ISBN 0-88344-557-3
ISBN 0-88344-556-5 (pbk.)

Contents

Foreword, by Vincent Cosmao   ix

Introduction   1

Part One
1492–1808: Colonial Christendom in Latin America   21

Chapter 1
A Colonial Christendom within a Capitalist Society   23
   *Latin American Underdevelopment: Rooted in Capitalism
        or Feudalism?*   23
      Production Relationships Based on Slavery   25
      Amerindians Defended   27
      Patronato Regio   28
      Reducciones   30
      Ecclesiastical Properties   30
      The Expulsion of the Jesuits   30
   Liberation Struggles during the Colonial Period   31
      Amerindian Uprisings   31
      Black and Mulatto Uprisings   32
      Creole Uprisings   33

Part Two
1808–1960: New Christendom in Latin America   35

Chapter 2
1808–1870: The Crisis in Colonial Christendom   37
   Why 1808–1870?   37
   Interpreting the Crisis   38
   Analysis of Latin American Society   40
      "Conservative" Sector of the Dominant "Classes"   40
      Liberal-Dependent and Liberal-National Groupings   41
      The Liberal Petite Bourgeoisie   42
      Dominated, Exploited, and Marginalized Sectors   43
   Social Groupings and the Independence Process   43

The Church and Independence   47
    Spain   47
    The Popes   47
    The Latin American Church   48
    The Bishops   49
    The Clergy   49
    Some Concrete Examples   50
Formation of the New National States   52
    Rejection of the Liberal-Conservative Interpretation   57
The Church and the New National States   58

Chapter 3
1870–1930: The Church under the Liberal Oligarchical State   61
Why 1870–1930?   61
Fundamental Contradiction between the Liberal State and the Masses   62
    Positivism in Latin America   63
    Popular Struggles against the State and the Liberal Oligarchy   65
    Socialist Movements of a "Messianic" Nature   66
    The Mexican Revolution and the End of the Oligarchical State of Porfirio Díaz   66
    The Rise of the Middle Classes against the Liberal State   67
    The Church vis-à-vis the Oligarchical Liberal State   67
    Secularization   68
Basic Options of the Church toward the Liberal State   70
    The Traditional Option   70
    The Option for Education, the Family, and Devotional Practices   71
    The Option for Europeanizing and Romanizing the Church   71

Chapter 4
1930–1960: The Church and Populist, Nationalist, and Developmentalist Movements   73
Latin America and the Socialist Alternative   73
    The Church and Nationalism, Latinamericanization, and Development   75
    Dismantling and Rebuilding New Christendom   76
Part Two—Conclusions   77

Part Three
1960–1985: The Crisis of New Christendom in Latin America   79

Chapter 5
The Crisis of International Capitalism and the Crisis of New Christendom   81
Keys for Interpreting the Present Crisis of the Capitalist System   83
    Transnationalization of Production, Capital, and Finance   83

    Restructuring of the International Market   83
    Reshaping Imperialist Domination   84
Three Historical Processes   86
    Church, Ruling Classes, and State   86
    Church and Popular Movement   88
    Church and New Model of Domination   89

Chapter 6
Argentina and Brazil   92
    Argentina   92
        From Conservatism to Populism   92
        Chronology of the Crisis Period for Nationalist-Populist New
            Christendom   96
        Reasons for the Crisis   97
        Priests for the Third World   99
        Short-lived Conciliar and Medellín Renewal   103
        Present Tendencies in the Argentine Hierarchy   106
    Brazil   107
        Birth of a Conservative New Christendom   109
        1930: Beginning of a New Stage   111
        1937: The Church and the *Estado Novo*   113
        1948: Birth of Specialized Catholic Action   115
        1950: The Church and the Agrarian Question   116
        1956–1959: The Church and the Problem of Underdevelopment   117
        Ação Popular   122
        Worker Catholic Action, 1966–1970   123
        Movimento de Educação de Base   125
        The Zenith of New Christendom   125
        Interpretive Recapitulation   128
        1964–1978: Basic Chronology   129
        The Alternatives Facing the Church after the 1964 Coup   129
        Characteristics of the Episcopacy Making It Vulnerable to State
            Manipulation   131
        Strategy of the Military Regime   132
        The Church and the National Security State   133
        Isolation and Repression of the Popular Church   136
        Evolution of the Brazilian Church, 1968–1978   138

Chapter 7
Latin American Theology, 1960–1985   142
    First Stages of a Latin American Liberation Theology,
        1960–1968   142
        Liberation Theology before Medellín   145
        From Pastoral Practice to Political Practice   146
    Spread of Liberation Theology in Latin America, 1968–1973   148
    Maturation and Growth of Liberation Theology, 1973–1978   152

viii *Contents*

    Liberation Theology and Other Theologies   153
    Positive Gains   153
Worldwide Recognition and Spread of Liberation Theology,
        1979–1985   *154*
    Central America   155
    Liberation Theology throughout the Third World   157
    Opposition to Liberation Theology   158
Part Three—Conclusion   *159*

Part Four
Church, Authoritarian State, and Social Classes in Latin America   161

Chapter 8
Differing Ecclesial Practices   *163*
    Ecclesial Practice of the Conservative Church   *163*
    Ecclesial Practice of the Social-Christian Church   *164*
        Rightwing Social-Christian Tendency   166
        Centrist Social-Christian Tendency   166
        Leftwing Social-Christian Tendency   167
    Ecclesial Practice of the Popular Church or the Church of the Poor   *172*
        Ecclesial Practice of the Popular Church under a "Democratic
            Opening"   176
        Ecclesial Practice of the Popular Church within Revolutionary
            Processes   177
        Theological Analysis of the Ecclesial Practice of the Church
            of the Poor   179
        Future Challenges to the Identity of the Church of the Poor   182
        The Historical Project of the Church of the Poor
            in the Popular Movement   183

Conclusion   *186*

Notes   *193*

Bibliography   *201*

Foreword

In presenting Pablo Richard's study *Death of Christendoms, Birth of the Church*, I would especially like to highlight the important contribution to theory that this economic, sociological, and political analysis of the church in Latin America represents. It points toward the kind of research that must be carried out if we are to have a better understanding of the role of the church in the development and liberation of peoples.

In his effort to comprehend how the church functions in Latin American societies, Pablo Richard has been led to rework the idea of "Christendom," which is indispensable for analyzing critically the history of Christianity in the West. Taking a new look at the question of the "end of the Constantinian era," which has enabled contemporary Christians to accept a critique that was indeed necessary, Richard has been struck by the fact that a "popular church" had appeared alongside the very system that the church had served to legitimize for centuries. His starting point is the historical importance of this "new church," which is acknowledged neither by authoritarian regimes nor by opposition forces. It has been theologians who have discovered its continuity with the origins of Christianity. Richard then asks to what extent this church born of the people, this church of the poor, is distinct from the ecclesiastical system that Europe had transplanted to Latin America, which previously had always found a way to adapt to changes in economic, political, social, and cultural systems. Striving to clarify the breaks with the past now taking place, Richard has shown that the dynamism and meaning of this new reality is to be found *in a rejection of any kind of alliance between the church and political society as a mediating factor between the church and civil society.*

Thus it becomes clear how a church born of the good news announced to the poor—in other words, born in faith—no longer means submission to the Law or to Caesar, whose power can be maintained only by being "divinized." Refusing to accept responsibility for the "civil religion" of a society that has considered itself Christian, this church is no doubt a threat to existing power. Jesus himself was such a threat, and after the resurrection of Lazarus, the priests and Pharisees said, "What are we to do with this man performing all sorts of signs? If we let him go on like this, the whole world will believe in him. Then the Romans will come in and sweep away our sanctuary and our nation" (John 11:47–48).

Clearly distinguishing his work from "theologies" of secularization or of the death of God, and from "messianisms without theology," Pablo Richard has found that the very rigor of economic, sociological, and political analysis has led him to question theologically the identity and historical meaning of this church of which he is both a critical observer and a believing and active member. Avoiding the trap of an interdisciplinary approach that could have led him to the silence of uncommitted scholarship, he has dared to become a theologian, to speak up and to work out a kind of language that witnesses to the faith of his church. He has thus risked being rejected by those observers whose reductive discourse is shaken by such an example. He is also likely to be rejected by the defenders of the kind of orthodoxy whose "normative" discourse is always in danger of replacing the kind of truth that is "done" in the ecclesial practice of faith. The guide for such practice is the Spirit, whatever may be the regulating function of the church built up in hierarchical fashion.

Inasmuch as I was a witness to Richard's austere, patient, and persevering research, undertaken in part to give an answer to many requests from scholars who wanted to know more about the Latin American church experience—"between faith and hope"—I should like to testify to the sense of faith I saw at work. This is the kind of theology that is returning to the path followed by the most faithful tradition of the church.

This work could have been more voluminous: it does not incorporate all the results of its author's research; the bibliography is a sign of it. Nevertheless, this is a masterwork in the sense that Richard's colleagues will no doubt discover how well he has mastered the skills of his trade. As they examine it calmly, some may be able to point out faults or rigidities, but as time goes on, readers will realize that one can scarcely question the basic structure or framework.

The Lebret Center, Paris, which is frequently suspected of being an "accomplice" of liberation theologians, had a key role in the fashioning of this work. The center feels honored to present to the public this work by a liberation theologian, a work dealing with his own practice and that of the church, and with his interpretation and practice of faith in Jesus Christ, dead and arisen.

It is obvious that analytical work is useful and even necessary. Its aim is not to "destroy the church" but to return it to the truth that characterized its origins and is still within its collective memory, a truth that no perversion seems to nullify: the promise of eternal life also refers to the ability of the church to overcome its own contradictions.

The church, which is ever to be built up anew in active resistance to the inertia that turns it into "Christendom," and which is "built through faith and through the sacraments of faith" as Thomas Aquinas was wont to say, is always being born, precisely where the good news is announced to the poor. That is how it is truly the church of the saints, whose blood is the "seed of Christians."

—Vincent Cosmao

Introduction

There are four main elements in this Introduction:

1. Establishing the object of this study.
2. Methodology.
3. Basic working hypothesis.
4. Reader's guide and overall outline.

I shall begin by establishing what the *object* of this study is to be. Its basic elements are noted in the very title of this book. That object itself will serve as the basis of the *method*, in keeping with the principle that "the method is determined by the object." I shall then set forth my *basic working hypothesis*, which will in turn guide and unify everything that follows. The Introduction ends with the presentation of an overall *outline* and suggestions for how this book should be read.

In order to make the task easier, I have added detailed summaries, which include not only titles and subtitles but "reading guides": short explanatory passages that appear at the beginning of almost every section in this study.

This Introduction is rather abstract and dry, and in places a bit obscure, particularly in the initial points about the way the object itself is established and the methodology employed. However, that obscurity will be dispelled in the course of the study itself.

1. ESTABLISHING THE OBJECT OF THIS STUDY

The vast and complex concept that best serves to mark off the object of this inquiry is that of "Christendom." I define Christendom as a particular kind of relationship between the *church* and *civil society*, a relationship in which the *state* is the primary mediation. Where Christendom is in place, the church seeks to safeguard its presence and expand its power in civil society, particularly by making use of the state. Hence, the object of this study is not the church in itself, but the *relationship* between the church, the state, and civil society. I am not going to make an abstract and generic study of this relationship, which is actually the essence of Christendom; I shall approach it as it developed in Latin America throughout its entire history, from 1492 until our own times.

It is not my aim to go into a lengthy treatment of the church, the state, and civil society in Latin America, but simply to specify the basic elements in the kind of relationship that constitutes Latin American Christendom.

I make use of the concept of "civil society" in both a broad and a strict sense. In the *broad sense*, I refer to the social totality taken in its entirety. In this broad sense, "civil society" includes the totality of the economic, political, cultural, and religious structures of a nation, and the prevailing consciousness of them. I use the term "civil society" in the *strict sense* to designate those structures whose function it is to create *consensus*—that is, those structures through which the dominant classes exercise their hegemony in a particular nation. Civil society in the broad sense is not something neutral or undetermined, inasmuch as every social totality is shaped or dominated by a consensus—that is, an intellectual, moral, social, and national unity imposed by the dominant classes. *Civil society* is distinguished from *political society* (the state) insofar as the latter utilizes coercion. The dominant classes exercise their domination on the level of *civil society* not through coercion, but by imposing *hegemony* of a moral, intellectual, cultural, political, and religious nature.

It is on the level of *political society*—that is, the state—that the dominant classes exercise their domination through the *coercion* of legislative, juridical, administrative, police, or military structures. I do not stop to give a precise definition of the state; I accept the usual and relatively concrete definition of it. In each section of my study, corresponding to the different stages of Latin American history, we refer to the historical forms that political state, or the state, has taken (the colonial "state," the liberal state, the populist state, the emergency state, etc.). This basic distinction between civil society and political society—the main lines of which have been taken from Antonio Gramsci—has been very useful in my research for interpreting the nature of Christendom and its present crisis, insofar as it has enabled me to go beyond the perspectives of other studies that have been too narrowly confined to the strictly *bipolar* church/state relationship. The notion of civil society, in both the broad and the strict sense, has enabled me to treat the church/state relationship as simply one mediation within the larger context of the relationship between the church and civil society. The concept of Christendom has enabled me to construct an overall framework for interpreting the *tripolar* relationship of church/political society/civil society (see Diagram 1, p. 3).

Having proposed these working notions of the concepts of civil society and political society, I must pause in order to come to a more detailed and more precise definition of the notion of the "church." When I speak of church in this study, I refer primarily to *ecclesial structures*, whether of hierarchy or base. If I subject these structures to historical and sociological analysis, I do not thereby reduce the reality of the church to its structures. I take it for granted that there is more to the church than those structures, and that it transcends those structures. Among the *hierarchical* ecclesial structures I include primarily, at the local level, bishops, priests, religious orders, and other ministries or responsibilities exercised by lay persons; at the national level, I have in mind episcopal conferences; and at the level of Latin America as a whole, there is the Latin American Episcopal Council (CELAM), the Latin American Conference of

Religious (CLAR), and so forth. Among the base structures I single out parishes, basic Christian communities, movements of Catholic Action, and other organizations that depend directly on the hierarchy. In dealing with both hierarchical ecclesial institutions and base-level structures, there are three dimensions or functions that must be distinguished: the cultural or symbolic function, the pastoral function, and the prophetic function (evangelization, catechesis, magisterium, theology). Each of these functions represents a structural dimension of the church.

Diagram 1

Church and . . . : Bipolar and Tripolar Relationships Distinguished

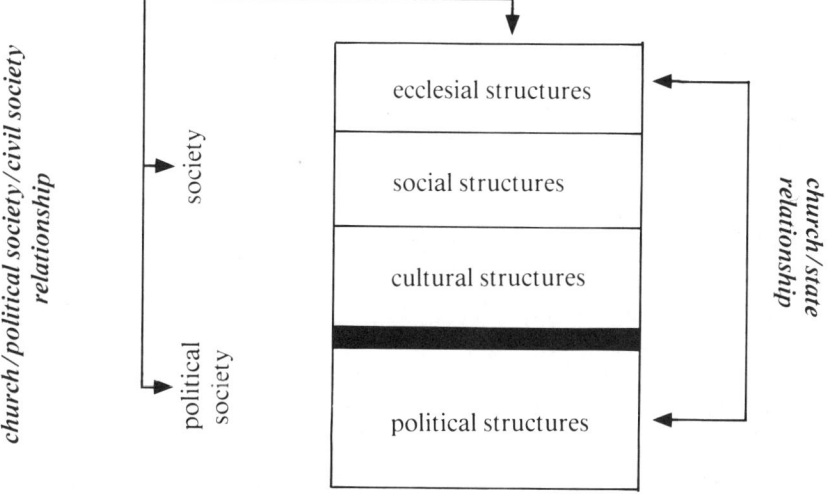

When I refer to the church in this study, what I have in mind, strictly speaking, are these *ecclesial* structures, and they should not be confused with those other structures that we normally call *ecclesiastical*. In themselves ecclesiastical structures already imply that there is a relationship between ecclesial structures and other structures of an economic, political, social, or cultural type. Thus we have, for example, ecclesiastico-political structures (concordats, ecclesiastical tribunals, military chaplaincies, etc.), ecclesiastico-social structures (Catholic charity work, church social organizations, etc.), and ecclesiastico-cultural structures (Catholic schools and universities, church media, research centers, etc.). When I speak of these *ecclesiastical structures* I refer directly to Christendom, and when I speak of *ecclesial structures* I refer directly to the church in the strict sense (see Diagram 2, p. 4). The contradiction between the ecclesial and the ecclesiastical, often mentioned today in Latin America, is a good expression of the underlying contradiction between church and Christendom, to which I devote particular attention in part 3 of this study.

Diagram 2

Church and Christendom Distinguished

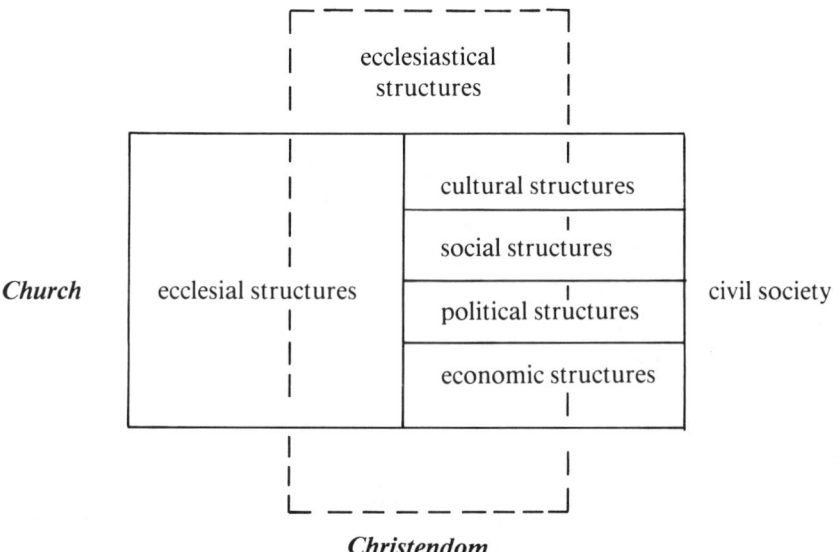

In addition to noting the distinction between church (ecclesial structures) and Christendom (ecclesiastical structures), I should give separate treatment to Christian structures of another kind, which we normally cannot identify either with the church or with Christendom. These structures (organizations, movements, groups, etc.) are explicitly confessional or religious, but *not* directly dependent on hierarchical *ecclesial* structures (as are basic Christian communities) and even less are they derived from, or representative of, a power relationship between an *ecclesial* structure and another power, whether social, political, or cultural (as is the case of ecclesiastical structures, the structures of Christendom). Under this category we could put structures as diverse as social or political institutions of Christian inspiration that do not depend organically on the church (e.g., Christian political parties, cooperatives, or labor unions), autonomous Christian groups or movements organized independently of the hierarchical church (e.g., Catholic integralist movements), and finally "popular religion" of the "Catholic" type. I do not intend to define these structures any further at this point. They represent, however, a place where the phenomenon of religion in the strict sense encounters other sorts of manifestations whose origins are economic, political, social, and cultural. Hence, these structures are largely outside the control or the direction of the hierarchical Catholic Church. We could use the term "Catholic movement" to designate all those confessional or religious structures that do not depend directly on the hierarchy or on Christendom.

The mainline Protestant churches (of European or North American origin) and the mass-based Evangelical churches (Pentecostals and others) are different in nature and follow a different sort of dynamic. Hence, we cannot assume that they have been similar, either historically or sociologically, to Catholic ecclesial structures, Christendom, or "Catholic movements." When I speak of the church or of Christendom in Latin America, I am basically referring to the Catholic stream. If I mention the mainline Protestant or Evangelical streams, I do so only to the extent that I discover some structural functioning similar or analogous to what is found in the Catholic stream. The situation of mainline Protestant and Evangelical churches in Latin America calls for a specific kind of analysis that goes beyond the limits of my research.

Now that I have finished an initial description or definition of the basic elements that go into the object of my inquiry—that is, Christendom, civil society, church-and-state (in the strict sense, as designating ecclesial structures, which I have distinguished from ecclesiastical structures, "Catholic movements," and Protestant churches), I must now undertake a historico-structural analysis of these same elements, and thus move deeper into the process of establishing the object of this study.

Historico-structural analysis is something basic for establishing this object and for understanding how that *object* subsequently (logically) determines my *method (methodus determinatur ab objecto)*. An insufficient or superficial grasp of the object could lead us to a wrong turn in the method (= the road) to follow. The relationship between working out the *object*, historically and structurally, and discovering the *method* reveals the dynamic character of the process of establishing the object. In saying "method" one is saying "way": discovering a methodology means "opening a way." Working out an object is not an abstract, static speculation but a process that is historical and dynamic, and is carried out and checked along the "way" that one gradually "traces" and "opens" (methodology). (As a Spanish poet puts it: "Traveler, there is no way; you make the way by moving ahead.") Working out the object and determining what methodology to use are inseparable processes.

In order to move ahead in this process of establishing the object I intend to study, I begin by situating the three basic elements of that object (ecclesial structures, the state, and civil society) within the broadest possible historical and structural framework. I will be extremely schematic for reasons of space. Indeed, the object will be worked out as we progress through this whole work.

I must first establish a basic distinction between *reality and consciousness*. This distinction is purely "methodological," inasmuch as *consciousness* exists and is reproduced within *reality*, as its inherent principle of knowledge and transformation; similarly, reality becomes consciousness insofar as it knows itself and becomes itself. When I speak of *reality*, I refer to *social reality*. The term "social reality" includes the historical reality of *humankind* as well as that of *nature:* human beings are transformed and are liberated in the transformation and domination of that nature of which they are an integral part. Within *social reality* I distinguish different levels or structural dimensions: the *economic* (production and the material reproduction of life), the *political* (political society, basically the state with its powers: legislative, juridical, executive, bureaucratic, police and military), the *social* (family, professional organizations, neighborhood, sports), the *cultural* (school and continuing education, art, mass media), and the *religious* (hierarchical or base-level structures, with their threefold dimension (cultural/symbolic, pastoral, and prophetic).

When I speak of *consciousness*, I refer to *social consciousness*, which is intimately connected to all the dimensions of social reality that I have just described. I distinguish social consciousness from ethical or moral conscience and from psychological consciousness. The social, ethical, and psychological dimensions of consciousness are intimately connected, but it is my assumption here that the basic dimension of consciousness is the social dimension and that it determines the other dimensions—the ethical and the psychological (which is not at all to deny that they are autonomous or to deny that ethical conscience and psychological consciousness can determine social consciousness). Social consciousness is structured fundamentally around values (for example, the values of liberty, equality, fellowship, democracy, order, development, justice, love, unity, etc.) and around projects (strategies, worldvisions, doctrines, theories, etc.). The dimension of social consciousness is not just a matter of the cultural or religious superstructure. Rather, it is related to the whole of social reality, and it is where that whole—economic, political, social, cultural, and religious—becomes conscious and intelligible, whether it takes place spontaneously or is sought deliberately. Social consciousness is not static or unhistorical, and it is not a purely passive reflection of social reality. On the contrary, the values, projects, and theories that articulate social consciousness have no existence and cannot be reproduced except within economic, political, and cultural history: within that history they become a way of knowing and a principle of transformation. I reject both the kind of fetishism of values that turns them into absolute and eternal beings, and the kind of mechanistic economicism that reduces values and other elements within social consciousness to the level of what is illusory and insubstantial.

The economic, political, social, cultural, and religious structures that make up *social reality*, and the values, projects, worldvisions, strategies, doctrines, and theories that go into *social consciousness* are not independent of each other, or juxtaposed to each other, or articulated in accordance with some historico-structural model that is always the same and valid everywhere. On the contrary, all such structures along with all their contents are intimately interconnected in a *social totality*. The meaning of that totality varies through history in accordance with the kind of social formation in effect, and in accordance with the origins, positions, and interests of the different human groups within that social totality. For some persons, the economic, political, social, cultural, and religious structures seem to be a reality that they have assumed and made their own; for others those structures represent a reality that is alien and imposed. For some there exists a total *cohesion* between social reality and the values of social consciousness; so much so, in fact, that they feel and think that holding onto that reality is an affirmation and a defense of the values of social consciousness, and "subverting" that reality means negating those values. Hence, for example, in their social consciousness, they feel and think that the preservation of private property of the means of production, or the preservation of present legal institutions, is the same as affirming and defending order, freedom, democracy, and justice. They also regard criticism or subversion of social realities as a disorder, an injustice, an attack on freedom or democracy.

For others, however, there is a total *contradiction* between the structures of social reality and the values of social consciousness, so much so that, in their experience and thinking, to preserve social reality is to deny the values of social consciousness, and to subvert social reality is to affirm those values. Whether the relationship between social reality and social consciousness is one of cohesion or of contradiction depends in each case on the objective situation, or on the subjective position of each subject within the social totality. This objective situation is basically determined by "class" origins or class situation, just as the subjective position is determined by "class" consciousness. It is social "classes" or complex blocs of social classes that are the subject in history of the economic, political, social, cultural, and religious structures of social reality and of the values, projects, strategies, or theories of social consciousness, as well as of the kind of relationship that exists between reality and consciousness. These classes have different interests, and that is what generates the dialectic of "class" struggle. These different interests, these conflicts and contradictions, and struggles between "classes" exist not only in the framework of social reality—that is, on the economic, political, social, cultural, or religious level—but also in the framework of social consciousness among different and contradictory values, projects, worldvisions, strategies, doctrines, and theories. The phenomenon of "classes" and "class" struggle runs all the way through the social totality, even if it is true that at each level it has its own specific characteristics. Contradiction between different "classes" does not have the same characteristics when it appears in the economic realm, for example, as it does in the cultural realm or the realm of social consciousness. Analysis of social "classes" and "class" struggle is extremely complex, and there is substantial variation between an industrialized country and a Latin American country. (That is why I have put the word "class" in quotation marks.) Here I cannot go into that complexity, but I have to highlight that phenomenon as an essential element for carrying out a historico-structural analysis of the social totality, such as I have done in its most basic aspects.

It is within this historical and structural framework of the social totality that I have to situate the object of this inquiry—namely, ecclesial structures, especially in their special relationship to the state and civil society (in both the strict and broad senses). The position of these three elements in the historico-social framework of the social totality and of the manifold relationships that we shall be able to discover in this framework lead me to a new understanding of the object of this study; an understanding now become more historical and more all-embracing. In order to summarize and to avoid the need to repeat things, I have schematized in Diagram 3, below, the major elements delineated in this section.

Diagram 3
Introduction, §1, Summarized

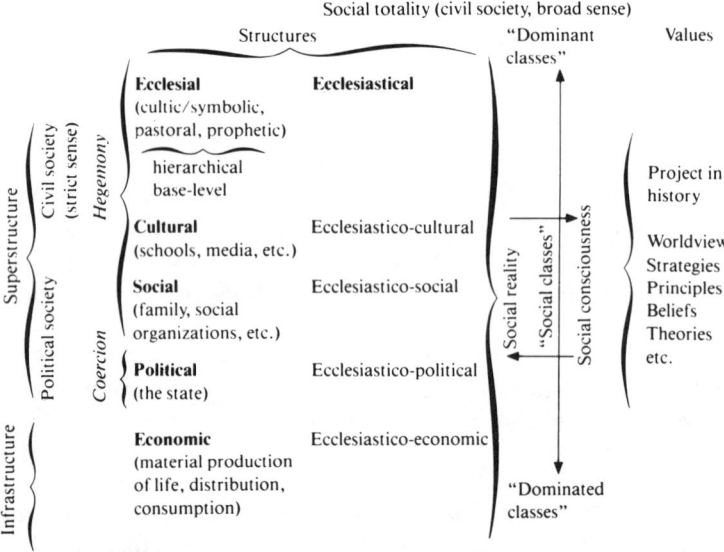

2. METHODOLOGY

The methodology of an undertaking is determined by its object. The process of precising the object of this study (§1) should serve as a basis for the reflection on methodology that I now turn to. By the same token, as the methodology is clarified, we shall also be getting further into the process of constructing the object of this study. Basically, I have been striving to define this object by situating it within a historical and structural framework. We saw that the object was structurally articulated within a *social totality*. Its constituent *parts* and the *relationships* between those parts have been briefly described. The point now is to see how this social totality "works" and, more precisely, how the object of this study "works" within that social totality. The methodology will be specified on the basis of how it works.

Two kinds of determinations present in the social totality will be analyzed: those of a *structural* nature, present within social reality, and those of an *ideological* nature, found in the relationship between social reality and social consciousness. After an overall analysis of these structural and ideological determinations, I shall look specifically at how they affect the object of this study and at the methodological consequences flowing therefrom.

Structural Determinations

Structural determinations are situated within social reality. I am not using the term "determination" in the metaphysical sense, as in the cause-and-effect relationship, but rather in the epistemological and historical sense; that is, I do not consider the determining subject as a *cause* but as a *condition of possibility* of the object determined, and as a *principle of knowing* that object. This means that the conditions necessary for producing that object and the rationality adequate for understanding it are found not in the object itself but in the determining subject. Furthermore, among the structural determinations a distinction will be made between some that I call *fundamental* and others that I call *relative*. When I speak of *relative* determinations I simply mean that such determinations do not exist in themselves and cannot be understood in themselves, but only *in relation to* fundamental determinations. The adjective "relative" merely expresses this logical or epistemological relativity; it in no way implies that it is subsequent in time, or that it is less powerful or important, or less significant in its impact.

Having made these two terminological clarifications, I proceed to spell out my methodological assumptions with regard to the *structural determinations* within *social reality* (for the moment I am leaving social consciousness aside). My *first methodological assumption* is that the thrust of the *basic* structural determination is from the economic infrastructure toward the political, social, cultural, and religious superstructure. This first assumption does not negate— but is dialectically articulated with—a *second methodological assumption*, to the effect that the structural determination of the economic infrastructure over the political, social, cultural, and religious superstructure is *relative*. It is in the economic infrastructure that the superstructure finds the very conditions that make possible its own unfolding in history, and the basic rationality that make it comprehensible. However, it is in the political, social, cultural, and religious superstructure that—*dialectically* and *in relation to* that fundamental determination—the economic infrastructure finds the very conditions that make possible its unfolding in history and the rationality necessary for making it comprehensible. The material reproduction of life (or its nonreproduction and the production of death) in the prevailing (capitalist) mode of production would be impossible, anarchic, and unintelligible, without the coercive structures of the state, or without the structures of civil society that play a hegemonic role (vis-à-vis social, cultural, and religious structures).

The fact that the political, social, cultural and religious spheres are *fundamentally* determined by the economic, and, on the other hand, the fact that the economic level is *relatively* determined by the other levels, constitute a historical and hermeneutical circle (Diagram 4, p. 10).

The first assumption—that the superstructure is fundamentally determined by the infrastructure—not only leads us methodologically to affirm the determining nature of the economic dimension (not as cause but as condition of possibility and principle of rationality); it furthermore leads us to uncover the economic and material basis for each dimension of the superstructure; that, in turn, implies a unified and all-embracing vision of the whole of social reality. That is why I can speak of the material and economic infrastructure of religion, or of an "infrastructural" religion (Enrique Dussel). We can situate religious issues and the theological dimension of the faith, hope, and love of the church community in a direct relationship with the vital, material, and economic problems involved in the production of life and death. The religious and Christian dimension takes on a new rationality in history when the starting point for interpreting it becomes economic and material realities such as work, bread, shelter, the reproduction of the body and of life itself, or their negation through unemployment, hunger, dire poverty, and all those oppressive and repressive mechanisms that produce death. In a similar fashion we can analyze the political infrastructure of religion ("political religion") and the social or cultural infrastructure of religion.

Diagram 4

The Historico-hermeneutical Circle in the Structures of the Social Totality

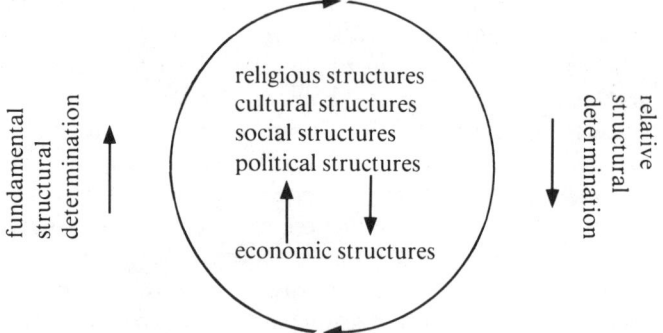

The second assumption—that the infrastructure is relatively determined by the superstructure—not only leads, methodologically, to the insight that there is a political determination of the economic dimension, and that there is a religious, cultural, and social determination of the political and economic dimensions; it further leads to the insight that the superstructure is *relatively autonomous*, as is each dimension of the superstructure. This relative determination (which may be as important or as historically significant as the fundamental determination) is made possible by the relative autonomy of each dimension: the autonomy of the religious dimension vis-à-vis the cultural, social, political, and economic dimensions; the autonomy of the cultural dimension vis-à-vis the social, political, and economic dimensions, and so forth.

With regard to the object of this study, I am saying that *religious structures—more precisely, ecclesial structures—enjoy a relative autonomy*: a dynamism, a nature, and characteristics that are *proper* and *specific* to them, which make possible, and explain, whatever direct determination there may be of the religious dimension over the cultural, social, political, and economic dimensions. Such a determination of the other dimensions within the social totality by the religious dimension may work in two ways: either by impeding or by liberating. The religious dimension may impede or block economic, political, social, or cultural change; or, on the contrary, it may have a liberating or transformative effect on those levels. In a similar fashion, we could say the same thing about the relative determination of the economic dimension, and about how the whole of social reality is determined, by the cultural, social, economic, and political dimensions.

Within this methodological option, I believe it is very important to know how to combine these two assumptions about fundamental and relative structural determinations. Although these two assumptions may appear to be contradictory, they are in fact dialectically complementary: each assumption is affirmed in what it denies of the other. The result is a synthesis that satisfies the demands of each.

This dialectical combination of both assumptions enables us to avoid two mistakes in methodology: on the one side, a *mechanistic economicism*, which applies only the principle that the political, the social, the cultural, and the religious spheres are determined by the economic, and denies the relative autonomy of these dimensions; and on the other side, an *abstract and unhistorical irrealism*, which takes up each dimension in isolation, as though it had an absolute autonomy and an unlimited capacity to determine the whole of social reality.

With regard to the object I propose to analyze (ecclesial structures, both hierarchical and base-level, with their cultural/symbolic, pastoral, and prophetic aspects), I maintain that the conditions that make it possible for this object to be produced *in history*, and that make possible the kind of rationality needed for understanding its meaning *in history*, are to be found in the cultural, social, political, and economic dimensions of the social totality. And I maintain that this object has a relative *autonomy*, its *own* substantiality, and a *specific* nature, that make possible, and explain, how this object exercises a direct and particular determination on all the other dimensions of social reality. This relative autonomy of ecclesial *structures*, as the object of *historical* and *sociological* analysis, is also consistent, on the level of *theological reflection*, with the autonomy of the church as a sign of faith, hope, and love. The ecclesial structures of the church, understood theologically as sign, transcend a purely historical and sociological analysis. But this transcendence, which sheds new light on the relative autonomy of the church, does not negate such analysis. On the contrary, it is borne out in the kind of historical and sociological analysis I am going to attempt.

Ideological Determinations

Ideological determinations are situated in the relationship that exists between social reality and social consciousness. The question of ideology is not a question of the superstructure within social reality, or a question limited to social consciousness. Rather, it is a question of the relationship between social reality as a whole (including all the infrastructural and superstructural dimensions) and social consciousness as a whole. What I have said in the previous section about structural determinations, about the meaning of the word "determination," and about the dialectical complementarity between fundamental and relative determinations, is also valid with regard to ideological determinations.

Ideological determinations are of two kinds: synchronic and diachronic. I must make clear what my methodological option entails with regard to each of these determinations. First, synchronic ideological determination. According to my methodological option, social consciousness is *fundamentally determined* by social reality, and social reality is relatively determined by social consciousness. The subject determining the production of the values, projects, strategies, and theories within social consciousness is social reality. It is social reality, not social consciousness, that makes it possible for values and theories to exist, and provides them with the rationality that makes them comprehensible. I reject the fetishization of values or of theory that turns them into eternal (unhistorical) and absolute (nonrelative) subjects, creating history and bearing responsibility for it. I believe the fundamental subject of history is the *concrete human being*, creator of economic, political, social, cultural, and religious reality, and responsible for his or her ongoing transformation, and not the *abstract human being* as defined by eternal and unhistorical values and theories.

The fact that consciousness is fundamentally determined by reality enables us to uncover the material and structural basis (of an economic, political, social, cultural, and religious nature) for the values and theories found in social consciousness. This methodological option goes along with an epistemological option that may be called "materialist." The term "materialist" is neither a metaphysical nor a moral attribute. The fundamental determination of consciousness by reality does not set up any metaphysical relationship of cause-and-effect. The term "materialist" does not connote any moral dimension: "material" is not opposed to "spiritual" but to "ideal." The "materialist" methodological option (as opposed to what is "idealist," but not to what is "spiritual") directs us back basically to an *epistemological* option; *knowledge* of reality, expressed in social consciousness, is rooted and grounded in the "material" (as opposed to the "idealist") transformation of that social reality. Reality is known, not through the acquisition of values or theories coming "from outside," but from the kind of practice that transforms reality. "Materialist" epistemology excludes neither theory, nor the cognitive and spiritual dimension of the human being. It understands theory and the cognitive and spiritual dimension of the human being as a dimension of social and historical practice (the transformation of the human being and of nature). Theory is developed and reproduced in the transformation of reality. It is not imposed on reality "from outside" like something abstract and eternal that has to "become incarnate" in reality in order to find itself verified there.

Everything I have just said about the *fundamental* determination of social consciousness by social reality does not rule out, but in fact dialectically affirms, the same point in reverse—namely, that social reality is *relatively determined* by social consciousness. In speaking of a relative determination, I do not mean a determination that is subsequent in time, less important, or of less impact or significance. I am merely stating that this determination stands *in relation to* another determination, the fundamental one. That means that the relative determination finds its very condition for being and its rationality in the fundamental determination. This is not, I must insist, a relationship of a metaphysical determination of cause-and-effect but an epistemological relationship, in the order of knowledge. The relative determination of social reality by social consciousness necessarily implies that we must recognize a *relative autonomy* of consciousness vis-à-vis social reality.

Consciousness (including what is found within it: values, projects, worldviews, theories, etc.) has its own internal consistency, its own nature, and its specific characteristics. Consciousness is not simply a "product" or a purely "passive reflection" of reality. It is a reality that is different and autonomous. In this sense I reject a materialistic and mechanistic kind of epistemology, or what may be called "vulgar materialism." I also reject any materialism of a metaphysical sort, along with its methodological consequences. There is no doubt that it is the transformation of reality that makes consciousness possible and enables it to discover the knowable content of ongoing history. That, however, does not mean that a process of conscientization, a transformation in consciousness, a process in which consciousness becomes clearer in principles or theory, cannot effect a significant and decisive determination on reality. Indeed, the transformation of social reality may even be preceded and influenced by the arrival of a particular kind of consciousness, or of a basic shift in consciousness with regard to principles or theory. Within the vision of a mechanistic materialism there is no way of explaining how consciousness and reality can be out of phase like this, but it can be explained coherently by the principle of the relative autonomy of social consciousness. My methodological option seeks to combine dialectically the assumption that consciousness is *fundamentally* determined by reality and the principle that reality is *relatively* determined by consciousness (and the consequent affirmation that social consciousness is *relatively autonomous*).

Thus, I am striving to avoid both the methodological deviation of a *mechanistic materialism* that considers consciousness to be a passive reflection of reality, as well as the methodological deviation of the *fetishization of consciousness* that transforms values, theories, and the other contents of social consciousness into abstract, eternal, alien subjects, off to the side of social reality or above it. For me to affirm sociologically and historically that social consciousness has a relative autonomy is coherent—on the level of theological reflection—with my affirming the autonomy (or the "gratuitousness") of "religious consciousness" or of "theological consciousness" (constituted by the experience of faith, hope, and love). This transcendent autonomy of "religious consciousness" does not negate the historico-structural dynamic of social consciousness within social reality. On the contrary, that is where it finds its verification and its true significance within history.

After this analysis of the kind of ideological determination that I have called synchronic, let us now go on to look at the *diachronic ideological determination* and the methodological option I have adopted with regard to that determination. The diachronic ideological determination has to do with the question of the *historical nature* of the relationship between social reality and social consciousness. With regard to synchronic determination, I stated that social reality was the *subject* basically determining social consciousness; now the question is that of the *historical character of that subject*. A consideration of this diachronic aspect follows logically and necessarily from the preceding consideration on the synchronic aspect. My methodological option focuses on the *coherence in history* between social *reality* and social *consciousness*. Such coherence exists when consciousness continually evaluates social reality in terms of past, present, and future: *present* economic, political, social, cultural, and religious reality is grasped as a reality that is historical, one that has taken place, that has been built up by human beings, which once did not exist and could be changed or replaced in the *future*.

Such coherence does not exist when reality is experienced or understood within social consciousness as an unchanging reality, a reality that has always been and will not change in the future, a reality with no past, present, or future. A consciousness that has not arrived at the point of recognizing the historical nature of social reality, or that hides that fact, I call an unhistorical or false consciousness (false not in a moral but in a sociological or epistemological sense). In that kind of consciousness there occurs a reversal: the *present* is experienced and conceived of in categories of the past (from the beginning, things have always been as they are now), and the *past* is experienced and conceived of in categories of the *present* (in the past, others had to deal with the same structures and contradictions as those existing today). To negate the historical character of social reality necessarily entails denying the future: to the extent that past and present are regarded as the same, the future can be nothing but the uninterrupted repetition of the present situation. That amounts to denying that there can be any future situation different from the present one. False consciousness is a consciousness with no future and no hope.

My general methodological option with regard to all ideological determinations, whether synchronic or diachronic, entails a *specific* methodological option for analyzing and interpreting the object of this study: *ecclesial structures*, both hierarchical and base-level, in their threefold dimension (cultic/symbolic, pastoral, and prophetic), and *the relationship* of these ecclesial structures to the *political structures* used by the church as a *mediation* in order to assure its presence and power within *civil society* (taken in the strict as well as the broad sense: the social totality where hegemony is imposed by way of social, cultural, and religious structures). It is this relationship of mediation that constitutes the basic structure of what I have called "Christendom." The specific methodological option made in order to synthesize the object of this study can be summarized under two basic principles:

First, all the structural and ideological determinations that constitute the whole (as I have analyzed them) are directly and essentially (not indirectly or accidentally) involved in elaborating the specific object we are studying: ecclesial structures, Christendom, and the social consciousness that the church and Christendom have of themselves.

Secondly, within the framework of ecclesial structures, Christendom, and the social consciousness that goes along with them, all the structural and ideological determinations that make up the social totality take on certain *specific* characteristics *of their own*.

The object we are studying is *part* of a social *totality*; it is not located "off to the side" or "above" this whole. Rather, within this whole it occupies a *specific place* and has *relative autonomy*. In using this methodology I have sought to avoid two basic errors: on the one hand, the error of interpreting the church, considered exclusively in itself and by itself, as though it had no historical or structural relationship to the other aspects of the social totality (economic, political, social, or cultural); on the other hand, the error of making a mechanical and general application to the church of the determinations that result from the economic, political, social, or cultural dimensions. Throughout this whole work, I have sought to be guided by these two principles in my methodological option and to avoid the two errors just indicated.

3. BASIC WORKING HYPOTHESIS

My general hypothesis deals with the crisis of Christendoms in Latin America, and in particular, the crisis of the New Christendom, which began during the 1960s. My definition of Christendom comes from the relationship encompassing the terms "church," "state," and "civil society." Within Christendom the relationship of church and civil society is mediated by the church-state relationship. A study of the crisis of Christendom in Latin America basically involves analyzing the crisis of the church/state/civil society relationship. It is my hypothesis that, beginning in the 1960s, this relationship has moved into an irreversible structural crisis in Latin America. My hypothesis is not directly centered on the crisis of the *church* but on the crisis of *Christendom*, which indirectly means a crisis for that form or type of church that has been linked to the workings (project) of Christendom. By the same token, my hypothesis is not directly concerned with the crisis of the state in Latin America, but with the crisis of the church-state relationship, as a mediation of the larger church–civil society relationship.

Consonant with the methodology adopted, one that is determined by the object under study, I have sought to provide an interpretation for the crisis of Latin American Christendom, starting from Latin American social formation. In analyzing this crisis I have centered on the processes that have a direct bearing on the church/state/civil society relationship. With regard to the crisis of New Christendom that began around 1960, I put forward the hypothesis that there are three basic processes at work in this crisis: the crisis of the state and of the dominant social bloc, the rise of the mass movement, and the appearance of a new model of domination. *Initially*, these three processes provoked a crisis in the church-state relationship, and hence a crisis in New Christendom, with the result that the church linked to New Christendom has been unable to retain its hegemony in civil society; *subsequently*, there has occurred a direct contradiction between New Christendom and a new kind of church that seeks to be set up outside any existing or possible kind of New Christendom and even in opposition to that kind of project. This direct contradiction between church and Christendom has had the effect of accelerating and deepening the process of crisis and dissolution affecting New Christendom.

It is my hypothesis that this process of crisis is of such a nature and is so great that the crisis of New Christendom is *structural* and *irreversible*. This means that there are two possibilities for the New Christendom that has prevailed in Latin America since the 1960s: one possibility is that there could begin a process of restructuring out of which would emerge a *new* model of New Christendom; the other possibility is that a decisive majority in the church could begin a process of once and for all ending New Christendom and going beyond it. For the first possibility to be realized, two things would have to take place. First, there would have to be set up a new relationship between the church and the new model of domination (more precisely, between the church and the new model of the state implied in this new model of domination), a relationship that constitutes the foundation for a new project of New Christendom. Secondly, it would be necessary to cut down, dominate, or suppress the form of church that stands in direct contradiction to any real or possible project of Christendom. On the basis of my analysis of the crisis of New Christendom during the 1960s and 1970s, and on the basis of my assessment that this church standing in opposition to Christendom has in fact come into existence, I propose the general hypothesis that the crisis of New Christendom in Latin America is *final* and *definitive*. The obverse side of that hypothesis is that a significant majority within the hierarchical church in Latin America has begun an irreversible process of dismantling New Christendom and moving decisively beyond it, and that that majority will continue to reject any model or possible project of New Christendom.

The proof for this hypothesis is found mainly in part 3 of this work. In order to carry out that proof I have chosen as representative cases those of Argentina and Brazil. I have chosen these two countries because it was there that the New Christendom prevalent around 1960 reached its highest level of development and expression and, as a result, it was in these two countries that the process of crisis of New Christendom manifested its essential and structural aspects most clearly and most deeply. In the course of my research I have studied the cases of Mexico, Chile, Peru, and Bolivia. The material gathered in the process has been very helpful for clarifying the process of how New Christendom arose in Latin America and how it entered into crisis, but for reasons of space I have had to set this material aside. The cases of Argentina and Brazil, moreover, seem sufficient for demonstrating the hypothesis formulated at the outset.

Certainly there is no question of making a direct and mechanical generalization of the cases of Argentina and Brazil to cover the whole of Latin America. I do believe, however, that in studying these two cases I have uncovered the key elements that enable me to generalize my interpretation of the crisis of New Christendom, while respecting the specific and proper characteristics of particular situations. In part 4 I have formulated a synthesis and an instrument of analysis that enable me to generalize for the whole of Latin America the results obtained from the cases of Argentina and Brazil.

The period beginning around 1960 is an *open period* in the sense that the structural crisis of the Latin American social formation, into which the crisis of New Christendom is set, has not yet encountered a stable and adequate resolution. The present situation prevents me from working out any finished and final thesis adequately corresponding to our hypothesis that New Christendom in Latin America is in crisis. This crisis is still in process. The results I come to in my analysis and interpretation cannot be a matter of jumping over history; I cannot define *with ideas* a process that still has not occurred *in reality*. My initial hypothesis poses a question, and the thesis I have proposed does not pretend to have provided a definitive answer, but simply to have improved the posing of the question and, in so doing, to have clarified the problems being raised. I am convinced that the basic elements of an answer are already present if the problem is posed correctly; conversely, a badly posed problem can never be answered adequately. This study seeks primarily to verify the basic hypothesis that New Christendom in Latin America is in crisis, but the interpretation of the possible final solution to this crisis in turn poses new questions and demands new hypotheses. A correct interpretation of the crisis of New Christendom must be the starting point for even a provisional initial effort to respond to these new hypotheses and questions.

My basic hypothesis deals specifically with the crisis of New Christendom that began around 1960, but this hypothesis cannot be formulated and verified without analyzing the *formation* period of this Christendom, and analyzing the formation and crisis of the earlier colonial Christendom. In carrying out this prior study of colonial Christendom and New Christendom, I have paid particular attention to the problem of *periodization*. A correct understanding of the factors and criteria underlying this periodization will be indispensable for understanding the change brought about by the crisis of New Christendom, starting in the 1960s. The crisis of New Christendom can be compared only with the crisis of colonial Christendom at the beginning of the nineteenth century. That is why I have devoted special attention to analyzing and interpreting that crisis. Making a comparative study of the two processes of formation and crisis in earlier Christendom and New Christendom has led me to formulate a general hypothesis on the periodization of the history of Christendom and of the church in Latin America. My hypothesis postulates that this history should be divided into three great cycles: one from 1492 to 1808, the second from 1808 to 1960, and a third that is considered to be beginning now, starting around 1960. This overall view of history and the elaboration of a periodization that corresponds to it have been important elements in my effort to formulate my hypothesis correctly and to seek to work out a thesis that measures up to the questions in my initial working hypothesis.

4. READER'S GUIDE AND OVERALL OUTLINE

The first three parts of my study follow in chronological order (part 1: 1492–1808; part 2: 1808–1960; part 3: 1960 to the present). The core of the proof of my thesis is found in part 3, but that should not be taken to mean that the first two parts are merely an introduction. The chronological order I have adopted follows from a methodological option. In the first place, I have taken very seriously the problems of periodization: such a division of history is utterly necessary for dealing with the question of the relationship between church and state, because it is basically a historical relationship. Any change of period, or age, or historical cycle entails a moment of crisis, a break or a shift in that relationship. The meaning of the church-state relationship depends largely on the overall interpretation of the historical period that is the setting for that relationship.

A general periodization of the history of Christendom and of the Latin American church has been especially important for grasping the nature and depth of the crisis in New Christendom that opened up around 1960. In my interpretation of history, as it is reflected in the periodization I have adopted, the crisis that opens around 1960 is analogous to the crisis that appeared around 1808. In 1808 the first cycle of the history of Christendom came to an end, as did the second cycle in 1960. To my mind, other moments of crisis and change, such as those that occurred around 1870 and 1930, are only relatively important, and only amount to subdivisions within my scheme of periodization. In each part and each chapter in this work I have dedicated a significant amount of space to theoretical justification of the periodization I have adopted.

In addition, the chronological order of the first three parts of this work will make it easier for me to draw a comparison between the formation, development, and crisis of colonial Christendom and of New Christendom. The model and structure of New Christendom originate in colonial Christendom. Studying the crisis of colonial Christendom, which occurred basically between 1808 and 1870, was a decisive help in my approach to understanding the crisis of New Christendom that emerged around 1960. Acquiring a historical understanding of the nature of colonial Christendom was likewise indispensable for interpreting the basic structure of New Christendom. For all these reasons I have organized the presentation of my argumentation in chronological sequence. It summarizes the way I have divided history and the way I understand the history of Latin American Christendom and the Latin American church.

Part 4 of this study, "Church, Authoritarian State, and Social Classes in Latin America," offers a synthesis. I have sought to work out a theoretical framework and instrument of analysis for interpreting the different forms or modalities that the church/state/civil society relationship assumes at present. It is particularly in part 4 (although also throughout this work) that I have sharpened the expression "civil society" with the idea of "social classes." In using the term "classes" I am fully aware that the reality of "social classes" in *dependent* and *underdeveloped* social formations is qualitatively different from what it is in industrialized countries. Within the limits of this study there is no possibility of clarifying this set of issues and taking a position on it. When I use the terms "classes" and "class struggles," it is in an analogical sense, making only a *generic* distinction between those classes, fractions of classes, or blocs of classes that express most clearly distinct *interests* and social *contradictions*. At some points I speak in rather general terms of "rich and poor," or "dominant and dominated"; at other points I am more precise, yet without any pretense of carrying out a scientific, rigorously elaborated "class analysis." Thus, I make distinctions between the agrarian, commercial, mining, industrial, and other bourgeoisies, or I speak of the oligarchy, the middle strata, the petite bourgeoisie, workers, proletariat, peasants, subproletariat (shantytown dwellers, or the marginalized), and the like. In any case, the most important and most decisive element is that my analysis of the social totality—of Christendom or of the church as part of that totality—be set within the perspective of the basic contradiction: that of "oppression-liberation," and not in the perspective expressed in the terms "backwardness-modernity" (Domingo Sarmiento spoke of "barbarism or civilization" in the nineteenth century). The opposition between these two perspectives will be developed throughout this present work.

PART ONE

1492–1808:
Colonial Christendom
in Latin America

CHAPTER 1

A Colonial Christendom within a Capitalist Society

My theoretical standpoint for understanding colonial Christendom is an overall analysis of Latin America interpreted in light of the categories of social formation, mode of production, and production relationships. In such a procedure, church history takes as its context the economic, social, political, and ideological reality of Latin America. This methodology enables me to sketch a history of Christendom and of the church whose basic reference point is the reality of the poor—Amerindians, blacks, and the poor and oppressed population as a whole. The other way to do church history is to take ecclesiastical institutions—bishops, dioceses, parishes, and so forth—as one's reference point. I do not exclude such elements, but I interpret them within a broader and more all-embracing context and horizon.

LATIN AMERICAN UNDERDEVELOPMENT: ROOTED IN CAPITALISM OR FEUDALISM?

A first point to discuss, one that is widely debated in Latin America today, is whether the social configuration in which colonial Latin American Christendom emerged was of a "feudal" or "capitalist" nature. This discussion is important for understanding colonial Christendom and the crisis it underwent in the nineteenth century. The position I adopt here is that Latin America was inserted into the expanding worldwide capitalist trading system ever since the Spanish and Portuguese conquest. From the very beginning, starting with its discovery and conquest, Latin America has developed with a *capitalist social pattern*.[1]

If my hypothesis is correct, I must refute other common opinions that misrepresent the reality of Latin America. For example, there is a theory that seeks to explain Latin American underdevelopment—and North American development as well—by pointing to the fact that Spain and Portugal transplanted to Latin America the archaic institutions of decadent Iberian feudalism, whereas North America benefited from having the institutions of progressive English capitalism transplanted there. Others draw a contrast between the entrepreneurial, Protestant spirit of those who colonized the North and the backward, Catholic spirit of those in the South.[2] These explanations conceal the colonial exploitation of Latin America and distort the specific character of colonial Christendom. The decisive factor for that Christendom is not any alleged Catholic-feudal historical backwardness, but rather the economic, political, and social structures of colonial exploitation. If South America had been discovered and colonized by Protestant Anglo-Saxons, would the basic character of colonial Christendom have been changed and would ours be developed countries today? Our enormous wealth in natural and human resources has condemned us, from the beginning, to a dependent export economy. From the very beginning, our ruling classes arose and became wealthy as local dependent agents of the exploitation carried out by European colonial powers. In that role, they brought Latin America to economic, political, cultural, and religious underdevelopment. It was where the wealth was greatest—in South America, not North America—that the greatest dependence and the greatest exploitation were established. The result was a class society that has generated our dire poverty and our underdevelopment. We have not been exploited because we were weak; rather, our weakness is a consequence of our original wealth. Dependence, class structure, and underdevelopment are thus rooted in the fact that the Latin American economy was inserted into European mercantile capitalism in our very origins. It is this perspective that must be the starting point for an examination of the nature of the "evangelization" and "christianization" of the Americas, and the rise of all the institutions of Latin American colonial Christendom.

It is within the social and political context I have been describing that the way evangelization had to confront the "domination/liberation" option takes on its full historical meaning. It is these polar terms that stand at the heart of the Latin American church from the very beginning, rather than the "feudal/captialist," "archaic/modern," or "traditionalist/progressive" alternatives. When some sectors of the church defended the Amerindians, as far back as the sixteenth or seventeenth century, they were always striving to defend the poor and the exploited, and to delegitimize the system of domination. The aspect of "exploitation" may even have been more basic than that of "paganism." Bartolomé de Las Casas, for example, believed that "an infidel Indian who is alive" is of more worth than "an Indian who is Christian but dead." Colonial exploitation imperiled the salvation of the "Christian colonizers" more than it did that of the "pagan Indians."[3] Given the capitalist and dependent nature of Latin American society, evangelizing and building up the church in Latin America would take place under the pressure of, and be structured by, the dialectic of oppression/liberation, justice/injustice, death/life, development/underdevelopment, and so forth. That is where our *specificity* lies, and that is what makes our Christendom *different* from other Christendoms, both in Europe and elsewhere. This *original* and "modern" situation must be the starting point from which we, as church, evaluate our weakness or grandeur, our fidelity to, or betrayal of, the gospel, and of our history as Latin Americans. "The Christendom of the West Indies is the first peripheral and dependent social formation introduced by modern Europe, prior to those of Africa and Asia."[4] Because it is dependent and peripheral, both the Christian and the social identity of our colonial Christendom is found in the polar terms "oppression/liberation." In that sense, our present "liberation theology" is as old as colonized Latin America.

Production Relationships Based on Slavery

Colonial Christendom emerged and developed within a capitalist social formation. That explains how this Christendom could have a "modern" character from its very origins, and how the contradiction of "oppression/liberation" runs right through it. It is this contradiction that faced colonial Christendom from the outset, not the contradiction of "backwardness/progress"—as though this Christendom had been feudal in nature and resisted being integrated into the capitalist system. Although this much is certainly true from the viewpoint of the capitalist character of Latin American *social patterns,* the widespread and harsh reality of slavery throughout Latin America is equally true when seen from the viewpoint of *production relationships.* It is widely recognized that the original accumulation and the industrialization of the centers of capitalism were made possible by the exploitation of Latin American natural resources (especially gold and silver) and that this exploitation was accomplished through production relationships based on slavery. This fact of slavery in Latin America is as obvious as the fact that Latin America was integrated into the world capitalist system. Thus it is that we find a social configuration that is *capitalist,* by being integrated into the center, and *slave-based,* because of its production relationships on the periphery:

> Without slavery there would have been no cotton, and without cotton, no modern industry. It is slavery that has made the colonies valuable, it is the colonies that have created world trade, and world trade is the necessary condition for large-scale mechanized industry.[5]

What is said of cotton can be said just as well of Latin American gold, silver, cocoa, sugar, and so forth. The same capitalist system was producing the disguised slavery of wage workers in Europe and the undisguised, backbreaking slavery of Latin America.

Two modes of production can be distinguished within this single capitalist society that was colonialized, peripheral, and dependent: one based on the exploitation of the Amerindian labor force (especially in Andean America, in what today is broken up into Mexico, Central America, Peru, Bolivia, and Chile), and another based on the exploitation of the labor power of slaves brought from Africa (especially in the West Indies, the Guyanas, and a significant part of what is today Brazil). Where the economy was more intensive, it was the work of black slaves that was used; where the economy, and particularly the export trade, became less intensive, it was possible to resort to nonslave labor power. Slavery in Latin America was a direct consequence of the integration of the peripheral economy into the capitalist development taking place in the European center.

This colonial situation, which I have described from the angle of slave-based production relationships in a capitalist society, allows me to analyze and interpret the economic and politico-social reality of Latin America from the perspective of Amerindians and blacks, who made up the most exploited sectors throughout the colonial period. It is also from the perspective of Amerindians and blacks that one must interpret the colonial Christendom that arose in that context. This is the perspective of the poor that enables one to uncover the deep historical meaning of Christendom and the real challenge of liberative evangelization in Latin America.[6]

In Latin America there was a structural relationship between *dependence* on the world capitalist system (an external factor) and *slave domination* (an internal factor), which in the end led to our *underdevelopment* and poverty. An external dependence and an internal structure of domination and underdevelopment are different aspects of the same reality. By the same token, it is within this situation that the struggle for independence, the struggle for the liberation of the poor, and the struggle against poverty and underdevelopment are to be identified. To become liberated from dependence, from slavery, and from poverty made up a single liberation process. This liberation process arose from a *fundamental contradiction* within Latin American capitalist, colonial, and dependent society.

Christendom was integrated into this dependent and slave-based social configuration. The contradictions generated by the whole process of resistance or liberation ran through this Christendom just as they ran through the system as a whole. When certain sectors of the church in the sixteenth century defended the Amerindians and consequently had to face the colonial political power, their action exposed a contradiction within the system of domination and represented a liberating current deep within it.

There is an old liberal theory that interprets all resistance of the church to undevelopment and capitalist integration as a consequence of its feudal character. Thus, any contradiction between the church and political power is interpreted as a consequence of the contradiction between feudalism and capitalism. This might be true of Europe, but it is fundamentally false with regard to Latin America. In Europe it is clear that the capitalist system arose and developed outside feudal Christendom, but in Latin America colonial Christendom at its very birth was already an integral part of the expansion of the mercantile capitalist system. The conflict between the church and political power in Latin America had a liberating sense within the capitalist system, and did not necessarily represent a contradiction between feudal Christendom and capitalist development.

In Latin America colonial Christendom had some feudal traits of course, particularly when this Christendom was integrated into marginal sectors—sectors that were not part of capitalist development, which was tied to exports and slave labor. Such was the case, for example, of lands under ecclesiastical ownership or passed on by inheritance, which were not exploited in a capitalist manner, as well as work involved in domestic service or other social relationships that bore the mark of the feudal tradition of castes, inherited by traditional landholding oligarchies, and similar situations. All this generated a contradiction that can certainly be interpreted in terms of certain feudal traits within colonial Christendom and of the capitalist integration of the Latin America system as a whole. But although there was such a contradiction, it was clearly a *secondary contradiction*. The basic fact about colonial Christendom is that it was integrated into the colonial capitalist system with its slave-based production relationships.

The church shaped by colonial Christendom was a church that bore the marks of dependence, slavery, and underdevelopment, and shared the responsibility for these three serious flaws in Latin American society. But in this situation—Christendom integrated into the dominant system—it is also true that any contradiction between the church and the dominant political power, especially the kind of contradiction that resulted from defending the Amerindians, was a liberating contradiction and a basic contradiction that challenged the church in its task of liberative evangelization. The presence or absence of this kind of liberating contradiction must be the basic criterion for evaluating and judging colonial Christendom: whether the church was or was not committed to the liberation of Amerindians and black slaves. In a word, one must interpret the history of the church, from its very origins in Latin America, from the perspective of liberation/oppression, life-or-death, especially the life or death of the Amerindian and the black slave.

In a *liberal* reading of church history, the fact that the church was not integrated into the colonial system is seen as a problem; in a *liberative* reading, however, the problem is just the opposite: the church was too much a part of the colonial system. Liberals have always judged the fact that the church was not integrated into the system as reflecting a conservative stance. That is the case when the church defended its traditional privileges, but not when it defended the interests of the poor. Today we are discovering that there were many "conservatives" in history, as it has been written by liberals, who were true "liberators"—and that by the same token those who are presented as "liberals" were really "oppressors." In order to avoid falling into the liberal trap, one must keep returning to the fundamental criterion for judging the church: the life of the Amerindian and of the black slave in Latin America.

Amerindians Defended

One must regard as a fact of the greatest importance the way a generation of Latin American bishops in the sixteenth century defended the Amerindians.

This fact implies a deep and radical questioning of Christendom and of the whole colonial system, and constitutes a foreshadowing of what in our own century is called liberation theology and the church-of-the-poor model.

Among those bishops we must place Bartolomé de Las Casas, bishop of Chiapas (1544–1547), Antonio de Valdivieso, bishop of Nicaragua (1544–1550), Juan del Valle, bishop of Popayan (1548–1560), Diego Medellín, bishop of Santiago, Chile (1574–1593), Antonio San Miguel, bishop of La Imperial, Peru (1569–1590), and many more.[7] It was not only bishops who spoke out. Missionary orders like the Dominicans and Franciscans also protested courageously during the sixteenth century.

It is from this perspective of liberation in history that the two great provincial councils of Latin America should be reinterpreted: the Third Council of Lima (1582–1583) and the Third Council of Mexico (1585). As said above, defending the Amerindians amounted to defending the "poor," denouncing the system of colonial exploitation, and questioning the missionary endeavor, and this from a theological standpoint.

Defending the Amerindians involved many kinds of activities. By way of example one may look at the case of Chile in the sixteenth century. Churchmen denounced the injustices and cruelties committed against the Amerindians; there is evidence that they promoted active resistance against the policies of the governors; they pressured for "hearings" so that Amerindians could be legally defended; they denounced the war against the Araucans as an unjust war and denounced the torture and murder of Amerindians taken prisoners of war, and so forth. The Jesuit Luís Valdivia wrote to the king that of the two million Amerindians present at the time of the conquest, there were not more than thirty thousand left (1610). He went so far as to state that the armed resistance of the Araucan people was just. The bishop of Santiago, Diego Medellín, analyzed and denounced the forced labor of Amerindians in the mines for eight months of the year, plus two months for going and returning, so that they had no time to work their own land. In addition, the Spaniards stole their harvests.[8]

Patronato Regio

In analyzing colonial Christendom, the *patronato regio,* "royal patronage," is one of the most important factors to take into account.[9] The *patronato* of the Indies had the effect of placing in the hands of the Spanish crown the responsibility for the evangelization of America. It was the Catholic kings who sent missionaries and had the right to collect tithes in order to finance evangelization and worship. They were also granted the right to set up new ecclesiastical foundations and to choose and present candidates for the episcopacy and other ecclesiatical honors. All correspondence and all relationships between the Latin American church and the pope had to pass under the strict surveillance of the Spanish crown. The situation in the Portuguese colonies was quite similar.

The king exercised the privilege of *patronato* alongside all the normal institutions of colonial power: the Supreme Council of the Indies, the "royal audiences," the viceroys, presidents, and governors. The practice of *patronato* generally went considerably further than the written legislation. Those who held power in the colonies could get to the point where they controlled the internal life of the hierarchical church and of the religious orders in an abusive manner. Both the legislation and the use and abuse of *patronato* resulted from the fact that evangelization, the building up of the church, and its educational and social works were an integral part of the enterprise of capitalist-colonial exploitation of Latin America. The fact that it delegated the right of *patronato* to the kings of Spain and Portugal shows great weakness on the part of the church of Rome, which during the seventeenth century was absorbed with the Protestant Reformation and the wars of religion. It was its weakness that pressured it to entrust the christianization of America to the civil power.

Patronato illustrates and provides a confirmation of what was stated previously. On the one hand, it becomes clear how absurd is the "liberal" position: the church (and colonial Christendom) was a separate or marginal entity, feudal in character, whose social function was conservative or divisive, and which was incompatible with the normative capitalist development of the Latin American social system. The situation was just the reverse: colonial Christendom was only too well integrated into capitalist development. On the other hand, the many tensions and fissures between evangelization and colonial exploitation, between some church authorities and civil authorities, took on a new liberating dimension in history, challenging the church to question the legitimacy of the social system as a whole. When it failed to do so, colonial Christendom lost its legitimacy. The integration of the church into the colonial system—an integration mediated by *patronato*—meant that, from the very beginning, the church and its work of evangelization were faced with the oppression/liberation alternative.

There was always conflict between *patronato* and some sectors of the church. It became sharper in the seventeenth and especially the eighteenth centuries. The reason for this conflict can be found in the fact that Latin American society was more and more integrated into European mercantile capitalism. The decline of Spain, beginning in the early 1700s, and the Peace of Utrecht (1713–1715), by which Spain and Portugal lost their dominance over the seas, opened the way for England to dominate Latin America more directly. Strengthened by the Industrial Revolution, England needed to gain new markets. It began to monopolize trade in slaves and merchandise, and moved into large-scale piracy. The Bourbon reforms at the end of the eighteenth century accelerated these changes, and Latin American integration into, and dependence upon, European mercantile capitalism was deepened. As a result, the formation of social classes accelerated, and confrontation between the classes heightened, and meanwhile the economic, political, and ideological underdevelopment of Latin American society deepened. In a situation where the church is an integral part of a colonial system that is ever more dependent, more class-structured, and leading to greater underdevelopment, the contradiction between the church and *patronato* took on a liberative social and political dimension. The main opponents of *patronato* were the Jesuits. The establishment of the Propaganda Fide in Rome in 1622—intended to bring all missionary work under Vatican control—also served to reinforce the contradiction.

Reducciones

There were in Latin America missionary institutions of the church known as the *reducciones* [Spanish; in Portuguese, *reduções;* self-sufficient settlements of Amerindians administered by religious orders]. They took on a positive liberating sense in the context of the contradiction between the church and colonial Christendom or between the church and Latin American society. These *reducciones* flourished in the seventeenth and eighteenth centuries in the areas of present-day Paraguay, Brazil, Peru, Bolivia, Ecuador, Colombia, Venezuela, Mexico, and as far as northern California. They were administered by Franciscans and Dominicans, though mostly by Jesuits. In these missionary institutions defense of Amerindians became concrete and real. Opposition between missionaries and settlers often became violent. Around the middle of the eighteenth century the Jesuits had more than eighty thousand Guaranis organized in *reducciones,* thus enabling them to withstand colonial exploitation. There were sharp differences between the *reducción* and the *encomienda* and other forms of colonial exploitation.[10] Amerindians in *reducciones* were not only taught Christian doctrine, but were provided with structures that enabled them to become organized economically, socially, politically, and even militarily.

Ecclesiastical Properties

The economic organization of ecclesiastical properties underwent—not always but in some cases and in particular situations—a development that was autonomous, independent, and in contradiction with the capitalist development of Latin American social configuration, dependent on European mercantile capitalism. These properties were not a feudal kind of obstacle to capitalist develoment; on the contrary, they laid the foundations for a national kind of development, and as such, they played a role that was liberative, in opposition to structural tendencies that were generating underdevelopment. They were not the social power base for conservatism, as maintained by the "liberal" position, but on the contrary they were the economic foundation for a "socio-national" power base, in contradiction with the dominant social pattern.

The Expulsion of the Jesuits

One of the most important events in the history of the Latin American church during the colonial period was the expulsion of the Jesuits, in 1767. This event was closely connected to the situation discussed above. Some twenty-two hundred Jesuits left Latin America. The significance of this event is both ecclesial and political, and it should be analyzed on the basis of the economic and social context of the eighteenth century and of the work of the Jesuits. The expulsion of the Jesuits was not due simply to certain "currents of thought" in Europe; rather it represented a victory of the European colonial power over the organization of national and popular interests that was already gaining momentum in Latin America during the eighteenth century. Many of the economic and missionary enterprises of the church were linked to those national and popular interests. Those who benefited from the expulsion of the Jesuits were precisely the groups and ruling classes that were tied to the colonial exploitation of Latin America. Among those ruling sectors were also found some other important sectors of the church—sectors that benefited from the way colonial Christendom was integrated into the colonial system.

LIBERATION STRUGGLES DURING THE COLONIAL PERIOD

One can appreciate more fully these efforts on the part of certain sectors of the church to resist and oppose colonial power to the extent that one becomes aware of how colonial Christendom was integrated into the Latin American social system. This integration constituted the normative context within which liberating pressures were manifested. This liberation movement, which existed within the Latin American church from the start, was extremely important for subsequent history. This importance has been overshadowed and even forgotten by the classic liberal analytical framework, which pits "conservatives" against "liberals." There is little study or analysis of the enormous influence the liberation currents of the colonial period had on Latin American social formation and on colonial Christendom. This primary contradiction between the currents of liberation and the system of colonial domination was also present inside the Latin American church from its very beginnings. This is what gives the Latin American church its own original character, and what distinguishes it from the European church from its very birth.

Amerindian Uprisings

To close this chapter, I want to note some of the liberation efforts during the colonial period that should enter into the historical framework for interpreting the Latin American church.[11] Among the Amerindians who put up the stiffest resistance to Spanish domination, there were the Araucans in Chile, the Calchaquis in Argentina, the Charruas in Uruguay, and the Caribs in the West Indies. From 1700 onward insurrections were more frequent and more significant.

In 1723 there was a violent Araucan rebellion in Chile (the Araucans were not defeated until their last insurrection, 1880–1883). Between 1735 and 1750 Juan Santos Atahualpa inspired and led a number of Amerindian insurrections in Bolivia and Peru. Revolutions by Amerindians working in the mines were typically social-minded and anticolonial. They occurred in almost every place where minerals were extracted for export. The year 1752 marked the beginning of a four-year war between the Guaranis and their Spanish and Portuguese overlords. The Guaranis had been organized into *reducciones* by Jesuit missionaries. They won the war—the only instance of a victorious Amerindian uprising. In the eighteenth century there are numerous insurrections in which Amerindians and blacks, mulattos and mestizos, joined forces, a fact that reveals the social, and not merely ethnic, nature of those conflicts. They arose within and against the economic and political structure of the colonial capitalist system of exploitation.

The war that broke out in November 1780, led by Tupac Amaru (José Gabriel Condorcanqui), the cacique of Tangasuca, was the most important in Latin American history. The war lasted until 1783 and spread throughout areas of present-day Peru, Bolivia, Ecuador, and northern areas of Chile and Argentina. The meaning of this war came out clearly in the words that Tupac Amaru addressed, on the eve of his death, to the viceroy's representative: "You and I are the only conspirators: you as the oppressor of the people, and I as one who has striven to liberate the people from this tyranny." Tupac Amaru's revolution brought out the antagonistic and irreducible conflict between the exploited masses and the system of oppression, and as such it has remained a symbol of all liberation movements in Latin America up to the present.[12] The bishop of Cuzco, the capital of the Inca empire, not only condemned Tupac Amaru's war, but personally directed the military defense of the city, and even had the seminarians in his diocese become organized militarily.

Black and Mulatto Uprisings

Next, the revolutions of blacks in Latin America should be mentioned—revolutions that showed a social dimension and a more developed political dimension. The insurrections of *cimarrones* (black escapees) during the colonial period numbered in the hundreds. The high degree of organization among black revolutionaries guaranteed that their resistance would be relatively successful against the system of colonial exploitation. The best known case was that of the organization of the "Republic of Palmares," a kind of free state made up of a federation of villages *(quilombos)* of escaped black slaves in the region between Pernambuco and Bahia, Brazil. It lasted from 1630 to 1695. Establishing the *quilombo* as a method of revolutionary organization was an accomplishment that earned it a place of honor in the Latin American liberation tradition. Black insurrections kept occurring in Brazil until 1888, the year when slavery was abolished.

An important fact, one forgotten by the "liberal" historians of Latin America, is that the ideas of revolution, republican government, and independence were first cultivated in Latin America by blacks and mulattos, particularly in Brazil, Uruguay, Venezuela, and the Caribbean. The mulatto plot led by

Alferez Tiradentes (Joaquin José da Silva Xavier) is paradigmatic. In 1789 he tried to prevent Brazilian gold from the being sent to Portugal. The movement spread in Minas Gerais, but on April 21, 1792, Tiradentes was executed. The plot took its inspiration from the ideas of the Enlightenment.

The uprising of workers in Bahia, Brazil, in 1798 was of the same nature. It was a popular movement made up mainly of mulattos. It proclaimed the "Republic of Bahia" ("a government that is republican, free, and independent, in which all may have access to political positions and public ministries, with no distinction between Creoles and blacks").[13] Historians regard this uprising by artisans to be the most clearly "political" social movement of the colonial period.

Creole Uprisings

Finally, there were the uprisings of Creole whites, not the earlier ones aimed at obtaining greater rights to exploit Amerindians, but the later ones aimed at liberation from the colonial system. The two best known revolutions were those of Asunción (Paraguay) and Socorro (New Grenada). The "rebellion of the commoners" of Asunción, led by the magistrate José Antequera against the viceroy, broke out in 1721. The rebellion was put down. When it flared up again in 1730 under the leadership of Fernando Mompo, it was democratic and revolutionary in nature.

Even more important was the "revolution of the commoners of Socorro" (contemporaneous with Tupac Amaru's revolt). The "commoners" organized an army to march on Bogotá. The movement expanded to towns in Colombia, Venezuela, and Ecuador. The participation of Amerindians and mulattos gave it a clearly social and political cast. Archbishop Antonio Caballero y Gongora played a disastrous role: he persuaded the commoner army to dissolve with promises that he subsequently refused to acknowledge. The viceroy unleashed a bloody repression. Nevertheless, the struggle continued under the direction of a mulatto ex-seminarian, José Antonio Galan. He was executed in January 1782.

PART TWO

1808–1960: New Christendom in Latin America

I use the term "New Christendom" in contradistinction to "colonial Christendom." The broad span of history under consideration is subdivided into three periods: the crisis of colonial Christendom (1808–1870), the rise of a New Christendom during the period of the liberal oligarchical state (1870–1930), and its transformation during the period of populist, nationalist, and developmentalist movements (1930–1960). At the beginning of each of the three chapters that make up part 2, I shall explain in more detail the periodization I have adopted.

The colonial crisis that broke out in 1808 (though its gestation began in the eighteenth century) led to a deep structural crisis for colonial Christendom. In terms of methodology, I intend to make the colonial crisis of the Latin American social system the starting point for my interpretation of the crisis of Christendom. This crisis did not affect simply the hierarchical structures of the church. That represented only one aspect or dimension of the overall crisis of the colonial system. Christendom had a relative autonomy and the crisis it underwent proceeded according to its own dynamic and logic, one that was proper to Christendom itself. But it is just as true that this very Christendom cannot be fully understood in itself, but only by starting from the economic, political, and ideological processes that shaped the social order.

In part 2 particular attention is paid to the 1808–1870 period, because it is during the crisis of Christendom that its nature and internal structure emerge most clearly. In my analyses throughout this study I generally put particular emphasis on the moments of crisis for the Latin American social system, for it is at such moments that the relationship of the church to political society and civil society is most obvious. The crisis of colonial Christendom during the 1808–1870 period is particularly important for comprehending the crisis of

New Christendom from 1960 to the present, the question to which I devote all of part 3. It is very beneficial to compare the two processes, and it is no coincidence that today throughout Latin America there is a widespread renewal of historical research. It is very difficult to grasp the significance of the present crisis of New Christendom unless an analysis of the crisis of colonial Christendom is kept in mind. No doubt there is an important difference between the two processes. During the nineteenth century the basic contradiction arose between colonial Christendom and New Christendom—that is, between two models of Christendom. In the crisis of today the basic contradiction is between New Christendom and a particular kind of church that arises on the margins of (and opposed to) any conceivable project of Christendom or New Christendom. This contradiction between church and Christendom will provide me with the key for interpreting the present period, which begins around 1960.

In part 2 I do not intend to portray the whole history of the social order and of the church in Latin America, but simply to provide an interpretation of the advent of New Christendom *on the basis of that history*. If I understand Christendom to mean that a fundamental element in the relationship between the church and civil society is the mediation of political society, then the way Latin American political society developed in history, and particularly the way church-state relationships unfolded during the 1808–1960 period, will obviously be essential for understanding New Christendom.

In dealing with church-state relationships it is essential to establish a "periodization." That is why I have made a sustained effort to limit my analysis and focus my concern on differentiating the three periods between 1808 and 1960. More precisely, I have sought to draw out the essential elements characterizing the evolution of the Latin American state during each of these three periods and the way this evolution modified church-state relationships, around which New Christendom revolves. This periodization of the historical evolution of the state in Latin America, and of church-state relationships, has been worked out on the basis of an analysis, primarily of economic developments, but also of political and ideological evolution, of the Latin American social system. Hence, the pivotal element of part 2 of this study is the periodization or division into the different historical periods of the process of gestation of a New Christendom in Latin America. The logical and methodological order involved in working out this periodization involves three basic aspects:

1) an economic, political, and ideological analysis of the Latin American social order,

2) an analysis of the relationship between church and state,

3) an overall interpretation of New Christendom considered in itself.

My conclusion in part 2 with regard to the advent of a Latin American New Christendom will provide me with a basis for analyzing in part 3 the crisis of this New Christendom after 1960.

CHAPTER 2

1808–1870
The Crisis in Colonial Christendom

WHY 1808–1870?

I begin this section by explaining my reasons for demarcating this historical period. The 1808–1870 period began with the struggle for political independence from Spain (1808–1824),[1] continued with the process in which the new national states asserted themselves (a process marked by instability, civil wars, and the political phenomenon of *caudillos*), and ended around 1870 with the appearance of the liberal oligarchical state in Latin America.

In the Portuguese colonies, the period began in 1807 when King John VI and all his court fled from Lisbon to Rio de Janeiro; then the ports were opened in 1808; formal independence came with the "cry of Ipiranga" in 1822 (Pedro I). The period ended in 1889 with the proclamation of the republic.

On the international level, the Napoleonic wars, and especially the 1807 invasion of the Iberian peninsula, had a decisive impact on Latin America. In 1808, King Carlos IV of Spain reversed his previous abdication in favor of Prince Ferdinand and instead granted all his rights over Spain and the Americas to the French emperor. On June 4, 1808, Napoleon proclaimed his son Joseph king of Spain. As to the end of this period, I locate it between 1870 and 1880—the great crisis of international capitalism out of which will arise modern imperialist monopoly capitalism, the most advanced form of capitalism.[2] Starting in 1880 the superpowers struggled over how to divide up the world, and it was English imperialism that prevailed and achieved hegemony. An important milestone in the history of the international working class movement was April 1871, when the Paris Commune issued its manifesto: the first attempt of a proletariat to take over a state. In May the Commune suffered cruel repression and many Communards migrated to Latin America.

Both the Napoleonic wars at the outset of this period and the crisis of international capitalism at the end gave rise to profound changes in the colonial relationships between European metropolitan centers and Latin America.

Napoleon's invasion of the Iberian peninsula weakened the colonial hold of Spain and Portugal over their colonies, allowing struggle for the independence of Latin America to begin. In many countries the liberal reforms that led to the liberal oligarchical state in Latin America coincided with the period of growth and stabilization of the Latin American raw materials export economy, which in turn was dependent on the modern monopoly capitalism and imperialism that arose out of the crisis of the 1870s. There is no single date for all Latin American countries, but it seems that 1870 can be chosen as the approximate reference point for the beginning of this process of economic and political stabilization of Latin American states, now dependent on this new stage of international capitalism.

An equally significant event for Latin America as a whole was the end of the war of the Triple Alliance (1865–1870): Brazil, Argentina, and Uruguay crushed Paraguay, the only country in Latin America that had undertaken a genuinely nationalistic and autonomous kind of development after independence. If Latin America had followed the Paraguayan model, which was cut off by triumphant oligarchical liberalism, there would not be an underdeveloped Latin America today.

In conclusion, I believe the dates 1808–1870 are the most appropriate for marking off this subperiod.[3] The second subperiod, that of the Latin American liberal oligarchical state, began in 1870 and continued until 1930, the date of a new and deeper structural crisis within international capitalism.

INTERPRETING THE CRISIS

All historians agree that it was during the 1808–1870 period that the Latin American church and Latin American Christendom experienced their deepest and most widespread crisis. Ever since then, the Latin American church has retained a memory of this as the crisis par excellence. Hence the interpretation of this crisis is vitally important for understanding subsequent history and the present crisis of the church, which started around 1960.

The interpretation of the crisis of colonial Christendom during the 1808–1870 period has generally been that of a conflict between the *church* and *liberalism*—a position that has blocked efforts at in-depth interpretation. As long as things remain at that level, one cannot come to any theoretical deepening capable of getting beyond the claims of conservative apologetics and liberal anticlerical dogmatism. The first group reduces the crisis to a breakdown within the church caused by the expulsion of most of the bishops in Latin America and a political division among the clergy over the wars for independence, or, later on, by persecutions of the church launched by the first liberal governments and by the positivist and secularist sectarianism of the liberal state. However, this breakdown was not the cause of the crisis in the church, but one of its effects.

Liberal ideologies, on the other hand, reduced the crisis of the church to a crisis of feudal society, which they regarded as incompatible with modern development and nation-building in Latin America. In the liberal view, the church, as a conservative and monarchical institution tied to the colonial past, had to change and submit to new forms of civil government; above all, it had to give up the social and political power it had enjoyed during the colonial period.

I believe both interpretations are partial and insufficient, though both express an element of truth. Neither the conservative hypothesis about a breakdown in the church, nor the liberal hypothesis about the crisis of feudal society, can give us a sense of the deeper meaning of the crisis of the church and of colonial Christendom during the 1808–1870 period. In order to shed light on the meaning of this crisis, I propose rather to go to its deep historical roots, which are to be found at the level of the economic, political, cultural, and religious processes of the period. It is on the basis of that kind of historical depth that one will be able to come to comprehend, politically and theologically, the crisis of colonial Christendom and of the church that was bound up with it.

By the eighteenth century England had already been able to subdue Spain and Portugal economically, by preventing them from playing any dynamic and autonomous role within world capitalism. At the end of that century, Spain and Portugal reacted and sought to "modernize" their economies. Among other measures (those that are called the "Bourbon reforms"), the liberalization of trade relationships with their colonies may be singled out. The result, however, was just the opposite of what was intended. On the one hand, the Iberian countries found that their ability to participate autonomously in capitalist development was lessened, and they found themselves pulled into an even greater dependence on England. On the other hand, the Creole bourgeoisie in Latin America increased its economic power significantly. Liberalization expanded trade with Latin America and stimulated the growth of production of raw materials for export. The Creole bourgeoisie increased its profits, its ambitions, and its power.

But the bourgeoisie did not enjoy *political power,* which was monopolized by Spain and Portugal, and by the whole complex apparatus of colonial domination in Latin America. Political power meant controlling the market, taxes, customs, import and export records, and the power to direct surpluses and uncommitted capital to one's own advantage. Political power also meant control over the government apparatus and the army, and control over the church by means of *patronato:*

> This contradiction between economic power in the hands of the Creole bourgeoisie and political power monopolized by the Spaniards was the motivating force that set the revolutionary process of 1810 in motion. The interests of the local bourgeoisie conflicted with those of the Spanish empire. The former needed to find new markets, but the Spanish Crown restricted exports to suit the convenience of Iberian trade alone. . . . Transfer of power would not bring a transformation of society. The local bourgeoisie simply wanted to assume control of the commerce controlled

by the crown. This is the reason for the essentially political, formal character of the Independence movement.[4]

With Napoleon's invasion of the Iberian peninsula, and the consequent weakening of colonial relationships with Latin America, the stage was set for revolution; everything needed for it had been developing since the end of the eighteenth century.

Yet the change in the colonial relationships of dependence, the increased economic strength of the Creole bourgeoisie, and the resultant contradiction between the economic power of the bourgeoisie and the political power of the monarchy do not explain in full the revolutionary process of the first quarter of the nineteenth century in Latin America. There were still other processes, of a political and ideological nature, that were linked to the economic process, but whose role in the independence of Latin America had a dynamic that was relatively autonomous and distinctive.

ANALYSIS OF LATIN AMERICAN SOCIETY

In order to clarify this complexus of economic, political, and ideological problems, I will make an effort—tentative, as a hypothesis—at the difficult task of discerning which groups, sectors, or social "classes" played a role in the independence process (not only during the 1808–1824 period, when independence was achieved, but also during the previous and subsequent periods). It is quite beyond the limits of this work to carry out any extensive or intensive "class analysis." Such an effort would, moreover, require an explanation of what the regions of Latin America have in common and what is peculiar to each. What I intend here is simply to *begin* such an analysis and particularly to open the way (that is, a methodology) for analyzing colonial Christendom during the 1808–1870 period.

"Conservative" Sector of the Dominant "Classes"

Within the dominant classes, three sectors can be recognized.[5] First there was the sector usually called *conservative*. Here we find the monopoly trading bourgeoisie tied to the Spanish market and its colonies. This sector was opposed to independence from Spain, because it would be economically against its interests. Thus, it combats contraband and all trade relationships with the English. Ideologically, this mercantilist bourgeoisie was "conservative," because it benefited from keeping the system as it was (dependent on Spain). It is incorrect to regard all the merchant bourgeoisie as liberal. This sector was not liberal; on the contrary, its class interests inclined it toward an antiliberal "conservatism," and toward an alliance with those sectors of the church that rendered legitimacy to Spanish colonial power. When this mercantilist bourgeoisie opposed legal and contraband imports from England, and in general the liberal current of free trade, it found support among national producers and artisans, and it identified itself with nationalistic and protectionist sectors of the bourgeoisie. After independence this "conservative" mercantilist bourgeoisie sought to maintain the colonial model of economy within the new political forms. The Creole petite bourgeoisie, linked to the political and administrative bureaucracy of the Spanish colonial power, was also part of the "conservative" sector. This sector felt that the independence movement threatened its very life.

Another part of the "conservative" sector was the agrarian aristocracy (which was not yet a social class), linked to precapitalist forms of production. To this grouping belonged those who owned lands that were set apart from public use (by rights of primogeniture and other titles of nobility) and sectors of the church tied directly to the administration of ecclesiastical landed property. Also included was the "slaveholding" or "feudal" aristocracy, which used slave labor or forced personal labor. As already explained above, this sector did not constitute a feudal or precapitalist mode of production, but was in fact integrated into the Latin American capitalist social system (within which there was an unstable and contradictory combination of feudal, precapitalist, and capitalist production relationships). This sector tended to disappear toward the end of the eighteenth century, and especially after independence, insofar as the liberal Creole bourgeoisie that came to power struggled to suppress the rights of primogeniture, to abolish slavery, and to release land that was held in mortmain (land not subject to buying and selling; held by reason of inheritance or ecclesiastical privilege).

Liberal-Dependent and Liberal-National Groupings

Among the ruling classes we also find the so-called *liberal* sector. The term "liberal" is quite equivocal and ambiguous: "liberalism" in Latin America includes a whole mix of different and sometimes contradictory social sectors and class interests. In general, the liberal Creole bourgeoisie was divided into two main groups: the one can be called "liberal-dependent" and the other "liberal-national." Both were interested in achieving economic and political independence from Spanish colonial rule (that is why the Creole liberal bourgeoisie joined the struggle for independence). However, the first group struggled for independence from Spain in order to set up a new social system dependent on English capitalism. By contrast, the second group struggled for independence from Spain in order to set up an autonomous and national social system not dependent on a European base. Hence, the liberal-dependent group is called the "European party" and the liberal-national group is called the "American party."[6] The first group basically tended to advocate free trade, whereas the second was protectionist. Although the interests of the two groups overlapped to some extent during the wars for independence, when independence became a fact these two fractions of the Creole liberal bourgeoisie clashed for several decades, even unleashing long and murderous civil wars.

Which social "classes" or "class" sectors made up these two fractions of the

Creole liberal bourgeoisie? The *liberal-dependent* fraction was made up mainly of the agrarian, mining, and free-trade bourgeoisie. The liberal agrarian bourgeoisie was the bourgeoisie that owned larged estates that had been freed of previous obligations and were then mainly devoted to production for export.[7] The free-trade bourgeoisie was the export/import bourgeoisie struggling against Spanish monopoly and favoring free trade with England and other European nations.

The *national-liberal* sector of the Creole bourgeoisie asserted its class interests primarily during the period after independence. This national sector of the liberal bourgeoisie was on the losing side during the civil wars following independence, and hence has been a forgotten sector in the history of Latin America. Sometimes it is confused with the conservative sector and is called "antinational" or "barbarian." The only case where the national-liberal bourgeoisie was successful was in Paraguay, with Dr. José Gaspar Francia, and the Solano Lopezes, father and son, until the war of the Triple Alliance (1865–1870).

The national-liberal sector of the bourgeoisie was made up of the incipient national industrial bourgeoisie (not pursuing the industrialization that was directly linked to export). Independent craft workers (who were quickly proletarianized by the influx of foreign products) could also be included in this sector. Persons engaged in small business in the internal market also belonged to this national sector. To some extent, the commercial bourgeoisie formerly linked to foreign trade with Spain and then converted to protectionism after independence also belonged with this sector. The national fraction of the liberal bourgeoisie was normally tied to the interests of the provinces as opposed to those of the ports, which were dominated by the liberal-dependent free-trade bourgeoisie. The clearest case is that of Argentina where there was a long struggle between the provinces and the port of Buenos Aires (between the protectionist federalism of the provinces and the free-trade centralism of the port).

The Liberal Petite Bourgeoisie

An important sector of the national liberal bourgeoisie was that of the petite bourgeoisie (although its importance was more in the political, cultural, and ideological spheres than in the economic sphere). This group was made up of lawyers, doctors, technicians, teachers, and employees of the bureaucracies of the new national states. Throughout the nineteenth century there were several generations of liberal intellectuals from the petite bourgeoisie, including significant sectors of the Creole clergy. This liberal petite bourgeoisie included eminent men such as Echeverria, Alberdi, and Sarmiento in Argentina; Francisco Bilbao, Santiago Arcos, Eugenio Lillio, and, a little later, Andrès Bello and Victorino Lastarria in Chile; José María Mora and Mariano Otero in Mexico; José Antonio Seco in Cuba; José María Samper and José E. Caro in Colombia; Justo Arosemena in Panama; Francisco de Paula Vigil in Peru, and many more. These Latin American intellectuals were receptive to the ideas coming out of the European revolutions of 1848, the utopian currents of French socialism, and Bentham's utilitarianism. This intellectual opening of the petite bourgeoisie to the currents of European thought placed it in the camp of the liberal-dependent bourgeoisie, but in many instances what emerged was an independent and nationalist position. This liberal petite bourgeoisie of the early period went into decline after the liberal oligarchical state was established, starting around 1870, and after the positivist movement appeared on the scene.

Dominated, Exploited, and Marginalized Sectors

Alongside the three sectors of the dominant "classes" already mentioned ("conservative," "liberal-dependent-European," and "liberal-national-American" sectors), there were the enormous masses of the dominated, exploited, and marginalized. In this category we find primarily Amerindians and blacks, mestizos and mulattos, as well as a significant number of poor whites. We cannot yet speak of exploited "classes," because slave, feudal, and precapitalists relations of exploitations were still in effect, but the overall tendency was toward the formation of classes, given the capitalist nature of the Latin American social system. In their origins the dominated "classes" generally coincided with the ethnic groups mentioned, given the way colonial exploitation took place. In order to get a rough idea of the number and importance of these exploited masses, we may examine population census figures. These censuses were taken on the basis of race and not of social status or class. But these census figures give us a rough idea of the importance of the exploited masses around the end of the eighteenth and the beginning of the nineteenth century.

A few examples will suffice: in 1770 Lima counted 57,500 inhabitants, of whom 30,581 were black slaves. Buenos Aires in 1778 counted 24,205 inhabitants, including 4,115 blacks, 3,115 mulattos, 674 mestizos, and 544 Amerindians. In the French colony of Santo Domingo in 1789 there were 30,000 whites, 24,000 mulattos and free blacks, and 452,000 black slaves. In Venezuela the first census carried out by the government of the republic in 1811 gave the following (approximate) figures: 200,000 whites, 400,000 mulattos and mestizos, 60,000 black slaves, and more than 100,000 Amerindians. In Brazil in 1817 an official census lists 3,817,000 inhabitants, of whom 1,390,000 were slaves.[8]

SOCIAL GROUPINGS AND THE INDEPENDENCE PROCESS

I now turn to examine how all these sectors or fractions of "classes" took part in the struggles for independence (1808–1824), and during the subsequent period (1824–1870). I shall also analyze the overall role of the church in these historical processes on the basis of what has already been said. Throughout this analysis I will be seeking to grasp the *meaning* of the events that occurred and

Diagram 5

Social Sectors in the Late Eighteenth and Early Nineteenth Century in Latin America

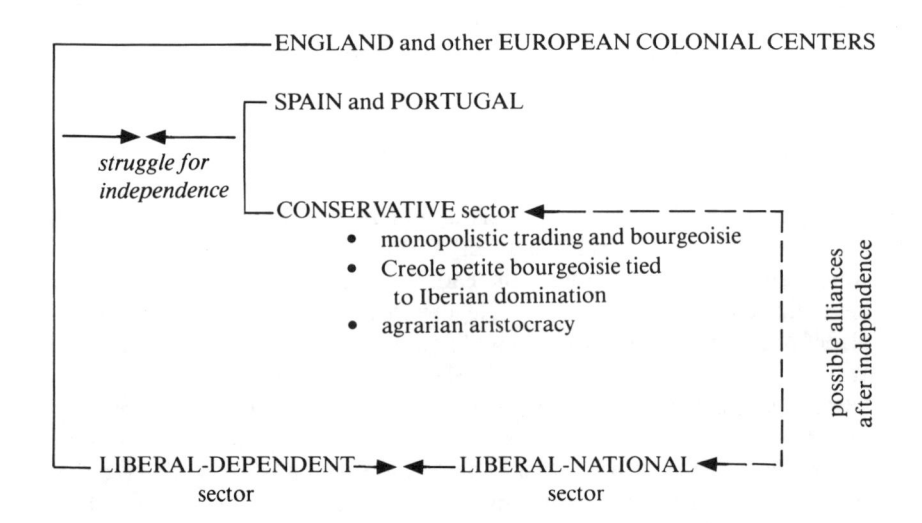

ENGLAND and other EUROPEAN COLONIAL CENTERS

SPAIN and PORTUGAL

struggle for independence

CONSERVATIVE sector
- monopolistic trading and bourgeoisie
- Creole petite bourgeoisie tied to Iberian domination
- agrarian aristocracy

possible alliances after independence

LIBERAL-DEPENDENT sector ↔ LIBERAL-NATIONAL sector

postindependence struggle

- agrarian bourgeoisie
- mining bourgeoisie
- free-trade merchant bourgeoisie

- artisans and national industrial bourgeoisie engaged in trade
- national commercial bourgeoisie working in the domestic market

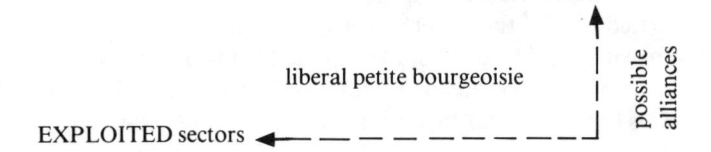

liberal petite bourgeoisie

possible alliances

EXPLOITED sectors

(slave, feudal, semifeudal, or free-labor; Amerindians, blacks, mestizos, mulattos, and poor Creole whites) thus to deepen an understanding of the nature of the crisis of the church and of Christendom during this period.

Most of the leaders of the revolution for independence belonged to the richest families of the landed, mining, and commercial bourgeoisie. I have already emphasized the contradiction between the *economic power* concentrated in this bourgeoisie and the *political power* monopolized by Iberian colonial powers. For the great property owners, the owners of the mines, and the merchants in Latin America, the purpose of independence was to enable them to take over complete political power in order to redirect the economy to serve their own "class" interests. Thus the Creole bourgeoisie as a social "class" was seeking to be politically independent instead of being subject to the Spanish or Portuguese monarchy. This "class" interest of the Creole bourgeoisie, which was the driving force in the political independence of Latin America, was able to identify itself with the interests of other social sectors, as well as with liberalism as an ideology, and thus to win over the allies it needed for the struggle against Spanish colonial domination.

Most Latin Americans wanted to be liberated from the exploitive colonial system, particularly because of its taxes and the tyranny of its political representatives. Everyone wanted independence, except those who benefited from Iberian domination, but each sector struggled for its own particular interests. The liberal bourgeoisie (landholding, mining, and merchant) sought independence from Spain or Portugal so as to negotiate a new, more favorable, economic dependence upon England. The national-liberal sector of the bourgeoisie struggled so that Latin America would be fully free, both economically and politically, from all foreign power. Finally, the exploited population struggled for the abolition of slavery and of forced personal service, for better economic conditions, for the possibility of landownership, and in general for greater social and political freedom and equality.

Insofar as it was motivated by the interests of wealthy property holders, planters, cattle ranchers, mine owners, and merchants, the war for independence was not in itself a social war rooted in the people. In 1814 the royal armies throughout Latin America had 95,578 men, of whom 73,178 had been born in the New World. "General Joaquín Posada Gutiérrez, a chronicler of the Independence movement, who was from Granada, notes that the cause of emancipation was not popular, that four-fifths of those in the Spanish armies had been born in [Latin] America, and that in general the Amerindians were on the side of the king."[9] The Creole bourgeoisie had to make many concessions and carry out social reforms benefiting other social sectors in order to unite Latin America against Spain and Portugal.

The set of circumstances that began to develop in 1808, with Napoleon's invasion of the Iberian peninsula and the weakening of colonial dependence, opened possibilities for liberation for both the dominant Creole sectors and the dominated sectors. The social demands of the dominated classes thus found expression in this situation and in some cases what broke out was a genuine social revolution that preceeded, accompanied, and followed the struggle of the bourgeoisie for political independence. Often it was the worst off who gave impetus to independence struggles. In some instances, those struggles were carried out precisely to control or suppress revolutionary pressures from the people (that was the case in Mexico where political independence meant the destruction of the popular revolution of Hidalgo and Morales).

However, even if the wars for independence had a social and popular character in certain cases, it was due to the need of the Creole bourgeoisie to subject a large sector of the people to its own "class" interests as a bourgeoisie. This social and popular aspect remained *foreign and extrinsic* to the basic thrust of the struggle for political independence from Spain and Portugal. There were exceptions, such as the case of Artigas in Uruguay, and in some other countries where certain individuals and particular segments of the forces fighting for independence had motivation other than political.

In terms of ideology, something similar could be said with regard to the "liberal" thought that inspired most of the independence leaders. This "revolutionary liberalism," acquired from England, the American revolution, the Enlightenment, and the French revolution of 1789, was quite *foreign and extrinsic* to the economic and social interests of the Creole bourgeoisie struggling against Spain:

> The liberal philosophy of the eighteenth century, which fathered the bourgeois-democratic revolution, was used in Latin America to attain only one part of this revolution: political independence. The arguments of the European bourgeoisie against feudalism were adapted by the Creoles in the struggle against the Spanish monarchy. In Europe liberal philosophy was the doctrine of the industrial bourgeoisie; in Latin America it was the ideology of the landholders, the mine owners, and the merchants. The vocabulary of liberalism was used in the service of different class interests. In Europe liberalism served as an instrument of the industrial bourgeoisie against the landowners; in Latin America it was utilized by the landholders and mine owners against the Spanish monopoly. There it served the cause of industrial protectionism; here, the interests of free trade.[10]

It is important to relativize the influence of liberalism and of the Enlightenment on the wars for independence and to put more emphasis on *the determining influence of the economic and political interests of the Creole bourgeoisie*. It is just as necessary to point out that almost none of the independence leaders had any overall set of social proposals relevant for the majority of the people. For the exploited "classes" independence did not mean any significant social or political improvement, even though those "classes" had participated broadly in the wars for independence as well as in all the seventeenth-century revolts and revolutions that paved the way for independence. It is important to grasp the nature and meaning of Latin American independence in order to get an adequate grasp of the attitude of the church toward independence and its role in it, as well as of the crisis of colonial Christendom.

THE CHURCH AND INDEPENDENCE

Spain

Let us now look at some events that will enable us to discern the meaning of the crisis of the church at the moment of independence.[11] First, it is important to recall briefly what was happening in Spain at that time. From the events of 1808 (when Carlos IV ceded all his rights over Spain and the Indies to Napoleon, who then proclaimed his brother king of Spain) until 1814, Spain was at war with France. During this period, colonial ties weakened, and the wars for Latin American independence began. In those circumstances, churchmen may well have entertained doubts about whether the Spanish government was legitimate and had to be obeyed. But in 1814 Ferdinand VII began to reign as an absolute monarch. He deported and imprisoned many Spanish liberals involved in politics. There began a period of absolutism that continued until 1820. The king recovered his full "legitimacy" and demanded complete loyalty from Latin American bishops. During this absolutist period (1814–1820) Ferdinand VII put men in whom he had complete trust into twenty-eight of the forty-two dioceses in Spanish America. The situation changed again between 1820 and 1823 ("Three-Year Constitutional Period") with the Spanish liberal revolution. The Madrid government initiated an antireligious and anticlerical policy: expropriation of ecclesiastical goods, expulsion of bishops, closing of religious houses, and so forth. This situation had a direct influence on attitudes toward Spain on the part of both Latin American bishops and of the pope in Rome. The situation shifted once more with the second absolutist period (1823–1833) when Ferdinand again repressed liberals and freemasons in Spain.

The Popes

It is in terms of this changing political context that we have to analyze the Roman position toward independence and toward the Latin American church, as it is expressed in these documents:

- 1816, Pius VII, Brief, *Esti longissimo*
- 1822, Pius VII, *Response to Bishop Lasso de la Vega of Merida* (Venezuela)
- 1824, Leo XII, Bull, *Etsi iam diu*
- 1831, Gregory XVI, Bull, *Solicitudo Ecclesiarum*

In 1816, with absolutism in full swing in Spain, and with the movement for independence in Latin America stamped out (except in the vice-royalty of La

Plata), Pius VII addressed himself to the church "of the Americas subject to the Catholic king of Spain" *(Etsi longissimo):*[12]

> We have no doubt that in the midst of all the disturbances that have taken place in those countries and that we have felt so bitterly in our heart, you have continually inspired your flock with the just and firm hatred with which such disturbances should be regarded. . . . the frightful and enormous harm of rebellion. . . . [The struggle for independence is] a sinister weed of disruption and of sedition, which the enemy has sown in those countries.

The revolution against the Spanish crown was presented as a revolution against the church.

When the liberal antireligious revolution broke out in Spain, the pope began to show himself more favorable to the new governments. This is apparent in his letter to Bishop Lasso de la Vega (1822). The pope remained neutral with regard to the war between Spain and its colonies; he made a distinction between "spiritual" and "political" interests.

This relatively favorable attitude changed again after the second absolutist victory and the restoration of Ferdinand VII, starting in 1823. Leo XII then indirectly declared wars for independence illegitimate; he described them as "dissensions," "resentments," "civil wars" that endanger the "integrity of religion" by disturbing the "peace of the country" *(Etsi iam diu).* This Bull was dated September 24, 1824—that is, a few weeks before the battle of Ayacucho (December 9, 1824), when external domination over Latin America was about to end. Latin Americans became aware of the papal declaration after the battle, and they were surprised and indignant. Some even doubted that it was genuine. The situation between Rome and the newly independent states began to return to normal around 1826. The pope gradually gave up the system of *patronato,* and entered into the process of rebuilding the church. With Gregory XVI's Bull *Solicitudo Ecclesiarum* in 1831, Rome finally recognized the new Latin American states.

The Latin American Church

As a *dependent* church and an integral part of a *dependent* capitalist society, the Latin American church found itself directly and fundamentally affected by the war for independence. It was not only the *patronato regio* that subordinated it to the Spanish colonial power and its local representatives as an integral part of that power; the church was integrated into the *whole* and into the *totality* of the dependent and capitalist Latin American social system.

When the conflict between the colonial power and the Creole bourgeoisie arose within this totality, Christendom and the church were deeply divided over it. The church was not attached to one of the poles of the conflict and opposed to the other; rather, the polarization within the social order was duplicated within the church.

This overall integration of the church into the Latin American social order took on forms that varied according to the social or political situation and the organic relationship or institutional function that one or another sector of the church had within society. The bishops were more directly aligned with the colonial power (the king and the higher colonial institutions). Then there were the sectors of the church more directly linked, socially and politically, either to the Creole bourgeoisie or to the exploited masses. Here we find essentially the clergy (Spanish or Latin American, secular or religious). The reactions of the bishops and clergy during the struggle for independence were not determined mechanically by the basic sectors to which they belonged, because secondary or relative factors likewise exercised an influence: their education and access to information, open or closed lines of communication, the attitude of the leaders of emancipation toward the church, and so forth.

The Bishops

The stance of the Latin American bishops toward the independence movement varied according to whether the bonds of colonial dependence were weakening or growing stronger. The political situation in Spain had a direct bearing on their weakness or strength, as did also the attitude of the pope. When these ties weakened (1808-1814 and 1820-1823), most of the bishops, after an initial negative reaction, strove for an attitude of neutrality, held back, or openly favored the independence movement. The pope did not take a stand before 1816, and in 1822 he assumed a relatively neutral posture. But when the bonds of colonial dependence were strengthened (especially between 1814 and 1820), most of the bishops openly opposed the Creole revolutionary movement. Pope Pius VII had taken the same position in *Etsi longissimo* (1816). With the position taken by Pope Leo XII in 1824 in the second period of absolutist restoration, Rome indirectly condemned the independence movement, but in so doing it showed how unfamiliar it was with developments in Latin America: for all practical purposes, colonial dependence on Spain was at an end.

The Clergy

Most of the clergy had a different attitude. Inasmuch as priests were only indirectly tied to colonial dependence, they were less dependent on the Spanish crown and on the legitimation deriving from the pope. In fact, linked socially and politically to the Creole bourgeoisie and to the "popular" sectors, most of the clergy were in favor of the movement for independence. If they played an important role in the revolutionary independence movement, it was due not only to their intellectual background or prestige, but primarily to the social and political position they occupied in Latin American society. Or, to put it more precisely, their prestige and education played a role in the independence process to the extent to which they played an integral role in the Creole society of the time.

Some Concrete Examples

Let us now look at *some concrete and typical cases* to illustrate what has been said. In Venezuela there was the case of Bishop Coll y Prat, in the archdiocese of Caracas, starting in 1810. Although his sympathies were royalist, he submitted to the new patriotic government and recognized independence. Yet when the royalist reaction took place in 1812, he welcomed it with enthusiasm. The Spanish authorities mistrusted him because of his previous stance, and he had to go to Spain to give an account of himself.

A little later, Bishop Lasso de la Vega was made bishop of Merida (Venezuela). His case was even more typical of the contradictions that the church was to experience during this period. Until 1820 he preached loyalty to King Ferdinand VII and supported the royal army in his pastoral letters and even financially. He regarded the independence movement as a divisive phenomenon and as a religious schism, because he saw the cause of the king and that of religion as one and the same thing. He believed the Spanish kingdom was the foundation on which the unity of the people and the unity of the church were built. But starting in 1820, with the liberal, antireligious revolution in Spain, he changed his mind and gradually shifted over to the camp of the patriots. On May 10, 1821, Simon Bolivar wrote to a friend about Bishop Lasso de la Vega and gave an exact summary of the bishop's situation (and indeed, the situation of the church itself): "He hates the liberals in Spain more than he hates the patriots, because over there they have taken a position against the institutions of the church, whereas we protect them."[13]

When a proposed constitution came up for discussion, Bishop Lasso de la Vega, in a way that was quite remarkable for that time, insisted that the article making Catholicism the official state religion be deleted. His attempt failed, for the republican government was not ready to give up the advantages of *patronato,* which it believed it should inherit from the king of Spain.

In 1822 this prelate published a letter favorable to the patriot government and, at Bolivar's request, also wrote a letter to the pope, explaining the situation of the church in Venezuela and defending the revolutionary movement. The pope's positive response to this letter, mentioned above, was spread throughout Latin America and patriotic revolutionaries everywhere were enthusiastic in their comments.

A remarkable case is that of Bishop José Cuero y Caicedo of Quito, Ecuador. From the beginning he supported the independence movement, and was also willing to be chosen president of the Second Revolutionary Junta. One writer on the royalist side said of him, perhaps exaggerating:

> The bishop has used revenues from the crusade and tithes for the support of the [revolutionary] army, and has required that both clergies [secular and religious] provide considerable economic support. . . . He has even gone so far . . . as to excommunicate certain clergymen who refused to go along with the national cause. . . . The procurator himself reports

that Caicedo raised a batallion of Amerindians and helped recruit soldiers.[14]

The posture of the bishop of Cuenca (Ecuador) was just the opposite. Bishop Quintián Ponte y Andrade was an outspoken and fanatic defender of the royal cause.

In Mexico all the bishops were on the king's side. It is said that, even though he had been born in Mexico, Bishop Manuel Ignacio González del Campillo of Puebla went so far as to prohibit priests from administering the sacraments to patriots involved in the insurgency. But starting in 1820, with the liberal revolution in Spain, the situation began to change and we find high prelates signing the Act of Independence. When Leo XII's unfortunate *Etsi iam diu* became known, the bishops, cathedral chapters, and religious communities raised their voices to defend Mexico.

Most of the other bishops—in Argentina, Chile, Peru, Colombia, Central America, and elsewhere—were hostile to the independence movement. As a consequence, they became marginal elements in the Latin American nations and churches. A good number of them were expelled by the new governments and many dioceses remained without a bishop for a long time.

By contrast, it was almost a majority of the clergy who participated in the process of independence. From the end of the eighteenth century, some sectors of the clergy were entertaining the new revolutionary ideas, especially in Argentina, Ecuador, Mexico, and Brazil. In Mexico during the eighteenth century there were a number of court cases against priests and religious who were accused of carrying out propaganda for liberalism and defending political ideas in opposition to the regime. The clergy organized meetings and revolutionary groups. Among other ecclesiastical groups in Mexico there was a concern for economic and legal reforms that paved the way for independence. In Brazil the clergy was very politicized and worked actively to spread liberal and revolutionary ideas. Many of the clergy participated in the Clube de Resistência, preparing for independence, and organized struggles against Portugal emanating from masonic lodges.

At the moment of independence itself the clergy played a decisive role in revolutionary juntas, and in writing manifestos and constitutions. Priests also spread the movement for independence among the people, organized fund-raising campaigns, accompanied the patriotic armies, and in some—exceptional—cases, took up arms to combat royalist troops. This patriotic role of the clergy stemmed from different motivations and had different emphases: in some instances members of the clergy were socially and politically connected to Creole bourgeoisies and in others to the popular sectors.

In Argentina the May 1810 independence movement enjoyed the decisive support and participation of the clergy, but that movement had a markedly "elitist" and "patrician" character. There was practically no presence or participation of the masses. In Mexico the situation was radically different. In its first phase the independence movement had a clearly popular and revolutionary character. It is well known that the parish priests Miguel Hidalgo and José María Morelos were leaders in this movement. They were not isolated cases. It is estimated that of the eight thousand priests throughout Mexico, six thousand supported the revolution. Around 1815 more than a hundred priests were executed for having taken part in armed struggle during the revolution. With their own independence movement, in which some sectors of the church took part, the Mexican Creole bourgeoisie combated and stamped out the popular uprising of Hidalgo and Morelos. Hidalgo was excommunicated by the bishop of Michoacan, Manuel Abad y Queypo, who had previously been involved in the movement for legislative reform measures in Michoacan; that movement is regarded as a precursor of Mexican juntas. Hidalgo faced a firing squad in 1811; Morelos in 1815.

FORMATION OF THE NEW NATIONAL STATES

With the consolidation of Latin American independence, during the period from 1816 (the Congress of Tucuman and the Proclamation of Independence of the United Provinces of Rio de la Plata) to 1824 (the Battle of Ayacucho, which ended Spanish domination in Central and South America, there began the period of the formation of the new national states. This period ended with the great crisis of international capitalism, the appearance of modern imperialism, and, in Latin America, the consolidation of the liberal oligarchical state (1870–1880).

As already noted, the political independence of Latin America was not of a social or popular nature. The masses of the poor and the exploited sectors, manipulated during the war for independence by both patriots and supporters of the king, did not experience any radical change in their situation. Hence, although we find a lot of talk about the state, constitutional monarchy, democracy, congresses, constitutions, parties, conservatives and liberals, and the like, after independence, it all referred basically to the Creole bourgeoisie, which means only 10 percent of the whole population. The remaining 90 percent made up the "forgotten" part of the history of Latin America.

I cannot go into details here. I must remain within the broad outlines of the history of the 1824–1870 period. That will enable me to cast some light on the deepening crisis of colonial Christendom in Latin America. This crisis became sharper and sharper after independence, despite all the efforts by the church to rebuild its internal structures and redefine its role in the new society. The historical significance of this period has often been misrepresented by a very one-sided and ideological exaggeration of the conflict between liberals and conservatives, and by an emphasis on the consequences that conflict had for the Latin American church. As a point of departure here, we shall pursue some observations by André Gunder Frank.[15]

The internal contradictions of the Latin American Creole bourgeoisie were intimately connected with relationships to Europe. Lord Canning's statement in 1824 is well known: "Spanish America is free, and if we do not mismanage our affairs, she is English." The Latin American Creole bourgeoisie was involved in carrying out this British colonial project. It split over its "class" interests: one faction wanted to seize the economic opportunity and prevail as the dominant "class" in its own country by establishing a new colonial pact with England; the other faction defended its economic and political interests by opposing the new British colonial power.

It was for this reason that as soon as independence from Spain was a fact, there arose a conflict between a *dependent* Creole bourgeoisie and a *national* Creole bourgeoisie. That was the underlying conflict that marked Latin American history during this period (1824-1870). It generated situations of complete anarchy, and often of civil war. The dependent bourgeoisie favored free trade and strove for an "outward-directed" development, creating new bonds of dependence on English capitalism. The national bourgeoisie, in contrast, was protectionist and strove for an "inward-directed" development, one that would be self-generating and independent, serving the interests of the nation.

In part 1 it was shown that the Latin American social system during colonial times had a capitalist character because it was an integral part of the single world system of commercial capitalism. The fact that Latin American society had this capitalist character does not negate the fact that feudal or precapitalist production relationships persisted within it. The result was a hybrid and contradictory situation, characteristic of dependent countries. The independence of Latin America did not mean that it moved from a feudal social system to a capitalist system; it was capitalist in nature even before independence. Hence, we should not liken the Latin American Creole bourgeoisie, struggling for independence, to the European bourgeoisie, struggling against feudalism in order to set up a democratic and modern capitalist system. The Creole bourgeoisie was made up primarily of large landowners, planters, cattle ranchers, mine owners, and merchants, all involved in exporting primary products. In contrast, the European bourgeoisie was primarily an industrial bourgeoisie, originally oriented to the internal market. Hence, Latin American revolution cannot be likened to European democratic-bourgeois revolution. The Latin American revolution for independence did not have the same character as the French Revolution of 1789. In Latin America the revolution took place within a capitalist social framework. When the colonies became free of the Spanish monarchy, and were quickly integrated into dependence on English capitalism, an internal reorganization of all production relationships took place. The fact that the Latin American social system became more deeply integrated into capitalism tended to destroy and dissolve those feudal and precapitalist relationships still remaining within it (I shall have more to say about this further on).

Once the struggle for independence was over, the fundamental dilemma of Latin America was not a "horizontal" dilemma, described in terms like "barbarism-civilization," "feudalism-modernity," "backwardness-progress," and the like, but the "vertical" dilemma between a fully autonomous kind of development and a dependent kind of development. Once political independence from Spain and Portugal had been achieved, the choice was: either to win economic independence and solidify political independence, or to be subject to a new economic dependence, this time vis-à-vis England, and thereby weaken political independence. Those who sought after this new dependence on English capitalism used one or another "horizontal" frame of reference as an "ideological" device to conceal and justify this new dependence.

The dependent bourgeoisie claimed that those who were seeking a self-sustaining national type of development were incapable of appreciating European civilization (see, for example, the essay *Facundo* by the Argentinian, Domingo Faustino Sarmiento). This new dependence, falsely presented as the way to "civilization," "progress," and "modernity," was not simply an "external" relationship, imposed "from outside," against the will of the Latin American Creole bourgeoisie. On the contrary, it served economic and political interests within that bourgeoisie. If the dependent bourgeoisie had been willing to struggle against dependence, it would have had to struggle against its own political and economic interests. When the bourgeoisie affirmed its dependence, it was also affirming its economic interests and its political interests as a dominant "class." The reverse was also true: when it asserted itself as the dominant "class," it was affirming its dependence. Thus, dependence was not only something external; it was a reality within dependent society, and the dialectic of "dependence-national autonomy" was intrinsically bound up with the dialectic of "class struggle."

Hence, the fundamental contradiction during the 1824–1870 period (the exact dates varied from country to country) was the one between the *dependent free-trade* bourgeoisie and the *protectionist national* bourgeoisie. These two sectors of the bourgeoisie struggled throughout this period for control of the state so as to be able to impose their own approach on development. The period ended precisely when the dependent free-trade bourgeoisie gained decisive mastery, and a primary export economy and a liberal oligarchical state gained firm control in Latin America (with Porfirio Díaz in Mexico starting in 1877, with Roca in Argentina, starting in 1880, with Guzmán Blanco in Venezuela starting in 1870, with Domingo Santa María in Chile starting in 1881, and so forth).

The dependency and free-trade approach increasingly led to the enrichment of the local oligarchy, the sharpening of "class" contradictions, and a general trend toward underdevelopment. An approach that focused on national interests and was willing to employ protectionism led to just the opposite kind of result, as was experienced in Paraguay from 1811 to 1870, until forces favoring a policy of dependence ended it all in the War of the Triple Alliance (1865–1870). Writing about Paraguay during its nationalist and protectionist period, André Gunder Frank says:

> In isolating his country from relationships which would result in dependence on foreign countries, Dr. Francia and his successors, the Lopezes,

achieved a Bismarckian or Bonapartist type of national development that differed from all other Latin American countries of the period. They built a railroad with domestic capital; they developed national industries by engaging foreign technicians but prohibiting foreign investment, as the Japanese were to do many years later; they established free, public, elementary education—almost eliminating illiteracy, according to contemporary sources; and furthermore, with the help of the Guarani Indians, they expropriated the great latifundia and merchant enterprises. Theirs was the most popular government in America.[16]

In Argentina there was opposition between Bernardino Rivadavia, who imposed a centralist constitution in order to subject the provinces of the interior to the interests of English capitalism, and Juan Manuel de Rosas, who respected the nationalist and protectionist federalism of the provinces. Rosas presented himself as a "restorer" because he preferred to reform the traditional order rather than import ideas and structures from overseas. With the fall of Rosas in 1852 this first effort to provide Argentina not only with political independence but with economic independence came to an end.

The civil wars that took place in Latin America between the dependent free-trade bourgeoisie and the national-protectionist bourgeoisie were analogous to the civil war in the United States. Between 1861 and 1865, Americans in the north, who were industrializing, nationalist, and protectionist, battled with Americans of the south who were farmers and planters, dependent on Europe, agro-exporters in favor of free trade. In the United States it was the industrial, national, protectionist bourgeoisie that won the civil war; in Latin America it was the dependent, free-trade, raw-materials exporting bourgeoisie that won. Indications of which side won are clear in both northern and southern halves of the hemisphere.

If the basic opposition between 1824 and 1870 was that between the dependent bourgeoisie and the national bourgeoisie, how are we to understand the opposition between *liberals* and *conservatives,* which enjoys classic status among historians? There is no doubt that the immediate effect of a stronger and more direct dependent integration of the Latin American social system into English capitalism—which was much more dynamic and more developed than Spanish capitalism—was the breakdown of all feudal and precapitalist production relationships. In this sense, greater dependence upon and greater integration into capitalism tolled a death knell for inherited property and for ecclesiastical mortmain properties. Land had to enter into the "free" circulation of money and capital. The process led by the agrarian bourgeoisie to "liberate" land entered into open contradiction with traditional forms of possession that had been monopolized by the land aristocracy and the clergy. The process of integration into capitalism (and the greater development of productive forces) similarly meant a crisis for all forms of slave labor, forced labor, and semiservile labor. Thus the Creole bourgeoisie fought to abolish slavery and other "traditional" ways of providing labor.

In this sense, the landholding bourgeoisie, the cattle growers, the mine owners, and the dependent and free-trade merchant bourgeoisie, for ideological purposes, took up a "liberalism" that they imported from the United States, France, and England. For their part, the sectors of the bourgeoisie tied to traditional forms of production—to slavery, to the "bonds" of the rights of primogeniture among the laity and mortmain among the clergy, which were attached to the titles, privileges, and the rights of the previous order—were regarded as "conservative." In this sense there was a *real* ideological opposition between the "liberals" who sought to end the Spanish colonial past once and for all, and the "conservatives" who remained attached to that past. But these "liberals" broke with the past in order to become part of a new dependence, which meant only wealth for them and greater misery for the majority in their national populations. In the name of "liberal" ideas, "progress," and "civilization," Latin America was subjected to a new colonial pact in which the "liberal" Creole bourgeoisie prevailed as a dominant *class,* and the process of underdevelopment became deeper and more irreversible.

There was a sector of the bourgeoisie that was genuinely conservative, but not everyone who opposed the new colonial pact, the new dependence, and the establishment of the "liberal" bourgeoisie as a dominant class, and opposed its policies of underdevelopment, was necessarily conservative and opposed to progress and civilization. Nor were all those conservative who were seeking an autonomous national kind of development and a policy of protectionism. Moreover, not even all those who remained anachronistically tied to the past were really conservatives. Being attached to the Spanish colonial past meant in some situations a certain resistance to new domination by England. Some other conservative sectors, tied to the previous Spanish colonial system, became genuine defenders of protectionism. That is what happened with the mercantilist monopoly bourgeoisie that had been tied to the Spanish colonial system, and with the coming of independence struggled tirelessly against English trade and contraband. There was also an incipient "industrial bourgeoisie," as well as craft workers who realized that their very existence was threatened by an uncontrolled flood of foreign goods. This very important national sector was protectionist, fiercely opposed to the economic policies of the "liberal" bourgeoisie, and yet it is obvious that it cannot be classified as "conservative."

In addition, the petite bourgeoisie took a nationalistic position, also in the name of liberalism, but a liberalism that was genuine and revolutionary. This sector opposed the "liberal" policies of the bourgeoisie that was seeking a new colonial pact with English capitalism.

Finally, and most importantly, there was the 90 percent of the population of Latin America, those who have always been the "forgotten" in history, that exploited mass of Amerindians, blacks, mestizos, mulattos, and poor whites, who were the main victims of the dependent colonial "liberalism" that intensified poverty and underdevelopment. If objectively these popular sectors made up the pole opposed to the "liberal" and "civilized" bougeoisie, the bulk of the people can in no way be categorized as conservative.

The fact that the dependent "liberal" bourgeoisie was seeking to establish a new colonial pact with England does not mean that in the opposite camp there could not be alliances between conservative sectors, nationalist and protectionist liberal sectors, and the popular sectors. In the countless internal struggles that took place between 1824 and 1870, there often were alliances between the national and protectionist sectors of the bourgeoisie and conservative sectors. There were also convergences and alliances between conservatives and popular sectors, insofar as those sectors were the direct victims of the economic policies of the dependent "liberal" bourgeoisie. Finally, in some very particular situations there can be found among the "liberal" dependent bourgeoisie some positions, values, or policies that were conservative. Antiliberals were often more progressive than the liberals, and anticonservatives were often more backward than the conservatives themselves, particularly if the perspective for examining "liberal" and "conservative" blocs is not merely ideological but economic, social, and political as well.

Rejection of the Liberal-Conservative Interpretation

In conclusion, it must be said that the classic usage of the terms "liberal" and "conservative" during this period (1824–1870) is:

- a false ideological mechanism created by the dependent bourgeoisie to hide and legitimize the neocolonial pact with England and other powers of the age;
- a false way to interpret history, an interpretation made in most cases by the ideological heirs of that dependent "liberal" bourgeoisie;
- a description that is partial, ideological, and confused, and hence unable to express the real and objective contradiction between capitalist and feudal or precapitalist relationships of production within the same Latin American capitalist social system;
- an ideological kind of polarity, one that, by concealing and falsifying matters, prevents a more scientific and objective analysis of the different sectors, strata, groups, factions, or social "classes" in the Latin American social system;
- a kind of polarity that does not cover all the segments or "classes" in the dominant bloc and completely ignores the oppressed and exploited majority.

Thus I believe that this labeling of the conflict ("liberal-conservative") ought to be rejected, or that it should be used only in reference to a certain historical usage—that is, a terminology used in the past by a particular sector of the dominant bourgeoisie. I believe it is more precise and more objective to use a terminology that expresses the economic, social, and political, as well as the ideological, reality of the different groups or social "classes" in Latin America. In speaking of the opposition between liberals and conservatives, it should always be made clear which group or which social "class" is under consideration. Above all, the "liberal-conservative" polarity should be situated in relation to the fundamental contradiction of the period between an economic, political, social, and ideological project that was dependent, pro-free trade, and pro-European, and another one that was national, protectionist, and Latin American in character. The terms "liberal-conservative" should also always be situated in relation to the opposed terms "dominator-dominated" and "development-underdevelopment," because dependence necessarily implied "class" domination and policies that produced dire poverty and underdevelopment.

THE CHURCH AND THE NEW NATIONAL STATES

After clarifying the nature of the basic contradiction in Latin America between 1824 and 1870, I now proceed to examine how the church fitted in. For all the reasons I have already set forth, it is obvious that positing that the basic opposition was that between "liberals" and "conservatives" has enormously misrepresented the history of the Latin American church.

Something immediately obvious is that all the governments that arose out of the struggle for independence wanted to claim the right of *patronato* that the kings of Spain had exercised over the Catholic Church until that time. They not only wanted to inherit the legal control of *patronato* but the abuses that went along with it as well—for example, in the late eighteenth century, King Carlos III's urging the church in Latin America to inculcate into the people veneration for the king and obedience to him. The independent governments believed that it was just as legitimate now for them to have the power to use the church in order to subject the people to the cause of the new governments. It was not just a matter of naming bishops, but rather of state control over ecclesiastical permission to preach and hear confessions, because preaching and hearing confessions were the most usual means for indoctrinating the people. If the king and the church had mutually agreed on using those means to serve colonial domination, there was no reason the new states should give up such a powerful instrument for legitimizing the state and indoctrinating the masses. In order to attain that objective, all the independent governments had no hesitation in declaring Catholicism the official religion of the state, and at first they repulsed any proposal for the separation of church and state.

After the end of the wars for independence, the church experienced a long period of disorganization, dispersion, and almost total breakdown: dioceses with no bishops, parishes and seminaries closed, a considerable drop in the number of clergy involved in pastoral work, doubt or questioning (at least until 1832) about the role the pope might play vis-à-vis the new republics, and especially a great deal of confusion over the role of the church in the Latin American society that had arisen out of the wars for independence. In this situation the Latin American church had to confront three basic tasks:

- rebuilding ecclesiastical structures
- reforming the church internally
- defining the specific role of the church in society vis-à-vis the state—that is, defining the position of the church with regard to the basic contradiction that I have pointed out, and with regard to *patronato* in the broadest sense.

It was very difficult to accomplish these three tasks. In the first place, the Latin American church was quite isolated from Rome. It was only in 1831, with Pope Gregory XVI (1831–1846), that Vatican relationships with the hierarchy in Mexico, Argentina, Uruguay, and Peru began to return to normal. With the pontificate of Pius IX (1846–1878) the situation worsened throughout Latin America as a result of his intransigent stand against any possible accord with "liberal" governments. Pius IX, author of the encyclical *Quanta Cura* and of the *Syllabus* (1864), where "modern society" was unconditionally condemned, could hardly comprehend the course of Latin American governments and the attitude of the Latin American church with regard to those governments. The only approach to solving church-state problems that he accepted was a concordat, but the situation was made more complicated insofar as Rome would sign a concordat only with those Latin American governments that had a "conservative" majority and where there had been a "liberal defeat." Such concordats were signed only in Bolivia (1851), Guatemala and Costa Rica (1852), Haiti (1860), Honduras, Venezuela, and Ecuador (1861), and Colombia (1887). But the conservative "majorities" were unstable and almost always transitory. Relationships with Rome were to take on a different character when the liberal oligarchical state became solidly established in Latin America.

In the second place, the practice of regalism in the new national states made it difficult to reform, rebuild, and redefine the church. This regalism resulted from the convergence of the weakness of the church in dealing with the crisis itself, and the responsibility the states took on for becoming involved in the internal life of the church, and their need to rebuild the church to suit their own political interests. Where the church had neither the will nor the capacity to restructure itself and carry out internal reform, the state felt a right and duty to become involved.

It is important to have a correct understanding of this regalism of Latin American governments during the period following independence. It was not a European-style ancien régime sort of regalism, of the kind that characterized Jansenism, Gallicanism, or Josephism. Nor was it a liberal, atheistic, antireligious, and anticlerical regalism or a regalism under a masonic, heretical, nationalist, or schismatic influence. It was another kind of regalism, usually called "republican." What this means is that once independence from Spain had been achieved, there was a need to be able to rely fully on the church for the task of rebuilding the nations and building the new republican states. The state took responsibility for church reform.

A typical case was that of the reform of Bernardino Rivadavia in Argentina.

Rivadavia was a devout, practicing Catholic, who had clearly felt the influence of the absolutist regalism of Carlos II, but who was now acting as a statesman in a Latin American context. In an authoritarian way, Rivadavia imposed his law of religious reform, without any anti-Catholic or anticlerical spirit, and without the least desire for "secularization." Rivadavia's law suppressed tithes and ecclesiastical courts and law, and changed the cathedral chapter into a civil body (the "senate of the clergy"); it made it obligatory for bishops to have pastoral conferences for the clergy; it provided for an annual budget with outlays for worship to be paid by the state; a minimum age of twenty-five was set for entering the convent, perpetual vows were suppressed, convents could not have less than fifteen nor more than thirty religious, certain orders were suppressed, and church goods that did not serve for worship were confiscated. The clergy and the hierarchy were divided over this reform.[17]

Finally, and most importantly, it was the three centuries of *patronato regio* that made it most difficult for the church to move ahead with the tasks of rebuilding itself, reforming itself internally, and defining its role in society vis-à-vis the state. The church could scarcely imagine how it could manage a thorough rebuilding, or how it could carry out internal reform, without the traditional tutelage and help from the state. The insertion of the church into civil society went by way of its integration into political society, and the state was the pivotal element. Moreover, the church was part of a social order where there had recently taken place a violent clash between two powers: the established and "legitimate" power of the king of Spain and the emerging power of the Latin American revolution for independence. It was not easy for the church to accept that the new republican state was automatically replacing its former patron and protector. Three centuries of the practice of *patronato* made a model of church reform without the mediation of the state unthinkable. Without mediation by the state, the church felt left out of Latin American civil society.

To the extent that this Christendom model went unquestioned, the fate of the church seemed to be inherently bound up with *patronato* and state tutelage. The crisis of the church during the wars of independence meant likewise a crisis for *patronato* and colonial Christendom, but by not questioning the legitimacy or validity of the Christendom model itself, the church made any solution to its internal and social crisis impossible. To rebuild the church and reform it internally called for radical questioning of the Christendom model, but such questioning seemed impossible during that period.

CHAPTER 3

1870–1930:
The Church under the Liberal Oligarchical State

WHY 1870–1930?

I have already provided a justification for my choice of 1870 as the date marking the end of the previous period and the beginning of this one. The date is not a precise point, but rather an intermediate reference point; exact dates varied from country to country. I have also noted that the year 1850, favored by many authors to date the beginning of this period, is too early (see note 3, chap. 2, above). The liberalism of the 1808–1870 period, which took its inspiration from the movement for North American independence, the French revolution, and the European revolutions of 1848, must be distinguished from the revolutionary oligarchical liberalism of the 1870–1930 period which took its inspiration from the English and French positivism of the 1880s. For example, in Mexico there is considerable difference between a Benito Júarez (1857) and a Porfirio Díaz (1877).[1]

The real reform, what is called the liberal reform, took place in Latin America during the last quarter of the nineteenth century when a raw materials export economy came to prevail, and the state was controlled by a dependent oligarchy able to defeat the nationalist bourgeois sectors and consolidate a second colonial pact, this time with England, and soon afterward, with the United States. This economic and political hegemony of the Latin American dependent oligarchy was also closely connected to the restructuring of international capitalism then taking place. Between 1870 and 1880 capitalism was in structural crisis, and monopoly capitalism and modern imperialism were on the rise.

After 1880 the great industrial powers struggled to control the sources of raw materials and markets. Between 1880 and 1914 there was a process of capitalist expansion. Both production and capital were increasingly concentrated, leading to monopoly capitalism, the effect of which was to reinforce the bonds of colonial domination over Latin America and over other Third World regions. The Creole oligarchies emerged as the dominant "class" in each of the Latin American countries by accepting a dependent relationship with imperialist monopoly capitalism. I cannot posit the formation of the liberal state, dominated by this dependent oligarchy, as being prior to this vital transformation of international capital and the new relationships of domination that flowed from it.

The fact that the Latin American economy came to be bound up with dependence on international monopoly capitalism during this period meant that Latin America was irreversibly headed toward underdevelopment. The centers of monopoly capitalism imposed a kind of development of the economic and social structures of Latin America that was based on exporting raw materials and agricultural products and importing manufactured industrial products. The connection between the new colonial dependence and the domination of the liberal oligarchy, which stood at the root of the increasing underdevelopment of the subjugated majorities, meant that from this period onward the struggle against underdevelopment was a struggle against the oligarchies and national dependence. The struggle against underdevelopment and for the liberation of the exploited masses was simultaneously an anti-oligarchical struggle and a nationalist, anti-imperialist struggle. This was likewise the context in which the Latin American labor movement began to develop during this period. The rebuilding of the church—its own reform, and redefinition of its role in civil society—likewise took on new and specific characteristics during this period.

As a closing date for this period I have chosen 1930, and almost all commentators are in agreement. It betokens the great crisis of international monopoly capitalism, and consequently, in Latin America, the crisis of the Creole oligarchies and the liberal state. Almost everywhere in Latin America, 1930 marked the beginning of a growing process of industrialization. Nationalist and populist movements and ideologies also appeared on the scene. Yet 1930 is not an absolute date. The crisis of capitalism reached its high point and became most spectacular with the depression in 1929, but the crisis as such extended from 1914 to 1945—that is, it embraced the whole period from the outbreak of World War I (1914-1918) to the end of World War II (1939-1945).

FUNDAMENTAL CONTRADICTION BETWEEN THE LIBERAL STATE AND THE MASSES

It was not the conservative sector of the oligarchy that constituted the only opposition to the liberal reform of the 1870-1930 period, nor was that even the basic polarity. I have already insisted on this point in connection with the 1808-1870 period, and I must make the point again here: the opposite pole of the liberal reform—indeed its main victim—was that of the poor and exploited population of Latin America—the campesinos, Amerindians, and mestizos, who were despoiled of their lands, who underwent political and cultural repression, and were often subject to genocide during this liberal period, as a consequence of the need to adapt agrarian structures to the demands of agro-export production. The liberal polemics against "conservatism" and "clericalism" on behalf of "freedom" and "progress" naturally made use of this "ideological disguise" to mask and justify the merciless exploitation of the poor majorities in Latin America.

During this period the church also experienced polarization and was also a prisoner of liberal reform, for it was little aware of the broad masses of the population experiencing repression and exploitation under liberalism and the church was becoming further removed from that population. Polarized by the liberal reform, and always fighting to defend its "legitimate rights" in connection with the liberal state, the church became separated from the people, most of whom continued to regard themselves as Catholics. Further on, I shall examine why the church strayed from its true path socially, politically and pastorally, and examine the consequences of that straying for the process of restructuring, reform, and redefinition. First, however, an understanding of the effects of the liberal reform during the period of the oligarchical liberal state must be deepened, in order to better perceive the functioning of this ideological mechanism, which served to conceal and justify the neocolonial exploitation of Latin America, and which, among other effects, proved capable of leading the church astray, both socially and politically, disrupting it, and manipulating it ideologically.

Positivism in Latin America

Liberal thought during the period of the oligarchical liberal state (1870–1930) was basically dominated by what has come to be known as positivism.[2] In Latin America, this term is equivocal. In the strict sense, it designates the philosophical school of Auguste Comte. But in a broader sense it is used in Latin America to designate other currents of thought: Darwinian evolutionism, Herbert Spencer's historical evolutionism, which applied Darwin's ideas to society and history, and the thought of William Graham Sumner, who transformed this historical evolutionism into the credo underlying North American sociology. The term "positivism" is also used for the utilitarianism of Bentham or John Stuart Mill, which had a decisive influence on the Latin American intellectual bourgeoisie.

Positivism embraces not only these currents and those of other thinkers in philosophical schools; in an even broader sense, it distinguishes a certain *way of thinking* typical of the period under study, one that many other writers have described as "scientism." It is a way of thinking, a method, or indeed a whole culture, that seeks to be completely "scientific"—that is, seeks to apply the methods of the natural sciences to all branches of knowledge, and thus to the historical, social, and human sciences. Hence positivism is experienced in Latin America in an overall fashion as a "scientific" way of thinking, a "scientific" attitude, which seeks to guide and rule economics, politics (especially in countries like Mexico, Brazil, or Argentina), and civil society as a whole, and especially the realm of education. It is on the basis of this broad sense that positivism becomes a political ideology, a worldvision, and in some (not merely exceptional) cases, a certain kind of "secularized and enlightened religion."

If positivism in Europe represented a philosophical current that followed the scientific revolution of capitalism and whose particular purpose was to gain mastery of that revolution through thinking, in dependent and underdeveloped Latin America, where no scientific revolution had taken place, "positivism"(evolutionism, utilitarianism, scientism, etc.) became the theoretical and ideological expression of the practice of domination on the part of the "liberal" Creole oligarchies. That was no historical accident, for there was a close structural connection, on the economic and cultural level, between Latin American *external dependence* on the industrialized and developed centers of capitalism, and the *internal domination* exercised by Latin American local oligarchies. If the colonial exploitation of Latin America was carried out in the name of progress and modernization, it was only to be expected that the dependent Latin American oligarchies would seek to disguise and rationalize colonial dependence and internal class domination by likewise utilizing, in a dependent and "class" manner, the philosophical currents and schools of thought that had arisen in the centers of imperialism and monopoly capitalism. Latin American Creole oligarchies, having become disciples of Comte, Spencer, Bentham, or Mill, translated into a practice of exploitation what in the developed countries was an academic or philosophical practice, with no great political consequences. Economic and political neocolonialism could not help but create cultural, philosophical, ideological, and spiritual neocolonialism.

During this period the reaction against the positivism that prevailed among the liberal oligarchy was reflected from different perspectives: on the one hand there were nationalist currents, anti-oligarchical and anticolonial in nature (and here I must mention one of the greatest Latin American writers of all, the Cuban, José Martí, 1853–1895); and then there were conservative hispanicizing currents, represented by those who rejected Anglo-Saxon imperialism and sought to save Latin American culture on the basis of its roots in the Hispanic tradition. There were, in addition, those who sought to overcome positivism by moving within other philosophical horizons, such as the Brazilian Raimondo Farias Brito (1862–1917), and the Uruguayan José Enrique Rodo (1871–1917). With regard to the universities, resistance to the positivist oligarchies led to the astonishing reform in Argentina in 1918, and in Peru in 1919, which were efforts to democratize the university and bring it closer to the people.

This was also one of the most outstanding periods for Latin American literature, with the advent of the "modernist" movement (a very misleading term), which also expressed a reaction against the prevalent neocolonial positivist cluture. The most noteworthy writers in this movement are Julian de

Casal (Cuba, 1863–1916), Manuel Gutiérrez Májera (Mexico 1859–1895), José Asunción Silva (Colombia, 1865–1896), Rubén Darío (Nicaragua, 1867–1916) Amado Nervo (Mexico, 1870–1919), and Carlos Pezoa Véliz (Chile, 1870–1908).

Popular Struggles against the State and the Liberal Oligarchy

The most significant resistance to the domination of the liberal state and the Latin American dependent oligarchy is to be found among the popular "classes" whose organizations and political parties arose precisely during this period (1870–1930).[3] The great missing element in Latin American history books is always the popular movement. Here I recall simply some facts that are essential for reconstituting a minimal historical frame of reference that will enable me to examine and evaluate the development of the Latin American church during this period.

Among the precursors of the Latin American social and labor movement, there was the revolutionary liberal petite bourgeoisie of the nineteenth century, that spread what is called the "utopian socialism" of Saint-Simon, Fourier, and Proudhon. There appeared organized groups such as the "Association of May" set up in Buenos Aires by Esteban Etcheverria (1838), or the "Society for Equality" created in 1850 in Santiago, Chile, by Francisco Bilbao and Santiago Arcos. Associations with socialist tendencies were also in evidence in Brazil, Uruguay, Colombia, and Mexico. But this first stage was rudimentary and had little contact with the masses.

During the second half of the nineteenth century there began a second stage, when mutual-aid societies became important, as did groups of craft workers, societies of artists and professionals, and many other guilds and worker associations. During this period the anarchist and anarcho-syndicalist ideas of Bakunin (1814–1876), Kropotkin (1842–1905), and others had considerable influence. European immigrants played a key role in introducing socialist ideas, particularly after 1870. Many of them were refugees fleeing Europe after workers had been defeated (as in the case of the Paris Commune) or after persecutions of socialists (for example, in Germany under Bismarck).

A third phase of the social and popular movement began at the end of the nineteenth century. During this third phase (from 1890 to 1930, and running more or less parallel to the stage of the oligarchical liberal state), a significant working class took shape in Latin America, especially in Mexico, Brazil, Argentina, Chile, Uruguay, and Colombia. The popular movement began to get beyond the first phase of liberal radicalism and the second phase of anarchism and anarcho-syndicalism that characterized the nineteenth centruy. Marxist currents began to penetrate into the Latin American labor movement. The first Marxist-influenced national and continental political organizations made their appearance. Although the International Association of Workers (AIT), known in history as the First International, dated from 1864, its influence in Latin America comes only later.[4]

Let me now point out some significant examples. In Mexico around the 1870s there was a proliferation of working-class publications. A few translated titles reflect the character of this period: The Socialist, The International, The Son of Labor, The Commune, Strike, The International Worker. In 1872 the "Circle of Workers of Mexico" was founded, and in 1888 the first known Spanish translation of the Communist Manifesto was published. The anarchist movement still continued and found expression, for example, in the armed revolts of the Flores Magon brothers between 1900 and 1910 (with their famous slogan "Land and Liberty!").

In Argentina there was a direct connection with the AIT, especially among immigrant workers. As early as the 1870s there was a French, Italian, and Spanish AIT branch, and its influence was spreading to Argentinian workers. In Uruguay the process was quite similar. In Chile the influence of the AIT arrived later, although it was there that the labor movement, under the influence of socialist and Marxist ideas, expanded most fully during this period and was best organized. Two institutions were particularly important, the Labor Federation of Chile (FOCH) set up in 1909, and the Socialist Worker Party (POS), founded in 1912. Here I should note the work of one of the greatest Latin American labor leaders, Luis Emilio Recabarren (1876-1924).[5] There was also an interesting labor movement in Cuba, which also witnessed considerable immigration from Spain. These cores of an internationalist and revolutionary proletariat in Latin America, small as they were, were important, for they were the starting point for what would develop into a much more extensive labor movement.

Socialist Movements of a "Messianic" Nature

I cannot overlook the social movements of a popular-messianic nature taking place during this period. Religion was blended with social protest. The best known examples were in Brazil: the "war of the Canudos" in 1897, led by Antônio Maciel ("the counselor"), and the rebellions in Contestado (southern Brazil) lasting from 1910 to 1916, led by João Maria and José Maria de Agostinho (see the works of Maria Isaura Pereira de Queiroz). The fact that popular religiosity serves as a vehicle for insurrections of a popular character (something common in Latin America) raises the question of the ambiguity of religion as both *protest* and *alienation*. When the institutional churches seem to be too tied to the state and to the ruling classes, popular religion often takes on forms revealing a class content antagonistic to domination.

The Mexican Revolution and the End of the Oligarchical State of Porfirio Díaz

The most significant event among the popular classes in Latin America during this period was undoubtedly the Mexican revolution, 1910-1920, which put an end to the liberal oligarchical state of Porfirio Díaz. An examination of this revolution, still scarcely known in the rest of Latin America, could provide a key for understanding how the transition from a liberal oligarchical state to a populist state took place in Latin America, and what role the peasant and popular classes played in that process. As is the case with every revolution, this one clearly reveals those laws of history that remain hidden during normal times. Every revolution, whether victorious or not, is a privileged moment for the overall interpretation of the history of a people. The Mexican revolution is of very special interest for all Latin America because the nature of the different social classes is revealed with such clarity, as are their true interests, and the way they actually behave in history when decisive class contradictions are being manifested.

In the Mexican revolution there were several revolutions taking place at once: the revolution of Francisco Indalecio Madero, that of Venustiano Carranza and the "constitutionalists," and the revolutions of Pancho Villa and Emiliano Zapata. Studying the dialectic of these manifold revolutions going on at the same time and within the same revolutionary process would no doubt be the kind of research most relevant for understanding Mexico even up to the present. Such a study would also be illuminating for Latin America as a whole. Given the limits of the present work, however, I cannot go into such a study here.

The Rise of the Middle Classes against the Liberal State

During this period in Latin America there appeared other movements of resistance to the liberal oligarchy, tied to the incipient "middle classes." As an example I may cite "Battleism" in Uruguay, named after its founder, President José Battle y Ordoñez, who was the dominant figure in Uruguayan political life from 1904 to 1929. In Argentina there was the "Yrigoyenism" of Hipolito Yrigoyen, whose party, the Radical Civic Union, governed the country from 1916 to 1930. In several Latin American countries during this period some liberal parties developed a "left wing," giving rise to what were called radical parties, which normally represented the interests of the "middle classes." These social and political groups, under certain circumstances, managed to take *governance* out of the hands of liberal oligarchies, but they never took over *power*. As long as the liberal oligarchies were not in crisis and the popular classes were not on the rise, the social and political movements of the middle classes remained very weak and were not able to set up any alternative to the dominant system. That is why—as will be seen later—the church did not open itself to the middle strata before 1930 or even 1950, depending on the country.

The Church vis-à-vis the Oligarchical Liberal State

I can now examine, somewhat schematically but within the historical framework just sketched, the situation of the church and how it evolved during the period of the liberal oligarchical state in Latin America (1870–1930).

In order to make clearer what is peculiar to church-state relationships during this period, I begin by distinguishing three stages in the evolution of these relationships in the course of the nineteenth (and the beginning of the twentieth) century:

First stage, 1808–1824 (approximately)—the struggle for independence: conflict with the church to the extent that it seemed to be tied up with Spanish colonial power. There was no rejection of the hierarchical church as such, but simply of its colonial character. The basic value affirmed by the political power coming into being throughout this period was that of autonomy—freedom vis-à-vis colonial power.

Second stage, 1824–1870 (approximately): formation of new national states. The state did not regard the church as tied to Spanish colonial power (previous stage) but rather as a church that still retained considerable social and political power within Latin American society. Hence, the state did not seek to *decolonize* the church but rather to *utilize* it as a force for legitimizing the state. In order for the church to be able to carry out this role, the state felt it had the right and duty to restructure and reform it (republican regalism). The aim was to subject the church to the state so as to subject and unify civil society as a whole. At this point the basic value affirmed by the state was no longer freedom, but national unity, which actually meant the hegemony of one sector of the Creole bourgeoisie over another.

Third stage: 1870–1930 (approximately): the liberal oligarchical state. At this point the state did not regard the church as a colonial power (first stage), or as a potential agent for legitimizing the state (second stage), but as a social and political force contrary to the interests of the state and society. If during the previous stages the state sought to decolonize the church or to subordinate it to the state, now it tended to reject it as a social institution. The state was no longer seeking legitimation from the church. Republican regalism tended to disappear. The state was no longer interested in reforming the church but rather in breaking it up as a social institution. The basic value for the liberal oligarchical state was not freedom, but material progress. Such progress was understood, as I have pointed out, in a "positivist" or "scientistic" sense. The state now regarded the church not as an institution standing in the way of freedom and Latin American autonomy vis-à-vis colonial power, or as an element that threatened national unity, but as a social institution impeding the "scientific progress" of humankind for which the state felt responsible. For the oligarchical state and positivist liberalism, the church was neither a colonial power nor a power for legitimizing the state, but an institution that was "antiscientific" and therefore "irrational," one that was opposed to "progress" and "modernization." During this stage there was almost a breach between church and state, and it occurred precisely at the peak of the crisis of colonial Christendom.

Secularization

I believe it is profoundly erroneous to categorize this whole evolution of the state and civil society vis-à-vis the church, especially during the period of the liberal state, as a process of *secularization*. There may be some secondary secularizing effects, but the core of the process was not a secularization—that is, an affirmation of the autonomy of secular society over against the church as a religious and sacral power. What is called secularization in Latin America is another version of the ideological mechanism I have already described, the one used by the liberal dependent oligarchy in Latin America to disguise and rationalize neocolonial dependence, and the domination and exploitation of the bulk of the people. There is a direct and essential connection between the political use of "positivism" and "scientism" by the Latin American ruling classes, and those classes' establishment of a neocolonial, dependent, and exploitive social system. The agent of "modernization" and "secularization" in Latin America during this period was the liberal oligarchy. The problem is not that of the "autonomy of the temporal" vis-à-vis the religious power of the church, but the problem of the "political hegemony" of the liberal oligarchy over the whole of civil society.

There is a basic difference between positivism and secularization in the developed European countries and in a dependent and underdeveloped Latin America. In Europe the industrial bourgeoisie affirmed its economic and political autonomy against a feudal power in which the church played a hegemonic role. Thus, hand in hand with the bourgeois revolution (industrial, scientific, political, and cultural) went a genuine liberal revolution, serving as a process of secularization. The situation in Europe changed when the bourgeoisie lost its revolutionary character and became the ruling class. But in Latin America the process was radically different. To begin with, there was no centuries-old feudal past. Latin America did not arise out of a feudal past, but rather as part of the process of the expansion of mercantile capitalism. In Latin America the agent of modernization was not the industrial bourgeoisie, but landowners, mine owners, and merchants.

After attaining independence from Spain and Portugal, the Creole bourgeoisie struggled not for economic and political autonomy but, on the contrary, in order to establish a bond of dependence and subordination to European monopoly capitalism. What stood in the way of this dependent bourgeoisie was not the remainder of a feudal past, but the social and political forces victimized by this dependence and subordination. That is why the "antifeudal," and "anticlerical" discourse of the Latin American oligarchy, along with its "secularizing," "liberal," and "positivist-scientistic" discourse, had no material or social basis to support it. It was and is an ideological discourse, a false discourse. In a situation of dependence it sought to copy the discourse of the European bourgeoisie, but it did so in order to serve economic and social interests quite different from those of the European bourgeoisie. The discourse is the same, but the historical processes were different.

The Latin American bourgeoise, as a dependent bourgeoisie, never had its own thought, whether liberal or positivist, that could provide the basis for an authentic secularization. The dependent oligarchy simply made use of liberal-positivist-secularizing discourse—false and ideological discourse—in order to disguise and justify its own dependence and class rule. If there was any thought that was genuinely Latin American, it existed only among the anticolonial and anti-oligarchical national sectors and among the popular sectors, or sectors linked to the interests of the people.

When, for example, in Argentina during the 1880s (under the Roca government), the church was persecuted in the name of "science" and "progress," and when in May 1882 there was a national celebration in honor of Darwin in order to convince the people of contradictions between religion and science, that was not a "secularization crusade" but a campaign for ideological domination over the people. The ferocity of the anticlerical struggle in Latin America is not explicable as part of a secularization process like the one that took place in eighteenth- and nineteenth-century Europe, but only as part of an ideological process demanded by the economic and political contradictions emerging in Latin America during this period.

From another angle, an argument that can be brought forward is that of the strong antipopular character of positivism and liberalism, and how foreign they were to the reality of Latin America. It was the product of elites completely isolated from the reality of their nations and the popular classes. What is called the process of "secularization" was actually a process that estranged Latin America from its own autochthonous popular culture.

BASIC OPTIONS OF THE CHURCH
TOWARD THE LIBERAL STATE

After this summary examination of the attitude of the liberal state toward the church, it is time to consider the attitude of the church toward the liberal state and its dominant "positivist" or "scientistic" ideology. It would take another volume to study the situation country by country. Here I simply present the basic options taken by the Latin American church during the 1870–1930 period. There were of course important differences from country to country. Some processes moved further ahead, while others lingered behind. Historical processes took different forms in accordance with the economic, political, or cultural conditions in diverse regions. But these secondary differences do not obscure the basic options taken by the church. Those options were not made in a vacuum, nor did one simply evolve from another. Rather, they emerged from within complex and contradictory historical situations.

1. The Traditional Option

The church went on as it had during the previous period and as though there had been no basic change within the state. The church sought to defend and safeguard its legal, social, and political rights vis-à-vis the liberal state in two ways: *directly*, by signing a concordat (or some similar kind of agreement) with the state; or *indirectly*, by forming an alliance with the conservative Catholic oligarchy, which invoked the church in defending its own rights vis-à-vis the state.

2. The Option for Education, the Family, and Devotional Practices

The church stood up to the state and its positivist ideology, not only in the realm of political struggle, but also in the social realm of family and education. In this realm the church put the emphasis on the formation of conscience and on devotional practices. Rejected by the state, the church tended to withdraw into itself, and to privatize Catholicism, by reducing it to a purely individual and familial dimension. During this period, the church dedicated most of its energies and its best resources to educational and devotional activities.

It should be kept in mind that, like the previous option, this one aimed at reconquering a dominant position within civil society as a whole, and it looked for support primarily among the ruling "classes" and the state. This overall aim of the church was reflected in its educational and devotional practice, which was aimed at the wealthiest and most powerful social classes or sectors, and was usually limited to them. The church wanted to be able to stand up to the state and prevail, and to regain its social power by influencing those young persons who would later exercise political and social power. The purpose of private Catholic schools was to form Catholic elites that would defend the rights of the church within the state, and through them, within the whole of civil society. The fact that the church turned to the realm of education did not at all mean that it was giving up its Christendom model.

3. The Option for Europeanizing and Romanizing the Church

The Latin American church sought to rebuild itself socially and internally with the support and aid of European (Italian, French, Spanish) churches and especially the church in Rome. The estrangement of the Latin American church from the liberal state inclined it to become europeanized and romanized. Until (approximately) 1870 the church was tied to the state in the centuries-old tradition of *patronato*. As it moved beyond that tradition, the Latin American church sought to establish direct ties to the church of Rome. For its part, Rome tried to strengthen its direct influence on the Latin American churches. For that purpose Pius IX in 1859 set up the Collegio Pio Latinoamericano in Rome, for the training of future Latin American bishops, romanized and removed from the reality of Latin America. Roman centralism was reinforced with the First Vatican Council (1869-1870). The romanization of the Latin American church reached its high point with the celebration of the Latin American Plenary Council, held in Rome in 1899.

The situation of the church during this period (1870-1930) is highlighted by a twofold parallel development. First, there was the *dependence of the state* and of the liberal oligarchy on the centers of monopoly capitalism, and the increasing *dependence of the church* on its center in Rome during this same period. Secondly, there was the *imperialist expansion* of monopoly capitalism after 1880, which was paralled by the *expansion of the European religious orders* toward Latin America during this same period. The phenomena were strikingly parallel, although to treat them as cause and effect would be simplistic. Nevertheless, they shared much the same basic orientation.

CHAPTER 4

1930–1960:
The Church and Populist, Nationalist, and Developmentalist Movements

From 1930 onward a very radical economic, political, cultural, and ideological change took place throughout Latin America, caused by the structural crisis of the capitalist system, starting in 1914, peaking in 1929, and stretching into the mid-1940s. With the worldwide crisis there came to be a *reformulation of the relationships of dependence* on an imperialistic hegemonic center (which has now shifted from England to the United States) and an *internal reformulation of economic and class structures* in Latin America. The most obvious aspects of this transformation were: the beginnings of a process of industrialization aimed at "import substitution" in Latin America; wild acceleration in urban growth; a population explosion; broadening of internal markets to absorb internal production ("inward-directed" mode of accumulation); grassroots reforms (agrarian reform, electoral reform, educational reform, etc.) needed for broadening internal markets; the rise of a new hegemonic sector of the bourgeoisie (the "national-developmentalist" industrial bourgeoisie); the replacement of the liberal-oligarchical state by the interventionist, democratic, or populist state; the expansion, politicization, and mobilization of the "middle strata" and the popular classes; an alliance between the industrial bourgeoisie and the working class (populism).

LATIN AMERICA AND THE SOCIALIST ALTERNATIVE

The new element that entered history during the 1914–1945 crisis period was the fact that the bourgeoisie and imperialism no longer offered the only solution to the crisis of capitalism; with the Bolshevik revolution of October 1917, there appeared the possibility of a socialist solution to the crisis. The People's Republic of China was established in 1948; between 1945 and 1949 the East European bloc of socialist countries was formed; between 1950 and 1953 imperialism was halted in Korea; in 1959 the Cuban revolution was victorious; in 1962 the Democratic People's Republic of Algeria was proclaimed.

At the end of World War I, the Third Socialist International was set up, in the belief that the Russian revolution was going to spread over the world and that the International would lead that revolution. Between 1918 and 1928 there were insurrectionary situations around the world. In 1928 the Third International thought the end of capitalism was imminent, and that the main obstacle to "world revolution" was social democracy, which it must therefore combat. In 1935 the situation changed abruptly and the International decided to become allied with sectors of the bourgeoisie in order to combat fascism; popular fronts were formed.

At the end of World War II, after talks between the United States, England, and the U.S.S.R., the world was divided into two large spheres of influence. The only concern of the U.S.S.R. was to establish a broad security belt to defend Soviet space. The "proletarian internationalism" of the 1918-1935 period was dropped and the strategy became one of world revolution starting from the Soviet Union (national socialism). The Soviets also stopped supporting the revolutionary circles that had been springing up around the world, and the "Cold War" began. China, Korea, and Southeast Asia turned away from the rest of the world. Capitalist reorganization and recovery during the 1945-1967 period was aided both by developments within the international socialist movement after 1935, and by the ability of capitalism to control and restrain the labor movement.

All these events would have a direct and important influence on Latin America. To a great extent, they explain how popular and leftist movements unfolded throughout the area (and particularly the aversion of the industrial bourgeoisie vis-à-vis populist and nationalist objectives).

The 1929 crisis of capitalism in the industrialized centers of Europe and the United States, and the consequent weakening of the bonds of dependence, created economic and political conditions in Latin America that "resulted in the beginning of the area's strongest nationalist policy and the biggest *independent industrialization* drive since the post-independence 1830s and 1840s."[1] This effort at *independent national industrialization* did not take place evenly throughout Latin America. It was especially important in those countries where, when the crisis broke out, the Creole bourgeoisie held control over the main export products and also where the internal market had expanded to a certain point and was well organized (as was the case in Argentina, Mexico, Brazil, Chile, Colombia, and Uruguay). In the other Latin American countries the process of "national" industrialization was a result of the expansion and integration of international monopoly capital, especially after 1950. In these countries foreign capital had such complete control over the raw materials export sector that the exploitation of national wealth benefited only the neocolonial metropolis and *never provided a thrust for the overall economy and society of the nation*. That is why in these countries there did not arise a "national bourgeoisie" capable of transforming, modernizing, or democratizing them. There was instead a parasitic bourgeoisie getting rich by serving foreign capital.[2]

If differences in the industrialization process from country to country are set aside, a common element can be seen in the fact that the *process of crisis* in the countries of the imperialist center meant that the Latin American periphery had a chance at a more autonomous and more "inward-directed" *development*, and that the process of *recovery and expansion* of transnational monopoly capitalism meant that Latin America was once more thrust toward rapid *underdevelopment* and the sharpening of the contradictions between a minority getting richer every day and a majority getting poorer every day. There was a direct connection between the *expansion of capitalism* in the industrialized centers, and the *reinforcement of relationships of domination-dependence*, intensification of *underdevelopment*, and sharpening of *class struggle* in the dependent countries. It was that direct connection that caused the struggle against underdevelopment, the anti-imperialist and national liberation struggle, and the struggle of the exploited classes against the Creole bourgeoisie and the capitalist system, to converge into a single movement in history.

This situation, which was *specific* to *dependent* and *underdeveloped capitalist* countries, provides me with the key for a basic interpretation of the 1930–1960 period in Latin America, and especially for interpreting the crisis of the populist, nationalist, and developmentalist movements during those years, as well as for understanding the *cause* of the political radicalization of the revolutionary movement of the 1960s and 1970s. All projects of *national liberation* (against economic, political, cultural *dependence*) and projects of development (against economic, political, or cultural *underdevelopment*) in the end were woven together into a *single project* to build a *Latin American socialism* within the dialectic of class struggle within history (against economic, political, and cultural *capitalist domination*). This maturation process, which by the 1960s and 1970s was *revolutionary, class-based,* and *socialist*, was the outgrowth of a slow preparation, starting with the *nationalist* and *developmentalist* movements of the 1930–1960 period. It is from this historical perspective that I shall seek to interpret and evaluate that period.

The Church and Nationalism, Latinamericanization, and Development

What has been said in the preceding paragraphs also provides me with a key for interpreting the New Christendom of the Latin American church during the same period. Starting in 1930, and especially after 1945, the church was deeply affected by the awakening to *nationalism* and *development* in Latin America. In the project of Latin American national liberation and proposals to overcome underdevelopment, the church saw a real possibility of rebuilding its own project, that of New Christendom, on a new foundation. The nationalist and developmentalist project enabled the church to advance in two directions: on the one hand, this project seemed to stand in contradiction, and as an alternative, to the *laicist-positivist liberalism* of the dominant oligarchies throughout the previous period (approximately 1870–1930); on the other hand, nationalism and developmentalism seemed to oppose, and to stand as an alternative to, the *atheistic* and *materialistic socialist tendencies* of the organized labor movement (against the international background of the October 1917 revolution and, after 1948, the "Cold War"). By opting for nationalism and panamericanism, and for the struggle against underdevelopment, the church was able to distance itself from "laicist positivist liberalism" and from "atheistic materialistic socialism." This option was not purely ideological; its social basis lay in the church's break with the old oligarchies and an alliance with the incipient bourgeoisies that were linked to industrialization and to regional and national interests; its political basis lay in the church's alliance with the state, and with parties or movements of a populist, nationalist, or developmentalist nature.

Dismantling and Rebuilding New Christendom

This conversion of New Christendom to the aims of nationalism and development enabled it to get beyond a series of limitations and contradictions characteristic of the period before 1930 (see the preceding chapter).

First, the church managed to free itself, or to move out of, the polarization between conservatism and liberalism. That polarization limited, falsified, and nullified the church's action, because the ideology of the period falsely presented and interpreted its opposition to liberalism as opposition to "progress," "science," and "modernity." The church moved beyond the "conservative-liberal" polarization, to a polarization of "national (or Latin American) liberation vs. foreign domination or dependence," and "development vs. underdevelopment." Henceforth, the church could stand up to positivist liberalism on the basis of a nationalist-developmentalist position that could hardly be interpreted as conservative.

Secondly, the nationalist and developmentalist project forced the church to move beyond its generally europeanized and romanized manner. From 1930 onwards, there was a slow process of nationalization and latinamericanization of the church, and a positive appreciation of Latin American identity and of its own particular culture.

Thirdly, the option of the church with regard to national and Latin American problems, and with regard to social problems and the problems of underdevelopment, made it move out of the purely devotional, familial, and educational atmosphere in which it had been immured during the period prior to 1930.

Finally, the nationalist, populist, and developmentalist project enabled the church to expand its social base beyond the narrow circle of the oligarchical elites in which it had been enclosed, toward the "middle strata" and the broad masses. In doing so, not only did it not have to break with the state and the dominant classes but it could even use their support and improve its own relationships with them.

In a word, the church was able to change and to strengthen its presence and power within civil society by dismantling conservative (antiliberal) Christendom, and by restructuring a New Christendom, which could be called "populist, nationalist, Latin American, culturalist, and developmentalist" (but antisocialist). The key for interpreting the transformation of the church during the 1930–1960 period lay in the *opposition between these two models of New Christendom*. (There is no question yet of the phenomenon I shall examine further on in dealing with the period from 1960 to the present, when the contradiction is no longer between two models of New Christendom but between Christendom and church, between the new developmentalist Christendom and a church that is beyond, and opposed to, any conceivable project of Christendom, and which I shall call the "popular church.")

The restructuring of New Christendom during the 1930–1960 period led directly to the crisis of this New Christendom during the 1960s and 1970s. Yet the hierarchical church had difficulty realizing that it was leading New Christendom toward its own crisis and possible dissolution. Starting especially in the 1950s and into the period of the Second Vatican Council (1962–1965), the Latin American church restructured New Christendom with relative ease, security, optimism, and even some triumphalism. This attitude and mind-set on the part of the church was rooted in history and was political, social, and ideological in nature. Politically, the church enjoyed excellent relationships with populist, nationalist, or developmentalist states; socially, the church broke with the older liberal oligarchies and quickly extended its influence among the emerging bourgeoisie, and to the middle and popular sectors; ideologically, the church found its own clearly defined identity, which differed both from "positivist and laicist liberalism" and from "atheistic and materialistic socialism." Nevertheless, this "social consciousness" of New Christendom concealed the longer-term process of its own crisis and destruction.

In part 3 of this work I shall analyze the basic elements in this crisis process (from 1960 to the present), but it is essential to understand that these elements were already in place when New Christendom was being built up during the 1930–1960 period. The crisis was implicit in the very identity of New Christendom, whose basic option against underdevelopment (and for development) and against dependence (and for national liberation) led inevitably toward an option against the capitalist system itself (and for a certain kind of socialism). The reason why things moved this way, as shown above, lay in the fact that underdevelopment and dependence were rooted in capitalism—that is, in the dependent and underdeveloped character of the capitalist system in Latin America.

PART TWO—CONCLUSIONS

As I finish my analysis of the crisis of colonial Christendom and the advent of a New Christendom in Latin America between 1808 and 1960, I draw two general conclusions.

1. Throughout all these years, the model that the church adhered to for its structure was that of colonial Christendom.

2. The church's success in building up a New Christendom, especially between 1945 and 1960, was only apparent; my examination of history has shown that the crisis of colonial Christendom, which began in 1808, had never been overcome.

On the basis of these conclusions I could put forth a third: the basic reason why New Christendom was unable to respond to the crisis of colonial Christendom lay in the church's own inability, up to around 1960, to subject the structure of the Christendom model to a radical, critical analysis. The church sought to rebuild a New Christendom without undergoing the prior and basic effort of subjecting the Christendom framework itself to an overall critique. That is what led me to state that the process of crisis in colonial Christendom, which began during the nineteenth century, is not yet over; moreover, the gradual rebuilding of New Christendom, because it was an insufficient response to the crisis of colonial Christendom, more and more concealed the root of the crisis. By legitimizing the Christendom framework itself, it also stood in the way of a solution.

Thus I believe that, because it was an inadequate response to the crisis of colonial Christendom, New Christendom undoubtedly sharpened the direct contradiction between *Christendom* and *church* throughout the whole 1808–1960 cycle. Throughout the preceding analysis of history I have shown that the underlying structure of Christendom—always maintained and never critiqued—followed the lines of the twofold relationship of church-state and church-society. The church sought to extend its influence and power in *society* by taking advantage of the mediation of the *state*. The relationship of the church to civil society passed through the relationship of the church to political society. Hence, Christendom necessarily implied that the church enter an alliance with the system and with the ruling classes.

Certainly, even during the colonial period (especially during the sixteenth century) and during the neocolonial period (especially during the first half of the nineteenth century) there was something of a church (with minority status, of course, and not very well organized) standing in contradiction to political power, whether colonial or neocolonial, and hence already tending to appear as a church outside—and in contradiction to—the model and structure of Christendom. Yet this contradiction between Christendom and church did not come to constitute a decisive and fundamental contradiction until the 1960s. Nevertheless, it is clear that the rise of this New Christendom helped pave the way to this contradiction and to the development of its essential elements.

PART THREE

1960–1985: The Crisis of New Christendom in Latin America

It is my hypothesis that during the 1960s there began a structural crisis that affected both Latin American Christendom and the church bound up with that Christendom. Such was the nature of this crisis that it opened a third large cycle in the history of the church in Latin America. I have dated the first cycle from 1492 to 1808 (from the discovery of the Americas to the beginning of the independence struggles), and the second from 1808 to the 1960s. During the first or colonial cycle (first colonial pact), Latin American Christendom was set up (part 1 of this study); during the second or neocolonial cycle (second colonial pact), which I have subdivided into three periods (1808–1870, 1870–1930, 1930–1960), New Christendom was established (part 2 of this study). The crisis of Latin American New Christendom began with the advent of the structural crisis within the capitalist system, the crisis of Latin American dependent capitalism, and the internal restructuring of economic, political, and ideological relationships starting during the 1960s (heading toward a third colonial pact?).

This period may lead one way or the other: either the New Christendom characteristic of the pre-1960 period will be radically transformed into a new model of New Christendom (in line with the new model of domination and with the authoritarian states), or a process of the final breakdown and dissolution of this New Christendom is now underway. The results of my inquiry incline me toward this latter possibility, because in most Latin American countries today there is beginning to appear a church that is either beyond the New Christendom model or has clearly broken away from it. It is during the 1960s and 1970s that for the first time in the history of Latin America there is a direct contradiction between Christendom and church: *one will be able to survive only if the other disappears. This process of contradiction is out in the open, but it might take some decades for the outcome to be decided one way or the other.*

However, the very process of crisis in New Christendom and the fact that New Christendom and church are in conflict justify the periodization I have adopted. In chapter 5 I examine the basic lines for interpreting the crisis of the capitalist system and the historical processes that have a direct bearing on the crisis of New Christendom, and the advent of a church standing in opposition to that Christendom. In chapter 6 I examine these same processes concretely in the cases of Argentina and Brazil. In chapter 7 I analyze the awakening and the concomitant theoretical reflection that took place during the 1960s and 1970s in Latin America as an outgrowth of these processes.

CHAPTER 5

The Crisis of International Capitalism and the Crisis of New Christendom

I should first like to state in general terms what the present crisis of international capitalism entails and, in particular, to draw out the processes that have a direct bearing on the crisis of Latin American New Christendom.[1] The crisis I am referring to is the structural—that is, long-range—crisis of the international capitalist system that began during the 1960s (in 1967 according to Frank, dos Santos, Danel, and others) and is likely to last for several decades more. I am not referring here to circumstantial or short-range cycles of recession and recovery in the world economy. The present crisis can be compared only to the crisis of 1873–1896 and to the more recent crisis of 1914–1945 (between the two world wars) whose high point was the 1929 crisis.[2]

In structural crises the survival of the capitalist system is assured by means of a thorough reorganization of the structures and mechanisms of production (particularly of the mode of accumulation and of the international division of labor). Crisis means that a particular model of economic growth or of political domination is worn out or has come to a standstill, but it does not necessarily entail the end or death of the capitalist system. The crisis of capitalism means only that its internal contradictions are accentuated. Capitalism survives the crisis if it manages to create the new structures within which the contradictions that the crisis produced can be resolved. The struggles of the popular classes and their political representatives play an important role in the resolution of these contradictions.

Finally, I believe the present crisis of the capitalist system is not only economic; it is a political, ideological, and cultural crisis as well. One of my initial assumptions has been that the crisis of New Christendom does not stand outside the present crisis of the international capitalist system, as I have defined that crisis here.

In part 2 I have shown, in overall terms, how there was a direct connection between the crises that arose in the colonial or neocolonial center, and the internal economic, social, and political restructuring of the dependent Latin American periphery. Changes in the relationships of dependence have always meant a change in the relationships of domination within the Latin American social system. All this had a direct bearing on Latin American Christendom. I have shown the close connection between Napoleon's invasions of the Iberian peninsula, the wars for independence, and the crisis of Latin American colonial Christendom.

I have also examined the connection between the 1873–1896 crisis of world capitalism, the establishment of the liberal, oligarchical state, and the restructuring of a New Christendom. When monopoly capitalism and imperialism made their appearance during the last quarter of the nineteenth century, a new division of labor was laid down. Latin America joined it by centering its economy on the export of raw materials. This mode of accumulation ("outward-directed") entailed the consolidation of a class structure in which the "traditional" landholding, merchant, and financial oligarchy held hegemony. This hegemonic bloc worked out its domination institutionally through the liberal state, and was expressed ideologically in "positivism."

This was the context in which New Christendom, conservative and oligarchical, developed: it was dependent on the European churches, and especially the Roman church, and it was removed from the reality of Latin America, in particular from popular culture and religion.

Next, I looked for the connection between the crisis of worldwide capitalism from 1914 to 1945, the new restructuring of the mode of accumulation and its class structure, and a shift from conservative New Christendom to another kind, one that was progressive (populist, nationalist, and developmentalist). With the crisis of 1914–1945, the world economy was integrated and internationalized. During this period the model of accumulation was based on industrialization as the basic structure for economic growth, although raw materials export also took a firmer hold.[3] On top of economic dependence came technological dependence: obsolete industrial technology was exported from the center to the Latin American periphery, thus maintaining control of industry in the dependent countries. This new mode of accumulation ("inward-directed") accordingly led to a reorganization of class structure in Latin America: hegemony came to be exercised by the national industrial bourgeoisie, although subordinated to foreign capital. Industrialization brought rapid urbanization, and an expansion of internal markets. The middle strata of salaried employees experienced a significant rise in social and political terms, and the industrial bourgeoisie sought to establish an alliance with them (the era of populist and nationalist projects). The liberal oligarchical state was replaced by the interventionist and protectionist state, which often had a populist character.

All these changes in Latin America during the 1914–1945 crisis of international capitalism had a direct bearing on Christendom and the church in Latin America. It was within these economic, political, and social processes that a transformation of Christendom took place. Such a historical perspective will provide me with the perspective needed for interpreting the advent of the New

Christendom, which I have described as populist, nationalist, or developmentalist, as well as open to the reality of Latin America and to the middle strata and popular sectors.

KEYS FOR INTERPRETING THE PRESENT CRISIS OF THE CAPITALIST SYSTEM

In the past, the crisis of the colonial system and the great crises of the capitalist system had a far-reaching impact on the structures of Latin American Christendoms. Similarly, the present crisis, which began during the 1960s, is bound to shake the foundations and vital structures of the New Christendom that was established during the 1930–1960 period. The present crisis of New Christendom and the present crisis of the capitalist system are simply two different elements of a single process—so much so that the former can be understood only on the basis of the latter.

I shall now look at the overall import of the present crisis of international capitalism, especially as it affects Latin America, in order to then go on to examine the crisis of New Christendom. I describe the overall meaning of this crisis on the basis of three keys for interpretation, although I cannot study them in detail here. These three keys provide me with a minimal framework for analyzing the crisis of New Christendom.

1. Transnationalization of Production, Capital, and Finance

A first key for interpretation is the internationalization or transnationalization of *production* in Latin America brought about by a rapid expansion of transnational companies, particularly during the 1955–1965 period. To that fact should be added the internationalization of *capital* or the transnationalization of finances in Latin America, spearheaded by international banking or by international finance centers—a process that became most accentuated between 1965 and 1975.[4]

2. Restructuring of the International Market

A second such key, closely connected to the first, and one that was to have a deep impact on the Latin American social system, was the restructuring of the international market. The overall tendency of this restructuring was toward better coordination and better "balance" between the industrialized countries, to the detriment of the underdeveloped countries. The first step was the restructuring of the markets of the United States, Europe, and Japan. Then, trade relationships were established with some socialist countries. Finally, some underdeveloped countries rich in natural resources were integrated into the worldwide system—Brazil, Venezuela, and Mexico. The result, of course, was a tighter control over prices, mounting transfers of surplus "from the poor to the rich," a steadily increasing division among Third World countries, and a growing imposition of models of trade, production, and consumption, and of development goals.

3. Reshaping Imperialist Domination

A third and final interpretive key is the gradual refashioning of imperialist domination. In this connection, I must mention two basic tendencies. One tendency gives the political dimension primacy over the economic—namely, by organizing counterinsurgency and national security on an international scale (with a network in the United States and a strong impact on Latin America);[5] the other tendency holds that the economic dimension has primacy over the political and is embodied in the Trilateral Commission.[6] The policy of counter-revolution was worked out particularly by John F. Kennedy and his secretary of defense, Robert McNamara, in the early 1960s. It amounted to a major reformulation of John Foster Dulles's "Cold War" (1948-1958). For Kennedy and McNamara the greatest danger to the "free world" came not simply from the "socialist" world, but also from "insurrection" (guerrillas, liberation movements, popular insurrections, etc.) in Third World countries. The enemy was to be found not only in the East, but was growing and becoming stronger in the South, in the poorest and most underdeveloped zones of the U.S. "sphere of influence." Kennedy planned to transform the military, political, and social power of imperialism to serve "nonconventional" wars of "counterinsurgency." The Vietnam war and the Alliance for Progress were the first attempts at counterinsurrection. I shall not pause to look at the well-known ideology and doctrine of "national security," but its logic is little different from that of counterinsurgency.[7]

It was in 1973 that the Trilateral Commission was formed at David Rockefeller's initiative. To understand its influence I must mention two prior initiatives that constitute, in a sense, the prehistory of the Trilateral Commission.[8] In the course of the twentieth century in each of the four great Western powers (England, France, Germany, the United States), commercial, industrial, and banking capital were linked together on a national level (the connection commonly being called "finance capital") in order to develop a "political economy" capable of resisting the demands of the rising labor movement. In the United States this linkage was carried out through the National Civic Federation. The effects of this agreement were felt in Latin America in successive U.S. invasions of Mexico, the Caribbean, and Central America.

The second initiative took place between 1959 and 1979 when the main economic political, and intellectual figures of the United States and Europe met in the Bilderberg Hotel in the Netherlands. Thus was born what was called the "Bilderberger Group," whose objective was that of a "closer collaboration to protect the moral and the ethical values of democratic institutions and independence in the face of a growing communist menace."[9] Among the Bilderberg Group we find men like Dean Rusk, David Rockefeller, McNamara, Kissinger, Mondale, Rothschild, Pompidou, and intellectuals like Samuelson, Rostow, Raymond Vernon, Raymond Aron. From such a concentration of economic, political, and intellectual power was to come a great number of initiatives such as the establishment of ALALC, AMECEA, ECLA (Economic Commission for Latin America), the program for industrializing Latin America through import substitution, the Alliance for Progress, "aid" organizations such as the International Monetary Fund (IMF), Inter-American Development Bank (IDB), Agency for International Development (AID), and so forth.

The Trilateral Commission took its place within this tradition and sought to coordinate the most representative forces in the United States, Europe, and Japan. In one sense it arose in reaction to the "primacy of the political over the economic" and against the bellicose, pragmatic, and brutal character of counterinsurgency and national security as represented by Nixon, Ford, and Kissinger. The ideologue of the Trilateral Commission was Zbigniew Brzezinski and its most representative politician was Jimmy Carter.[10] Most of the men in the Carter administration were "Trilateralists." The international vision of the Trilateral Commission was not centered on East-West military polarization (communism vs. capitalism) but on the socio-economic polarization between North and South (rich countries vs. poor countries). The United States wanted to break out of its international isolation and, by uniting with Europe and Japan, to organize a united front against the economic demands of the Third World, and in particular against the demand of those striving to defend prices for strategic raw materials (such as was being organized in institutions like OPEC) and against the demand for a New International Economic Order. The First World was organizing itself to deal with a Third World that might unite and become independent. The Trilateral Commission also tried to set in motion a new division of labor in which the role of the Third World would be basically that of providing raw materials and consuming manufactured goods.

One aspect of an ideological nature, very important for my analysis, was the "defense of human rights" that the Trilateral Commission took up as an "alternative" to the repressive approach of military dictatorships. There were *economic* and *social* reasons for "Trilateral humanism": "repressive militarism" was regarded as a double obstacle to the expansion of internal markets that the Trilateral Commission aimed to carry out in the underdeveloped countries within the framework of a "restricted democracy." Militarism was thought to generate an excessive politicization, the consequence of which would be a social and economic breakdown of the plans of the Trilateral Commission to develop the Third World and bring some Third World countries (including some socialist countries) into the "free market" controlled by the Trilateral countries.

There were, moreover, reasons of an *ideological* and *moral* nature: the "defense of human rights" sought to make up for the crisis of "legitimacy" affecting the capitalist system, and to cover over the most brutal contradictions between "rich and poor" and thus to neutralize the demands for a New International Economic Order, or demands expressed in the Charter of Algiers on the Rights of Peoples in 1976. Within the domestic context of the United States, Carter sought to restore its self-confidence and its confidence in the role it had to play at the international level. The "social morale" and "national identity" of the United States suffered a dangerous deterioration with the Vietnam war, Watergate, scandals involving the CIA, transnational corporations, and the like. When the Trilateral Commission defended human rights, and especially when Jimmy Carter did so, it was not a "spontaneous messianic-religious impulse" but an "ideological strategy" aimed directly at supporting the economic, political, and military interests of imperialism.[11]

The three interpretive keys I have outlined provide a *minimal historical frame of reference* within which I can seek to interpret the crisis of Latin American New Christendom and of the church tied to that Christendom. This crisis of Christendom, which began in the early 1960s, has continued and became more evident through the 1970s and up to the present.

THREE HISTORICAL PROCESSES

On the basis of this interpretation of the general thrust of the structural crisis of the dependent and underdeveloped capitalist system in Latin America, I should like to single out *three specific processes* that have a direct bearing on Latin American New Christendom, in terms of both the crisis and a potential way out of the crisis. The analysis of these three processes will be brief and in outline form. I shall be more detailed when I examine the cases of Argentina and Brazil.

1. Church, Ruling Classes, and State

I have stated more than once that the essential element of the project of New Christendom is the alliance between the hierarchical church, the ruling classes, and the state. In its effort to "christianize" society, the church relies primarily on *political society* (specifically the state) and on those classes that have *hegemony* in economic, political, social, cultural, and ideological life in a particular country. The aim is to guarantee the church presence and missionary activity by christianizing those "on top," those "in charge," the elites, the social and political leaders of a nation. This New Christendom church regards any break with the state or the ruling classes as a grave danger, as cutting the church off from society. Church survival seems to depend on whether the state guarantees its "rights and interests," whether laws and institutions have a "Christian" thrust, whether the future leaders of the state or the political figures of the ruling class receive a "Christian education." Hence, it is also bound up with the survival of schools, universities, mass media, political parties, unions, and other social works of a "Catholic" character.

After 1930, and especially after World War II, this alliance between the church, the ruling classes, and the state worked relatively well. Populist or nationalist governments during that period (such as those in Argentina, Brazil, and Mexico), which had replaced liberal governments, sought to establish a "loyal collaboration" with the church (even in Mexico where Lazaro Cardenas was able to improve relationships with the church after the difficult days of the revolution and the anticlerical policies of Plutarco Elias Calles). Although the church had never been able to accept the *laicist and positivistic liberalism* of Latin American oligarchies, it found that it could readily accept the *populist and nationalist* projects of the industrial bourgeoisie, in which it saw a real possibility for reconstituting New Christendom. When populist or nationalist leaders actually went so far as to profess that they were *Christians*, the process of rapprochement between church and state became that much easier and faster. This process moved even more rapidly during the "developmentalist" period that followed the populist and nationalist period in most Latin American countries. Generally speaking, "developmentalism" explicitly made reference to Christian social thought (especially after 1955 and during the 1960s). The most noteworthy cases were those of the Christian Democratic governments in Chile and Venezuela.

Starting in the 1960s with the overall crisis of the dependent Latin American capitalist system and even more with the crisis of projects and development models of a populist, nationalist, or developmentalist nature, with the crisis of the social classes on which they were based, and with the crisis of the "representative democracy" state that had been set up after World War II, the very basis of the New Christendom of the 1940s, 1950s, and the early 1960s also plunged into crisis. The greater the church's rapprochement or identification with the state and the hegemonic ruling classes of the previous period, the more violent was the crisis. The most extreme crisis of New Christendom was in Chile, where the church and Christian Democracy had been most closely identified. Here the expansion and decline of New Christendom paralleled the expansion and decline of Christian Democracy (expansion from 1960 to 1967; decline after that).

The crises of the national states during the nineteenth century and the crisis of the liberal state during the first half of the twentieth century did not have the same impact on Christendom, because church-state relationships were much weaker and much more conflictive during that period. What is new in the present situation derives from the violent and all-embracing nature of the crisis of New Christendom, due precisely to the character and nature of the relationship between the church, the state, and the ruling classes during the recent past. The *present* crisis of New Christendom can be compared only analogically to the crisis of colonial Christendom at the beginning of the nineteenth century. That is why in my proposal for a "periodization" of the history of Christendom and of the Latin American church there are three broad cycles: 1492–1808, 1808–1960, and 1960 to the present.

In the following chapters I shall expand this analysis of the process of crisis in the relationship between church, ruling classes, and state, which is the basis for the crisis of New Christendom.

2. Church and Popular Movement

A comparison of the 1870–1930 and 1930–1960 periods reveals a striking evolution in Latin American New Christendom. There was a remarkable broadening of the social base: the overall tendency was to move from a Christendom *enclosed* in the tight circle of oligarchical elites toward a Christendom *open* to the middle classes and popular sectors. There was a shift from a church on the defensive, struggling against liberalism, to a church on the offensive, struggling against underdevelopment. There was a progression from a romanized, alienated church centered on formal devotions and mass religious displays, and absorbed in issues of family and education, to a church open to Latin American and national issues, concerned about providing its most active members with a thorough formation, and attuned to social and political problems. New Christendom evolved from conservatism to reformist and developmentalist social Christianity.

Obviously, the basis for this new kind of social and political presence of Latin American Christendom and this significant expansion of its social base was an alliance the church made with the ruling classes and the state. Thus, an "ecclesiastical populism" enabled the church to win over large sectors of the "middle classes" and of the popular classes *without breaking its alliance with the ruling classes*. However, the situation changed and tended to become conflictive when these middle and popular strata began to become socially and politically involved against the system and against the ruling classes. Starting with the Cuban revolution in 1959 and throughout the 1960s and 1970s, there was a growing resurgence of the popular movement following on, and as a result of, the crisis of the capitalist system, and more particularly, when it became clear that populist, nationalist, and developmentalist models had reached their limits. Populist movements came to a halt, and in general the popular classes gradually asserted greater autonomy with regard to nationalist and developmentalist bourgeoisie. The process of resurgence of the popular movement was not uniform and continuous throughout Latin America, but its overall tendency was to expand and become deeper, both geographically and historically.

This growing resurgence of the popular movement in Latin America starting in the 1960s had a direct impact on New Christendom because of its very success in winning a significant place for itself among the middle and popular classes during the period immediately preceding. There had been numerous insurrections or movements among the most oppressed sectors in earlier centuries and in the first half of the twentieth century, but Christendom remained largely "outside" or "above" those movements. The newness of the present situation comes from the fact that it is the *very social base* of New Christendom that has become socially and politically involved. The conscious participation of a significant number of Christians in social and political movements during the 1960s and 1970s is well known: Camilo Torres and "Camilista" groups, the sweeping politicization of the "Christian intelligentsia," the rise of groups of priests taking up political positions; the Latin American movement of Christians for Socialism; liberation theology; and other similar phenomena. As things are at present, the popular movement has won over the social base of New Christendom within the Latin American population. The contradictions of class struggle are getting to the point where they affect New Christendom from top to bottom, and the result is breakdown and crisis.

I should make it clear that the contradiction is not between the church and the popular movement, but between a particular model of New Christendom and the popular movement. The church itself faces the challenge of an internal division between a church that remains tied to the New Christendom model and another church that rejects that model. This rejection of New Christendom is a result of the fact that this new sector of the church is being built up anew from within the popular classes and the liberation struggles taking place all over Latin America. The sector of the church that is opposed to New Christendom and that rejects any sort of alliance between church and state or between the church and the ruling classes is what I call the "popular church." I shall return to this contradiction between popular church and New Christendom in greater detail in the chapters that follow.

3. Church and New Model of Domination

At the beginning of this chapter I sketched out the process of restructuring the new model of domination, the basic elements of which have already emerged in the present crisis of the international capitalist system. As long as this crisis and the popular movement's reaction to it continue, the new model of domination will not emerge as a clearly defined and firmly established totality. In this sense the period beginning in the 1960s is *open* and will end up either with the capitalist system being surpassed or with the overall restructuring of a new model of capitalist domination. To speak even now of this model as a foregone conclusion would be to deny the reality of the ever deepening crisis of the system and the ever growing resurgence of the popular movement. But, wherever this deepening crisis and this resurgence of the popular movement may lead, and indeed as a response to these two processes, it is certain that the basic elements of the new model of domination have begun to take shape.[12]

Although I have no intention of completely covering all aspects of this new model of domination, let me recall its major agents and elements: transnational companies, transnational banking, militarism, counterinsurgency, the national security system, the Trilateral Commission, and the like. The higher the profile these agents or elements assume, the greater grows the contradiction between them and the bulk of the Latin American church. It is not only small groups of radicalized Christians who have become aware of these elements and criticized them, but also a significantly large proportion of the hierarchical church in Latin America (with the possible exception of the Argentinian and

Colombian episcopacies). Thus there is a growing awareness that Christianity and the ideology of national security stand in direct contradiction, and that the policies of military dictatorships, the transnational companies, and the Trilateral Commission are incompatible with the action of the churches in favor of human rights and a "liberating evangelization."

Throughout the history of Latin America, the hierarchical church has always known how to adapt to new political systems of domination. When Spanish or Portuguese colonial power crumbled, the church eventually came around to being reconciled to the new national states. Thus, the crisis between the liberal oligarchical state and the hierarchical church could have been settled satisfactorily after 1930 with populist, nationalist, or developmentalist governments. At present, however, it is difficult to see how the bulk of the hierarchical church can adapt to, or be reconciled to, the new model of economic, political, social, cultural, and ideological domination. The church's prior experience of the two processes just described (crisis of the relationships between church and state, and church and ruling classes, and the political radicalization of the social base of New Christendom and the church) makes such an adaptation or reconciliation impossible. Of course some small groups in the hierarchical church have already worked out such a reconciliation between the church and a new model of domination, a development that could enable a new model of Christendom to emerge. In such a case, following on conservative New Christendom (1870–1930) and populist-nationalist-developmentalist New Christendom (1930–1960), there could have emerged a third model, which I could call "ecclesiastico-military, national security, or trilateralist New Christendom." Nevertheless, most of the hierarchical church in Latin America rejects such a possibility.

The three processes I have sketched out here, and which I shall examine in more detail in the cases of Argentina and Brazil, react in a convergent and simultaneous manner on New Christendom, and hence lead to its crisis and breakdown. The impact of these three processes comes precisely from the fact that they are simultaneous, and that they have interacted and reinforced one another during the 1960s and 1970s. The crisis of the state and of the ruling classes, which brings about a crisis in the church/state/ruling-classes relationship (upon which New Christendom is founded), is a process that is particularly critical for New Christendom because it takes place simultaneously with a growing political radicalization of the social basis of New Christendom. The two processes are intertwined and dialectically reinforce one another: the crisis in church/state/ruling-classes relationships creates a power (and leadership) vacuum within New Christendom, and that smooths the way for an accelerated process of political radicalization within its social base. From the opposite end, this radicalization process hastens the process leading to a split between the church, on the one side, and the state and ruling classes on the other. Added to this situation, which has rapidly become critical, there is a growing contradiction between the church and the new model of domination. Not only is there an objective contradiction; Latin Americans have become aware of the incompatibility, for example, between Christianity and the doctrine of national security or militarism, or between Christianity and the ideology of transnational companies or that of the Trilateral Commission. In analyzing the crisis of New Christendom it is essential not to neglect these three processes, because it is the fact that they are simultaneous and convergent that reveals how deep and far-reaching the crisis of New Christendom is.

The period of 1960 to the present is not homogenous in terms of time or space throughout Latin America. I divide the period into subperiods in chapter 6, with regard to the cases of Argentina and Brazil, and in chapter 7, with regard to Latin American theology. In general, I single out three stages from 1960 to the present:

First stage, 1960–1968. The second general conference of the Latin American Episcopate took place in Medellín, Colombia, in 1968. During these years there was a growing general awareness that the dominant system was reaching its limits and was in crisis, and hence that New Christendom was also in crisis (the Medellín documents clearly reflect this awareness).

Second stage, 1968–1973 (the 1973 coup in Chile is taken as a reference point for similar developments elsewhere in Latin America). Latin America underwent contradictory processes, of both liberation and domination. New Christendom experienced a political polarization around the minority of Christians who represented a solution to the crisis of both the system and New Christendom.

Third stage, from 1973 onward. The basic contradiction between New Christendom and the "popular church" was ever more apparent. The meeting of the third general conference of the Latin American Episcopate at Puebla confirmed and deepened this basic contradiction.

CHAPTER 6

Argentina and Brazil

In this chapter I try to deepen the general analysis undertaken in the previous chapter and test it by applying it to the concrete cases of Argentina and Brazil. I have chosen these two countries because it is there that the process of the crisis of New Christendom and the rise of a "popular church" has been most obvious. Because my primary aim is not simply to reconstruct the history of these two processes but to come to a theoretical interpretation of them, I made an effort to find the countries where these processes can be discerned and grasped most directly. What has happened in Argentina and Brazil cannot be applied mechanically to the rest of Latin America, but some theoretical conclusions drawn from the analysis of these two countries may be generalized, or at least they may serve as a reference point or analytical tool that may be useful for other historical situations.

I have taken 1930 as the approximate starting point for my research, and I base myself on the analysis set out in part 2, chapter 4, above. I cannot interpret the crisis of New Christendom in Argentina and Brazil without analyzing how it arose and reached maturity: the essential elements for explaining the crisis of New Christendom were already present there.

In part 4 (which deals with the church, the authoritarian state, and social classes in Latin America) I take up again in a synchronic and systematic fashion the most important theoretical conclusions reached in this chapter.

ARGENTINA

From Conservatism to Populism

The Argentine church provides a typical example of the evolution of a church through all the historical stages through which most Latin American churches passed in the course of the twentieth century: the *oligarchical* stage, the *populist-nationalist* stage, the *developmentalist* stage, and the stage of confronting an *authoritarian-miltary* system.

Between 1916 and 1955 the Argentine church slowly and hesitantly underwent a passage from an oligarchical to a populist stage. During these years the church broke its social and political alliance with the conservative oligarchy and established a new alliance with the populist industrial bourgeoisie. Throughout this process the church retained its aim of rebuilding "Christendom"—that is, it sought to renew its internal structures and to assert its presence and power within civil and political society—essentially by relying on the state and on the ruling classes.

Schematically, the 1916-1955 period can be divided into three phases:

• 1916-1930 "Prepopulist" period, with Presidents Hipolito Yrigoyen and Marcelo Alvear of the "Radical Civic Union."
• 1930-1943 Conservative period, called the "decade of infamy" because of corruption and the abandonment of the country to imperialism.
• 1943-1955 Peronist populist period. Juan Domingo Perón, president from February 1946 to September 1955.

At first the church was reluctant to break with its oligarchical past because of the "laicist" thrust of "Yrigoyenism" and because the *liberal* and *positivist* ruling oligarchy had only recently come around to desiring reconciliation with the church, after several decades of harsh confrontation. This "conversion" on the part of the liberal oligarchy was due to its internal weakness and to the fact that new and adverse social forces had appeared on the scene (the industrial bourgeoisie, the middle strata, and the proletariat).

Before 1930, the Argentine church had managed to reorganize itself internally and to consolidate its position in society. That is why the oligarchical governments of the "decade of infamy" sought the support of the church. President Agustín P. Justo (1932-1938) provided the church with significant support, thus enabling it to achieve an extraordinary expansion during the 1930s.

The triumphalism and optimism of conservative New Christendom reached its high point with the thirty-second International Eucharistic Congress held in Buenos Aires in 1934. The "laicist" and vaguely "socialist" character of pre-1930 populism and this oligarchical-Constantinian euphoria delayed the final break of the Argentine church with the oligarchy and its opening up to populism. Nevertheless, the church intuitively understood that the oligarchy was socially and politically weak, and it was especially aware of growing pressure from the middle strata and the popular classes. Moreover, the church knew that conservative New Christendom was weak: it was clear that behind the ostentation of its external forms, it had little content (no evangelization) and it was alien to the people (no connection with popular culture and religiosity).

If the church remained tied to its past, it would lose any possibility of gaining influence in the social sectors of the middle and popular strata. But if the church broke with the oligarchy and opened up to the nascent popular sectors, the result could be a social revolution that would be against the system and opposed to the ruling classes. The church rejected such an outcome: it was incompatible with its Christendom model. It was not the church that found a way out of the dilemma, but a sector of the ruling class, the industrial bourgeoisie, which offered the church a social and political project. This sector of the bourgeoisie proposed a break with the liberal oligarchy combined with a national and popular project that could both incorporate the new social sectors of the middle and popular strata and keep them under control, and could give rise to an organized popular political movement that would be led and controlled by this same bourgeoisie—a project not of liberal but of Christian inspiration. The bourgeoisie convinced the church that this project was neither laicist, nor socialist, nor Marxist. Everything came together around 1945 in the person of Juan Domingo Perón. The church's conditions for breaking with the conservative and liberal oligarchy were met, and it became willing to accept the populist and nationalist project of the emerging industrial bourgeoisie.

During the 1930-1943 period within the Argentine church this historic transition was already underway: its habitual antiliberal stance had little by little brought the church to work out in ideological terms a "Catholic nationalism" in which the ideas of "kingdom of God" and "nation" were mutually self reinforcing. Moreover, it was during this time that the struggle against liberalism and modernism in the church led to "integralism," a doctrine that sought to find the answers to all family, social, and political problems exclusively in the faith. This integralism gave the church political, if pseudo, leverage, making it feel politically secure and independent vis-à-vis the oligarchy. Catholic nationalism and integralism readied the church's social consciousness for the historically important shift from the camp of the oligarchy toward a national-populist alliance.

In 1945 and 1946 Juan Domingo Perón succeeded in getting most of the Argentine bishops to back him by using a time-honored method: guaranteeing the "rights of the church."[1] Perón opposed separation of church and state, prohibited divorce, and proposed that the teaching of religion be obligatory in public schools. There was nothing original in his taking this political tack; other presidents had already done so, including the "populist" Yrigoyen (1916-1922) and the "conservative" Agustín P. Justo (1932-1938). Perón's originality lay in how officially and explicitly "Christian" he made his own political project. In his speeches, Perón made use of papal social encyclicals and officially based his own position on Catholic morality and theology. Moreover, he involved the church in many government programs. The church seemed to be a part of any social action on the part of the state.

What most appealed to the church was that Perón stood poles apart from the three enemies it most feared: liberalism, laicism, and communism. Nationalism with a Catholic, social, and popular thrust was the ideological foundation for the alliance between Perón and the church. This nationalism was quite different from Christian social ideology or the kind of social Christianity that would provide inspiration for Christian Democracy in other countries such as

Chile, Uruguay, or Venezuela. This substitution of Catholic nationalism for social Christianity was typical of the more industrialized Latin American countries. Latin American social Christianity, which came from Europe, did not emphasize nationalism enough, and during this period seemed to be a weak ideology, inadequate for controlling the masses in countries like Argentina and Brazil which had experienced the greatest degree of industrialization and urbanization.[2]

With the advent of Peròn, church and state were reconciled in Argentina, thus supplying the basis for a New Christendom model. After the liberal reform, toward the end of the nineteenth century, the church had been cast aside by the state. For a Christendom church, that meant that its ability to rebuild and take its place in civil society was radically diminished. Most bishops saw in Peronism the possibility that Christendom might be restored. Only a few bishops and priests whose pastoral work was with the working class and with peasants took part in the Peronist movement as a popular movement that could open up possibilities to struggle for greater *social justice*, altogether apart from the Catholic and nationalist project of a New Christendom. In short, Peronism enabled the church to rebuild its social and political power within a New Christendom model that had the two characteristics it desired: it was a Christendom with a large social basis, especially among the middle strata and the popular classes, and yet it was a Christendom shielded from the dangers of laicism, liberalism, and socialism. It was a New Christendom that could be called populist-nationalist built top-down—that is, by the state and the bourgeoisie—and its central aim was to defend the "rights of the church" in civil and political society.

The populist character of this Christendom did not at all mean that the "rights of the church" would coincide with the rights and interests of the poorest and most exploited. Nevertheless, paradoxically, this new model opened a variety of possibilities for a greater rapprochement between the popular classes and the hierarchical church, a rapprochement that was later to bear fruit when Peronism lost support at the grass roots and the working class regained its independence as a class within the Peronist movement.

Because the basis for the alliance between Perón and the church was more political than ecclesial, the populist form of New Christendom was tied to the economic and political fate of the Peronist project. That project entered a crisis around 1953, and as a consequence there was a crisis in the alliance between Perón and the church. The break finally came in November 1954 and was quite violent. What happened is important to my thesis because it reveals the nature of this populist and nationalist New Christendom. From the time Perón broke with the church, he made divorce legal, suppressed religion classes in the public schools, and undertook a constitutional reform to bring about separation of church and state. Accompanying the break was a violent anticlerical campaign, orchestrated by the Peronist government.

As might be expected, the Argentine hierarchical church focused the conflict on the "rights of the church" and excommunicated government officials who violated those rights. It was most significant that in order to defend its rights vis-à-vis the state, the church became allied with the most reactionary forces in the anti-Peronist opposition, including ultraliberal, Masonic, and anticlerical sectors. Everything was sacrificed for the rights of the church, which were regarded as more important than the popular movement developing within Peronism. The conflict showed how the church used populism to defend its own rights instead of taking a stance within the populist alliance as a defender of the people's rights. The rights of the church and the rights of the poor were far from being one and the same. They could not be one and the same within a Christendom model.

The anti-Perón reaction of the hierarchical church provided a pretext and legitimation for the fall of Perón (1955), and for the conservative/liberal counterrevolution during the following period (1955-1973). Nevertheless, it must be added that during the conflict between Perón and the church, both participants had basically the same attitude toward the popular movement. It is typical of the populist bourgeoisie in Latin America to take advantage of the popular classes in order to seize power, and then to abandon them in moments of crisis. After 1952 the populist project had exhausted its economic and political possibilities. Perón no longer needed the people and he began to turn toward his former "enemies," the oligarchy and imperialism. Populist New Christendom headed toward the same sort of political stance, but less consistently: its social base had been won over by the mass movement that arose out of the Peronist movement.

Chronology of the Crisis Period for Nationalist-Populist New Christendom

From 1955, when Peronist populism lost its strength and entered its final crisis (though this was not true of Peronism as a popular movement) up to the present, Argentina experienced the three processes that I have been signaling as basic during the present period in Latin America: an economic, political, and ideological crisis affecting the dominant system, the rise of a mass movement, and the advent of a new model of domination. The following brief chronological table presents the historical framework that will provide a basis for an interpretive analysis of the church during this period:

I. *1955-1966: "Liberal Developmentalism"*
—September 16, 1955: "Liberating Revolution" and overthrow of Perón. President: General Eduardo Leonardi (Catholic nationalist).
—November 13, 1955: coup d'etat. Leonardi replaced by General Pedro Eugenio Aramburu (liberal, freemason).
—February 23, 1958: elections. President: Arturo Frondizi (developmentalist liberal).
—March 19, 1962: coup d'etat. President: José María Guido.
—October 7, 1963: elections. President: Arturo Illía (liberal).

II. *1966-1970: "Military Developmentalism"*
—June 28, 1966: coup d'etat. President: Lt. Col. Juan Carlos Onganía. "Argentine Revolution."
—June 8, 1970: Onganía replaced by Brigadier General Roberto M. Levingston.

III. *1971-1976: "Great National Pact"*
—March 16, 1971: Levingston replaced by General Alejandro Lanusse.
—April 1971: government beginning to negotiate with Perón.
—March 11, 1973: elections. President: Hector Cámpora (who resigned in July under pressure from right-wing Peronism).
—September 23, 1973: elections. President: Juan Domingo Perón.
—July 1, 1974: death of Perón. President: Isabel Perón.

IV. *1976-   : National Security State*
—March 24, 1976: coup d'etat. President: General Jorge Rafael Videla.

Reasons for the Crisis

Throughout these years the three underlying processes mentioned above spread and became more pronounced:

1. The ruling classes experienced an ongoing structural crisis: no sector of the bourgeoisie was able to establish its own hegemony and impose its own politcal project. The armed forces had to interfere as a power capable of taking over for a bourgeoisie in crisis (between 1955 and 1976, six presidents were overthrown by the military), the economic crisis continued, and there was an ideological split within the bourgeois elites.

2. The Peronist movement broke down at the grassroots level, provoking a process of political radicalization in the popular movement. New revolutionary political organizations developed (ERP, Montoneros, and others), the labor movement broke away from its own bureaucracy and from the tutelage of the state, and acquired a growing class autonomy, and so forth.

3. A new model of domination took shape, especially with Onganía (1966-1970) and Videla (after 1976), sustained by the ideology and doctrine of national security.

With this political context (1955-1978) in mind, and on the basis of the three underlying processes sketched out, I must now situate and interpret the development of the Argentine church. I must analyze:

1. The crisis of the New Christendom model and of the church tied up with it, and the crisis within the kind of social consciousness that had been shaped ideologically by nationalism, populism, and developmentalism.

2. The advent of a "popular church"—that is, of a church in the process of breaking away from the system of domination and the ruling classes, a church that has nothing to do with any model of Christendom, but is involved with the poor and the oppressed. The aim here is not to reconstruct the *whole* history of the Argentine church from 1955 to 1978, but simply to interpret *some* of the

breakthrough moments and some of the events that paved the way for a popular church.[3]

The Catholic hierarchy was destined to be marked by its active participation in the "liberating revolution" that overthrew Perón in 1955 and then by the fact that it was willing to be used by the ruling classes in the subsequent counterrevolution. After 1955 it was clear that the church had broken with the Peronist movement and was allied to the reactionary anti-Peronist forces. This was the kind of church against which revolutionary Christians would take their stand.

The official church, with guilt feelings vis-à-vis the bourgeoisie because of its former alliance with Perón, and fearing the popular and revolutionary currents developing within Peronism after Perón, drifted with the tide and accepted a subordinate role in the different political projects attempted by various sectors of the bourgeoisie that succeeded one another in power. First, it went along with the Catholic nationalism of the "liberating revolution" (which used the symbol of a "V" for victory crowned with a cross) and with the president, General Leonardi. Next, the hierarchy had to negotiate a forced reconciliation with the liberal, laicist, and Masonic regime of General Aramburu. Finally, it was pulled into Frondizi's neoliberalist developmentalism. Ten years of drifting led to splits within the institution, and an ideological explosion. At that point three tendencies appeared: "traditionalist-militarist," "liberal-conciliar," and "progressive" (or "Third World" in Argentine terminology [after the Movement of Priests for the Third World; see below]).

The ecclesiastical current that rested on the alliance between the church and the armed forces became particularly powerful with the presidency of the "Catholic" Onganía (1966–1970) and his "Argentine revolution." The prototype of this church was Cardinal Antonio Caggiano, vicar for the armed forces. The vicarate for the armed forces, only recently established, became very important. The Cursillo movement became a "cadre school" for selecting and training Catholic military officers who then went on to occupy strategic positions in the state and the armed forces. The myth of a "Catholic Argentina" enjoyed a resurgence and an important sector of the hierarchy sought to impose a project of ecclesiastico-military New Christendom.

For a short while, the postconciliar atmosphere, Medellín, and the Third World movement opened up a space for the conciliar and progressive tendency of the Argentine church, expressed in the episcopal conference of San Miguel, held April 21–26, 1969. The Declaration of San Miguel, which adapted the Medellín conference to the Argentine situation, acted as a brake on "ecclesiastico-military Christendom" for a while. Most of the bishops soon forgot this document, the best that the Argentine episcopacy had produced, but it struck a note at the grassroots level of the church, sounding a go-ahead to those who wanted to develop a church committed to the people.

The balance of forces between the militarist and conciliar tendencies of the Catholic hierarchy (and hence their mutual neutralizing effect), and the radicalization of the Argentine popular movement during the 1966–1976 period, gave rise to a popular and revolutionary current at the grassroots level in the

Argentine church. This current was best expressed in the Movement of Priests for the Third World (PTW).

The hierarchy was more concerned with the wider-ranging process of systemic crisis, the crisis of national-populist Christendom. The resulting doctrinal and ideological confusion on the part of the hierarchy created a power and leadership vacuum in the Catholic Church. It is within this context that I offer a brief interpretation of the PTW.[4]

Priests for the Third World

On August 15, 1967, five months after the appearance of the encyclical *Populorum Progressio* (March 26, 1967), the "Message of Third World Bishops" was published.[5] These two documents—and especially the "Message"—were to have a great impact on Argentina, at this point subject to the repressive dictatorship of Lieutenant Colonel Juan Carlos Onganía. A group of priests collected signatures in support of the "Message of Third World Bishops," and by February 1968 had 320 signatures on file.

Representatives from thirteen dioceses gathered in Córdoba in a national conference, held May 1-2, 1968. The purpose of the meeting was to examine the economic, social, and political situation in the country and to take a stand as pastors within that situation. The priests recognized the need for a minimum level of organization: they chose diocesan representatives, regional coordinators, a national secretariat, and general coordinator. Thus was born a *national organization of priests*, which the press named the Movement of Priests for the Third World. This movement arose not against the hierarchy, but in independence from it. It was a *priests'* movement, which explicitly and consciously situated its *pastoral practice* within the context of the social and political reality of the *popular movement*.

This was something new and original within the Latin American church, and had nothing to do with the kind of protest movements by priests, or "underground churches," springing up in Europe or the United States around the same time. The Medellín conference, which was held shortly afterward (August 1968), was to give a new impulse to the PTW, which would disseminate and interpret the documents of the bishops at Medellín.

On the basis of Medellín the PTW decided to orient its activity in three directions:

1. To do conscientization and provide information at all levels on the situation of exploitation experienced by most of our people.
2. To denounce the abuses and injustices of a society under the yoke of capitalism, the international imperialism of money, and neocolonialism.
3. To add to the urgency of denunciations and declarations the power of *deeds* that can prod persons to take stands and thus to seed change.[6]

From the outset the PTW insisted that priests should be *actively present* in the struggle of the popular classes against the Onganía dictatorship. It is that presence that led to what the movement called "prophetic deeds." Such deeds were multiplied during the 1969-1970 period, with repressive consequences for priests in the movement.

The second PTW national conference took place May 1-3, 1969, in Colonia Coroya (Córdoba). The final document, entitled "Our Underlying Convergences," stressed three important points:

1. The undeniable *fact* of injustice and repression, and the liberation process in Argentina;

2. The PTW *stance:* acceptance of the revolutionary process toward radical and urgent structural change; rejection of the capitalist system and of any kind of economic, political, or cultural imperialism; the search for a Latin American kind of socialism that would make it possible for a New Human Being to come forth, and the socialization of the means of production as well as economic, political, and cultural power. Socialism as imposed by socialist political parties was rejected.

3. Involvement with the poor, the *agent* of liberation.

These three points, and particularly the second, indicate the degree of political awareness present in the movement during this period. The option for socialism was intended to provoke a great deal of discussion, a point I will address further on.

A popular insurrection in Córdoba (called *el cordobazo* or Córdoba coup) took place in May 1970 and the PTW played an active role in it. On November 12 that same year President Onganía announced the consecration of the country to the Immaculate Heart of Mary, provoking vigorous protests from the PTW. These events publicly revealed how ecclesiastico-military Christendom and the popular church were locked into a head-on confrontation.

On May 1-2, 1970, the third national PTW conference was held in Santa Fe. Out of that meeting came the "Santa Fe Communiqué," which provides the best picture of the PTW.[7] Its political and ideological option was, like the one made in 1969, against capitalism and imperialism, and in favor of Latin American socialism. The statement accepted the "revolutionary process," and regarded the experience of Peronism as a "key element for incorporating our people into the revolutionary struggle." At the organic level, two underlying principles were laid down. These two principles would be accepted by all similar movements in Latin America during the 1968-1973 period:

1. *Identity as church:* "We do not want another church. We feel a deep solidarity with what we believe is the true church of Christ." But the hierarchy must undergo radical change if it was to put into practice what it had said at Medellín (1969).

2. *Political identity other than that of a political party:* "The Movement is not, does not want to be, and cannot constitute itself as, a *political party.*" As such the PTW did not take a position with regard to "the tactics, strategies, or tendencies of groups and organizations, respecting in these areas its members' freedom of choice." The revolutionary political option (socialist and anticapitalist) was thus lived and expressed as that of a church involved with the poor.

Participants in the movement's national conference in 1970 included Bishop Zaspe of Sante Fe, Bishop Devoto of Goya, and Bishop Brasca of Rafaela. The presence of these bishops confirmed the ecclesial dimension that the PTW maintained.

Between 1970 and 1973 the movement underwent severe repression. On August 12, 1970, the permanent commission of the episcopacy published a harsh statement alleging errors on the part of the PTW. The movement replied by publishing a book, *What We Think: Letter to the Argentine Bishops*. The tension between the PTW and the hierarchy never reached the breaking point. With this publication the PTW evidenced a high degree of Christian, theological, and political maturity. Under pressure from the hierarchy, the movement reflected on its own course, and radicalized its basic options.

During 1971 the PTW began a wide-ranging and deep reflection on the connections between Peronism and socialism. A document on the topic was discussed at the fourth annual conference (July 8-9, 1971) held in Carlos Paz (Córboda).[8] The thinking in this document already reflected the breakdown of Peronism as a populist movement. On the one side there was the kind of top-to-bottom populism set up by the political representatives of the bourgeoisie; confronting it was the populism of the masses, which in the crisis situation was breaking away from the bourgeoisie and moving in the direction of revolutionary forms.[9] The PTW saw this "class" split within Peronism very clearly, and it took up the issue of socialism in the context of that split. Its document, entitled "Peronism-Socialism," made a distinction between the revolutionary and the reactionary factors within Peronism. The revolutionary factor was:

> The people as present and active in the Peronist movement. The PTW does not opt for Peronism, but for the people as a whole, which, however, finds its expression in Peronism. It is not its doctrine or ideological expression that makes Peronism revolutionary, but the fact that it is a political movement that gives expression to the people.

The reactionary factors within Peronism were identified as the bureaucracies of the party and of the unions, the dogmatism of "orthodox" Peronists, and the "third position" in the ideological sense (as defined in the following paragraph).

The PTW pointed out a "third position," or "third way." Here there was a distinction between a third position in the *ideological* sense, which defined Peronism as a middle way between capitalism and socialism (such a third position was rejected as reactionary), and a third position in the *political sense*, which opted for socialism, but for a Latin American kind of socialism built up on the basis of the history and real situation of Latin America, and not subject to any foreign nation (it is this "third way" that was accepted as revolutionary).

The document also made distinctions between "the people," "Peronism," and "Peronist organizations." "The people" stood in contradistinction to the "antipeople," meaning, the oligarchy and imperialism. The prevailing distinction during this period was that of people/antipeople, and not that of people/elite, the kind of contradistinction that will *later* be imposed by sectors further to the right and more "top-downward" in the PTW. The 1971 document stated that there was no intention of dissociating the popular movement from Peronism, for Peronism was the historical expression of the people's aspirations and interests. To reject Peronism would entail moving outside the popular movement and against it.

In its 1971 documents the PTW was still speaking rather ideologically and had not arrived at a deeper economic and political analysis of the way things were. But in that year there began to develop a tendency to use the Marxist analysis of social classes and of class struggle, without ceasing to be Peronist. In 1972 and 1973 this became the prevailing tendency, especially in the provinces. Curiously, Christians played a major role in mediating the encounter between Peronism and Marxism. The Peronist writer with Marxist tendencies, Juan José Hernández Arregui, had considerable influence on Christian youth (he wrote a book *What Are We Entitled as a Nation? Ibero-American Historical Consciousness*). The Argentine Communist Party, which always stood outside the Peronist movement or against it, predisposed Peronism against communism or any other form of Marxism.

The high point for the PTW was reached in 1972. There were about eight hundred active members and two hundred sympathizers (out of some five thousand priests in Argentina). But more important than the number was the social and political impact of the movement. Its activities made the news and were the object of nationwide commentary. The whole church felt challenged and pressured by the PTW. In contrast to a hierarchical church, the bulk of which was tied up with the military, there appeared the image of a church that arose from the people's struggles.

In 1973 and 1974 the PTW split sharply into a minority that submitted to the bourgeoisie's top-to-bottom, official Peronism, and a majority that took its stand alongside the popular Peronist movement. This latter group was forced to go underground in May 1974, when Perón broke with the Peronist Youth, and, more generally, with grassroots Peronism. The military coup (March 24, 1976) initiated a new period for the Argentine popular church, one that was to deepen and radicalize the experience acquired between 1966 and 1976.

During the 1955–1976 period, when the Peronist popular movement was splitting into two mutually hostile class blocs, the church was polarized around two antagonistic positions: one position sought a solution to the crisis in a military regime tied to the dominant classes, and the other looked for a socialist type of solution, tied to the popular classes. Between these two *clearly defined* positions was to be found a *hesitant majority*. This was not a "centrist" majority, as it is customarily put, but a majority that was confused, buffeted by contradictory currents; it was a group that hesitated because it did not want to submit to military regimes, but did not want to sever its connections with the dominant classes either. And there was another hesitant group as well, one that wanted to be more deeply committed to the popular classes, but also rejected any kind of socialist or Marxist solution.

Short-lived Conciliar and Medellín Renewal

Social and political tensions and conflicts are not automatically reflected within the church, but in accordance with different specific conditions, because the church always retains a relative autonomy within civil society. In Latin America, the conflict within the church as such was more directly aligned with social and political conflicts in those countries where there had been a populist phase prior to the crisis. The connection is all the more direct where populism has had a "Christian" character during that phase, and where the government has clearly been tied to the hierarchical church. At the moment of crisis, the populism of the previous phase provides the impulse for a more broadly-based and deeper politicization, even within the realms of religion and the church.

The Argentine church provides a typical example. It was clearly one of the most *politicized* churches in Latin America, and hence one of the most politically *polarized*. Halfway groups, those that have not taken a clear position, have always been short-lived and insignificant; ultimately they became part of one or other of the opposing tendencies. That is what happened with the middle-of-the-road and progressive group of Argentine bishops that experienced a renewal thanks to Vatican II and the Medellín conference, but was also divided into two subgroups, one drawn to conservative interests, the other to the "Third World movement." The document of the bishops' meeting at San Miguel (1969), which was the best expression of postconciliar renovation, had a short lifespan and was soon forgotten by most of the hierarchy. (The Third World movement, however, disseminated and interpreted the document from a popular perspective.) The fact that Argentina experienced the post–Vatican II and Medellín period during the highly repressive Onganía dictatorship of 1966–1970—a dictatorship that claimed to be militantly Catholic—was obviously not irrelevant in this connection.

During the 1971–1976 period, the bourgeoisie tried to impose its hegemony by replacing repression with conciliatory policies (the "Great National Accord") and by pitting Perón against Peronism. The church continued to be so polarized, however, that it could not play the role so typically played by other churches in similar situations, that of being an "arbiter" or "mediator," standing "above" social and political scissions and tensions. During the period of the "Great National Accord" each sector of the church worked on its own political project. The promilitary sector of the church trained civilian and military cadres for its project of ecclesiastico-military New Christendom at the UCA (Argentine Catholic University) and in the Cursillo movement. Along with Fathers Menvieille and Sánchez Abelenda, it was Bishop Tortolo who provided leadership for this effort, and who then became president of the espiscopal conference in April 1970. At the same time, the church present in the popular classes became more deeply committed to the popular movement and leftist organizations, and deepened its political involvement, thoretical understanding, and organizational ties.

Set between these two clearly defined sectors of the church, the bishops who had no political analysis of the situation and no overall proposal for society tried to evade socio-political conflict by taking refuge in the strictly moral and religious realm. Despite their good intentions, the conservative and militarist bishops always managed to manipulate this religious moralizing on the part of the hesitant and indecisive majoriy. A typical document reflecting this timid and indecisive church, which serves the dominant ideology by default, is the one that came from the thirtieth plenary assembly of the Argentine episcopate (November 30, 1974), "The Moral Root of the Crisis."[10] This document understood the *political* situation in *moral* terms, placing morality on the side of the established system and "immorality" on the side of revolution. For example, the Argentine church ruled out Marxism, in moral, rather than political, terms, because it was "atheistic" and "materialistic." Moral terminology concealed a political judgment. The same thing was true where the document dealt with "subversion" and "violence."

From July 1975 onward it was no longer simply repression but an overall war that was unleashed against the popular movement and the left. This war knew no limits or prohibitions, and took on the nature of a crusade: the "enemy" was "atheistic" and "against the nation itself." General Jorge Videla took command of the army. The role of Isabel Perón in the government was simply to provide a Peronist cover in order to justify repression.

It was during these months that the president of the episcopacy, Bishop Tortolo, was also named vicar for the armed forces, with Bishop Bonamín as deputy vicar. From that point on, the promilitary hierarchical church, with Tortolo and Bonamín leading the way, began to take an active role in the political life of the nation. It coordinated all its activity with that of the armed forces, which had been called in to intervene directly in national politics. Since 1966 preparations had been underway for an alliance between the church and the armed forces, intended to serve as the basis for the project of ecclesiastico-military New Christendom; now that project moved into action. Bishop Tortolo provided public justification for the military antiguerrilla action in Tucumán.[11] In the presence of the highest officers in the army, Bishop Bonamín, in a widely publicized homily, stated, "The army is expiating our country's impurities. Would not Christ desire that the armed forces some day move beyond that function?"[12] A number of generals spoke of defending "freedom and religion," and of exterminating "traitorous and atheistic subversives." On December 5, General Luciano Adolfo Jauregui stated in a speech:

> Let Argentines have no doubt whether we will succeed. . . . We are going to move forward with this war and win it on the terrain they have chosen, in the countryside, the city, the factory, the university . . . or in any other

institution they might have infiltrated: in the church, against those who seek to change our God become man, for a man become God. We are not going to let up our attack in any way; we are going to annihilate them. We know our mission . . . and we cannot be fooled.[13]

Military officers were speaking "theological" language and the two vicars for the army were speaking "military" language.

The proclamation for the aborted military coup of December 19, 1975, included the following paragraph:

Before God, there can be no self-satisfaction, nothing lukewarm, no indifference, no anonymous hero. If there are no more just men in Argentina, we must accept the punishment. For our own part, we say, "I have fought the good fight, I have finished the course, I have kept the faith. In this month of the Immaculate Conception, long live the fatherland!"

When Bishop Tortolo celebrated Mass for the coup officers, he spoke of them in these terms: "admirable men with a high level of morality and a consistent and unbending attitude toward the faith and with regard to principles."[14] Other bishops, such as Bishop Antonio Plaza, archbishop of La Plata, joined with the promilitary bishops. Nevertheless, the episcopal conference and most of the clergy reacted against the ecclesiastico-military campaign, and publicly sought to restrain it.

Starting in March 1976 the more moderate part of the hierarchy reasserted its leadership within the Argentine church for a period of time. Its best known representatives were three archbishops—Primatesta, Aramburu, and Zaspe. The small group of "Third World bishops" (Angelelli, Brasca, Devoto, Scozzini, Hesayné, de Navares, and others) continued to struggle alongside the popular church. They were generally reduced to silence and calumniated. On August 4, 1976, Bishop Angelelli died as the result of a suspicious "accident," following a harsh confrontation with military officers after the murder of two priests in his diocese. Another bishop-martyr of the popular church in Argentina was Bishop Ponce de León, bishop of San Nicolás. As of 1978, more than fifty priests and religious had been murdered or had simply disappeared. The number of lay persons accorded the same fate is beyond calculation.

When the coup took place in March 1976, the position of the militarist bishops was one of public and unconditional legitimation. Most bishops, reflecting a conservative or conciliatory mentality, used more moderate language, giving "critical support" to the new government. At the thirty-third assembly of the bishops (May 10–11, 1976) the militarist group was unable to impose its viewpoint, but the more moderate majority did not speak out clearly and sharply either. On May 16, the "Pastoral Letter of the Whole Episcopate on the Situation of the Nation" was published. This document was confusing and ran counter to the thinking of most of the clergy and of grassroots Christian movements.

In their pastoral letter, the bishops provided a clear *legitimation* for the coup and the military government, attenuating it with a series of *conditions*. This *conditional legitimation* did not enable the bishops to go beyond advocating a "humanization" of the military dictatorship. This appeal to a regime regarded as legitimate put the Argentine church in a situation of dependence on, and subordination to, the military government. The church lost its "prophetic autonomy." The pastoral letter stated: "The historical justification for what is happening in our country is to be found not simply in the termination of a particular situation, but also in the provision of appropriate political action of the government in the pursuit of the common good of the whole nation."

By legitimizing the *origin* of the military government, the bishops opened the possibility of legitimizing its *exercise*. In other words, the military coup was legitimate in its overthrow of a bad government, but a legitimate government could arise out of that legitimate origin only if it was capable of ensuring the common good. The document had a very courageous paragraph condemning torture and human rights violations. But as positive as it was, this condemnation was relativized by its asking the people to bear all kinds of sacrifices, while leaving to the military a vast field of action, where one could not act "with the chemical purity found in times of peace." The problem was that these "impurities" tolerated by the bishops were precisely the human rights violations that were continually taking place. The bishops' good intention of "humanizing" the overall situation remained trapped in the relentless logic of military dictatorship.

The bishops in fact provided a legitimation both for the dictatorship itself and for its exercise. The militarist bishops would take advantage of this situation, translating the abstract and ambiguous language of the episcopal majority into concrete and well-defined language. The moderate bishops found themselves once more led by the minority favoring an ecclesiastico-military New Christendom. But outside this New Christendom, in the heart of the oppressed masses, the church was growing.

Present Tendencies in the Argentine Hierarchy

In closing this section, I should like to summarize an analysis of the present tendencies of the Argentine Catholic hierarchy, made by an Argentine priest in 1978.[15] According to this study, four tendencies may be found:

1. Bishops of the *progressive tendency* (8 percent) take the Medellín conference as their theological reference point and a "socialist project" as their political reference point.

2. Those of the *conciliar tendency* (50 percent), for whom the main reference point is Vatican II, do indeed denounce human rights violations and the poverty of the people. Nevertheless, their language is ambiguous: they defend the existing legal framework and are radically anti-Marxist. Archbishop Zaspe

of Santa Fe says the church is persecuted for defending the people, but adds immediately, "Marxism is an ideology that is inhuman, anti-Christian, atheistic by its very nature, and radically oppressive. It is not redemptive, does not bring salvation, and does not lead to liberation."

3. Those of the *conservative tendency* (30 percent) are still linked to the preconciliar church of Pope Pius XII. This group does not understand the Argentine political process, and does not try to understand it.

4. Those of the *pro-military tendency* (12 percent), by contrast, are not acting out of inertia or "conservatism," but out of a clear-sighted understanding of the military ideology. Bishop Bonamín, vicar of the armed forces, and a good representative of this tendency, has even gone so far as to say, "When blood is spilt, redemption takes place. God accomplishes redemption through the Argentine army. It may be that the military—a falange of honest and pure individuals—are to be purified in the Jordan of blood in order to be presented to the country" (March 24, 1977). This sector of the hierarchy provides the military dictatorship and its repressive action with an unconditional legitimation.

If I note that the promilitary sector of the Argentine Catholic hierarchy has succeeded in leading the conservative sector and the Vatican II sector to some extent, or at least has been able to interpret their ambiguous or conciliatory language within the terms of military ideology, I realize that 92 percent of the Argentine hierarchy has been unable to put up any *prophetic resistance* to the dictatorship, or to provide *gospel-inspired leadership* for the church as a whole. Thus, the Argentine episcopacy is among the most reactionary in Latin America. It has no equal anywhere but in Colombia, where the bishops' reactionary political stance is not promilitary but merely conservative. The attitude of the Argentine clergy and of most active grassroots Christians is utterly different. These sectors experience their identity as church in communion with those Argentine bishops who are linked to the popular church and who—something unique in Latin America—have among their numbers two bishops who have been made martyrs by repression. In no other country in Latin America can one find such a sharp separation between the bulk of the episcopacy on the one side, and the Christian people, clergy, and religious on the other.

BRAZIL

As I turn to the modern history of the Brazilian church, I particularly want to examine and interpret the process of crisis in a specific kind of new Christendom and of the church connected to it and the process of the birth of a popular church—that is, a church that has nothing to do with any Christendom model, one built up out of the people's struggle for liberation from oppression. As is the case elsewhere in Latin America, these two processes began in Brazil around 1960.

The stage that began in Latin America in the 1960s is still *open*: the bulk of the church has not given up the New Christendom model, even though that model is now in a process of crisis and breakdown. There are vigorous efforts to adapt this Christendom model so as to keep it in place. Some small sectors of the church seek a quick answer to the crisis by establishing a new alliance with national security (military) regimes, and thus project a model of ecclesiastico-military New Christendom. The stability of this model would be linked to that of the military regimes themselves.

Most of the church rejects such a project but without awareness of any alternative form of Christendom. The possibilities are still not clear, and the crisis is prolonged. Nevertheless, there is another minority group in the church that rejects *any* project of Christendom, and is seeking to build a church *beyond* any kind of alliance or connection with the prevailing system and with the dominant classes: a church that arises as a "sign of liberation" for the popular and oppressed masses. This church is growing, even though it is subjected to harsh repression from authoritarian or military states, and is likewise condemned and regarded as illegitimate by sectors of the church that have opted for the new model of domination.

The process that began around 1960 will be over when the bulk of the Latin American church has resolved its internal crisis, *either* by adapting to the model of ecclesiastico-military New Christendom or authoritarian New Christendom, which is structured into the new model of domination, *or* by being converted to taking the path already opened by the popular church, beyond any Christendom model. As long as this period has not ended, the main part of the church, not opting for one route or the other, will continue to experience a deepening internal crisis.

Although the church certainly has a dynamic of its own, and its own specific autonomy, the way it evolves in the coming years and decades will be closely connected to what happens economically, socially, and politically in Latin America. How the Latin American church solves its crisis, whether it opts in the directions already visible in some minority groups, will thus depend to some extent on the direction taken by Latin America itself: whether the present period ends with the definitive triumph of the present counterrevolutionary process and the new model of domination becomes firmly established, or whether, on the contrary, this period remains open and the tone is set by a significant and permanent step forward in the overall movement of liberation. The church will not evolve in a mechanical fashion, nor will its direction be automatically determined by socio-political processes. Nevertheless, this is the context in which the Latin American church will be transformed and will be seeking to resolve its present crisis. The fact that Christendom itself is in question—and the basis for Christendom is the alliance between church and state or between church and ruling classes—makes it all the more obvious that the church is situated within the socio-political crisis.

In the case of Brazil the options I have sketched are utterly clear. What I intend to do here is not to go through the whole history of Brazil and the

Brazilian church, but simply to propose some overall interpretations. In order to interpret the present crisis of the Brazilian church and the crisis of the Christendom model at its root, I must take a brief look at the past and examine the situation prior to the crisis; then, looking forward, I must make an analysis from the present vantage point to determine what possible solutions to the crisis may be seen to be taking shape.

During this present period (which started in 1960), the past, which remains in perpetual crisis, and a future, already present in embryo, exist side by side. Only a broad historical perspective will enable anyone to discern what aspects of the present are *in crisis* because they ought to die out, and what aspects are *in a critical situation*, because they are in a process of birth and maturation. The New Christendom church is a church *in crisis;* the popular church today is a church that is *in a critical situation* because it is searching for its own path and its own identity while resisting and being battered by repression, but it is not at all a church *in crisis*. It is not the whole church that is in crisis, but only a form or kind of church, one that is tied to a New Christendom model.

Birth of a Conservative New Christendom

After the period of crisis of colonial Christendom in Brazil (1808-1889), two overall stages in the formative process of New Christendom can be distinguished: a conservative, antiliberal stage and a populist-nationalist-developmentalist stage. Precise dates cannot be given, because processes in history make initial appearances in the form of promises, and later they strive for self-prolongation, when they are in a state of crisis. In general, however, the formation of conservative New Christendom ran parallel to the First Republic (1889-1930). At that time, Brazil was experiencing a coffee boom and the liberal-positivist reform carried out by the ruling oligarchy. That oligarchy succeeded in consolidating its internal control and deepened its external dependence on an agro-export economy, which fitted into the new international division of labor imposed by the advent of international monopoly capital (around 1880). On January 7, 1890, separation of church and state was decreed.

During that period, significant numbers of immigrants arrived (four million between 1890 and 1940 and, according to de Kadt, one hundred thousand a year between 1890 and 1900). At that time too Protestantism underwent significant expansion. It was in this context that the Brazilian Catholic Church carried out a renewal: it shared in the expansion and euphoria of the oligarchy as a result of the coffee boom, but at the same time it vigorously challenged the liberalism and positivism of the oligarchy. That is why the result was a church on the defensive, one that felt threatened by liberalism and Protestantism, in an unfamiliar situation of separation of church and state.

Even after being constitutionally separated from the state, the Brazilian church did not give up its Christendom project. On the contrary, it tried to rebuild itself institutionally and recover its power in civil society, by continually seeking recognition and support from the state. In order to assert itself as a power vis-à-vis the state, the Brazilian church looked to Rome for support. The church became romanized and europeanized, becoming further withdrawn from things Brazilian and further removed from popular Catholicism.

At first (1890-1900) the Brazilian church skillfully maintained its independence from the state, though not at all relinquishing its desire for recognition by and support from the state. That is why subsequently (1900-1930) the church's effort degenerated into "organizational triumphalism" (Hoornaert): the church sought the support of the state in its struggle against liberalism and Protestantism. It tried to win state support by multiplying ecclesiastical institutions and dignities, schools and shrines, religious celebrations and eucharistic congresses, and so forth. That is how there arose a formal kind of New Christendom, focused on externals, with no deep gospel substance, and utterly foreign to the culture and interests of the people. One of the signs of this conservative New Christendom, triumphalistic, formal, and foreign to the Brazilian people, was the statue of Christ the Redeemer, dedicated in 1931, overlooking the city of Rio de Janeiro. To this day, this statue of Christ reflects the contradiction between Christendom and the poverty-stricken residents of the *favelas* surrounding the city of Rio.

The Brazilian intellectual Jackson de Figueiredo typified this conservative New Christendom. In 1922 he set up the Dom Vital Center, and managed it until his death in 1928. For Figueiredo, the combat against atheists, freemasons, and Protestants made it imperative for the church to hold political power. The way to christianize society was to provide a Catholic education for the oligarchical elites and make use of the state to assure the "rights of the church." To achieve these aims, Figueiredo strove to set up a Catholic political party, but Archbishop Sebastião prohibited it. Leme, who occupied the see of Rio from 1921 to 1942, was just as representative of this period. As early as 1916, as bishop of Olinda, he stated, "The Roman church must become organized and united in order to be able to put pressure on the government."[16]

Catholic nationalism came on the scene late in conservative New Christendom, and paved the way for the transition to the next stage. This nationalism strove to have the state recognize Catholicism as the official religion of the Brazilian people and the Catholic Church as the national church. Catholicism was presented as an essential and necessary element in what made Brazil a nation. Atheism and heresy alike were tantamount to betrayal of the nation. This nationalism tried to use the state to combat liberalism, atheist humanism, and Protestantism, and thus to give the Catholic Church a hegemonic role within civil society. Jackson de Figueiredo, the ideologue of nationalism, believed that the spiritual and temporal powers should be united in order to guarantee that there be a "Christian order," which would provide a basis for finding solutions to all political and social problems. This movement can be traced to certain European writers such as Joseph de Maistre, Charles Maurras, and Donoso Cortés. The ideas of Catholic nationalism were circulated by the review *A Ordem*, set up in Rio in 1921 with Figueiredo as editor.

Catholic nationalism finally (and contradictorily) led to a rapprochement between conservative Catholicism and positivism, a development that should not be surprising: both expressed the ideology of the ruling oligarchy. This nationalistic and positivistic Catholicism was resurrected in the military ideology of national security, wherein "Christian order" was regarded as the basis of the nation. Thus Catholic nationalism, a current of thought differing from, and opposed to, social Christianity, sought to establish a new pact between the hierarchy and the ruling classes. That was destined to take place during the following stage, starting in 1930.

1930: Beginning of a New Stage

In 1930 there began a second stage in the history of Brazilian New Christendom and the church tied to it. Two moments in this stage can be distinguished—a *populist* period from 1930 to 1955, and a *developmentalist* period from 1956 to 1964. A brief historical outline will provide a basis for interpreting the development of the church during this period:

I. *1930-1955: Populist Period*
—1930-1945: (Second Republic), President Getúlio Vargas.
—1937: creation of the *Estado Novo*.
—1945: fall of Getúlio Vargas. New president, Eurico Gaspar Dutra (conservative, anticommunist).
—1951: elections. Getúlio Vargas reelected president.
—1954: after Vargas committed suicide, the vice-president João Café Filho, Presbyterian, took over power.

II. *1956-1964: Developmentalist Period*
—1956: president, Juscelino Kubitschek.
—1961: president, Jânio Quadros (who resigned in August).
—1961-1964: president, João Goulart.
—March 31, 1964: armed revolt. National security regime.

I examine briefly two phenomena of this stage (1930–1964): the movement of the Brazilian church from a conservative, antiliberal New Christendom to another kind of New Christendom, populist-nationalist-developmentalist, and then the beginning of its crisis during the early 1960s.

With Getúlio Vargas the Catholic hierarchy was able to make an alliance (based on the constitution and other legislation) with the state, which provided the foundation for the New Christendom that the church wished to inaugurate. In 1931 Cardinal Leme, accompanied by some fifty bishops, paid a visit to Getúlio Vargas to present him with a list of all the political and juridical demands of the church. To back up this petition, there were impressive demonstrations by Catholics. The church used the LEC (*Liga Eleitoral Católica*, Catholic Electoral League) as an instrument of pressure. The LEC was set up in 1932 with the approval of the cardinal of Rio. The Brazilian church, which had been opposed to the establishment of a Catholic political party at the end of the nineteenth century (under Bishop Antônio de Macedo Costa) and during the 1920s, now gave its approval to the LEC, which sought to be not a political party, but an instrument for political pressure, used directly by the bishops. All the demands of the LEC and the hierarchical church were included in the 1934 constitution.

What the bishops had not managed to obtain in 1925 with a Catholic president, Arturo Bernardes (1922–1926), they now obtained from Getúlio Vargas, who called himself an agnostic. Bernardes, who had been elected with the explicit support of the church and who enjoyed excellent relationships with the Catholic hierarchy and the Vatican, could not get the two-thirds majority vote needed to modify the constitution. Even though a "separation" of church and state was retained in the 1934 constitution, the church was now recognized as having the following rights: the state could give financial aid to the church "in the interest of the majority"; members of religious orders had the right to vote; the juridical situation of religious congregations was improved; military chaplaincies were permitted; religious marriage had the same force as civil marriage; divorce was prohibited; and, most important, the state could give financial aid to Catholic schools, and the church could teach religion classes as part of the public school curriculum.[17]

How to explain this shift in church-state relationships after 1930? It was not that the church had acquired more political power in such a short time, or that the bourgeoisie had suddenly converted to Catholicism. The basic reason is to be found in the crisis of the economic, political, and social basis for the conservative New Christendom of 1889 to 1930. With the crisis of 1929 the coffee boom halted (prices plummeted), the economic model based solely on agro-export came to an end, and there began a rapid expansion of industrialization-urbanization (especially after 1950).

The impact of the economic crisis was such that the large landholders were brought to ruin, and both the liberal and conservative wings of the oligarchy lost power. With the revolution of 1930, the incipient industrial bourgeoisie, allied to the cattle ranchers of Minas Gerais and Rio Grande do Sul, represented and led by Getúlio Vargas, seized political hegemony.[18] Vargas pushed forward a program of industrialization and economic independence, with growing participation on the part of the state, and the support of new social sectors: the "middle strata," and working-class sectors in the cities (promulgation of social welfare legislation and the formation of state-promoted labor unions).

In a word, in 1930 Brazil passed from an oligarchical to a populist stage. The process was not as quick as might appear nor were the changes as radical as might appear, but the revolution of 1930, with its political leader Getúlio Vargas, marked the end of one age in Brazil, and prefigured the beginning of another.

It is within this context that I must interpret the change in church-state relationships. In view of the crisis of 1930, the weakening of the oligarchy, and the pressure of the new middle strata, the church and the ruling classes believed that the time had come to open the way for reconciliation. Even the most liberal sectors of the bourgeoisie toned down their anticlerical language, and the hierarchy softened its aggressively antiliberal stance. The populist project, personified in Getúlio Vargas, needed the support of the church (or at least needed not to have the church as an enemy): most Brazilians identified themselves as Catholics. For its part, the church saw in the populist program—which was guaranteed to be neither liberal, nor laicist, nor socialist-Marxist—a chance to broaden its social base among the emerging middle and popular strata. Thus Vargas initiated the passage from a conservative antiliberal New Christendom to another kind of New Christendom, one that was populist-nationalist and, after 1956, would take on a "developmentalist" character.

Breaking with conservative New Christendom turned out to be a slow and difficult process. It was only after 1945, at the end of Getúlio Vargas's first presidency and the end of World War II, that there was any significant change in the mentality of church leaders.

In keeping with the Christendom mentality, the Catholic bishops tended to use their alliance with the populist state (after gaining official recognition in the constitution of 1934) in order to expand and safeguard their power and influence in civil society, especially in terms of institutions, schools in particular. The church was now able to put into practice what had been proposed by Catholic nationalism—to utilize political power to combat the enemies of the church: liberalism (positivism, laicism, secularism, naturalism), Protestantism (especially broad-based Protestantism), and spiritism (Umbanda and other forms). The 1934 constitution signaled a victory of Catholicism over Protestantism. Some sectors of the church took advantage of the official government nationalism to characterize Protestantism as foreign and contrary to the very ethnos of the Brazilian people. It was typical of this kind of New Christendom that it preferred to use political power in this fashion rather than work at catechesis and evangelization.

1937: The Church and the Estado Novo

So important did the hierarchal church regard its alliance with the populist state as the basis for New Christendom that this alliance was not severed in the crisis of 1937. In November of that year Getúlio Vargas dictatorially canceled elections and extended his presidency under the pretext of a proposed new constitution and the creation of the *Estado Novo,* "new state." This was to be a corporatist state, which would make the Catholic Church an integral part of the republic. In addition, Vargas suppressed political parties and put limits on democratic freedoms. Most of the Brazilian church accepted the *Estado Novo*, particularly because it promised to hold back the "communist threat." The reaction of Archbishop João Becker of Porto Alegre was the most enthusiastic, yet quite typical of a Christendom mentality. He publicly lauded the constitution of 1937, pronouncing it democratic and in line with the social doctrine of Pope Pius XI. The bishop's political argument was that the *Estado Novo* was the only alternative to "chaos," a position that justified state use of violence in the general interests of the nation.

The most important aspect of *Estado Novo* for the church was that it guaranteed the civil rights of the church, especially in the domains of family and education. The "Christian order" and the "order and stability of the state" were practically one and the same. Moreover, the church was seen as fitting into the social programs of the populist state. The state sometimes utilized and financed social and educational structures of the church, and the church made use of state structures (public schools, military institutes) for its pastoral work.[19]

With the aid of the state, the church rebuilt its institutional apparatus, and enhanced its social and political influence in civil society. The New Christendom model, with backing from the state and its laws, guided civil and political society in a "Christian" direction.

But the church could not reform itself internally or carry out any genuine evangelization by means of such methods. Evangelization is inherently incompatible with a Christendom model. Christendom "produces" unevangelized Catholics. In fact, the apostolic and lay movements during this period (1930-1945) were insignificant. The Catholic Action founded by Cardinal Leme in Rio in 1923, which was extended to the national level in 1935 along the lines of the Italian model, was a meaningless institution in terms of apostolic and evangelizing activity. Given its view of the church and pastoral activity, Christendom had no need for a strong and extensive lay movement. That situation changed after 1945.

The first stirrings of renewal came before 1945 from the Dom Vital Center. In 1928 the nationalist intellectual Jackson de Figueiredo died, and Alceu Amoroso Lima took his place. This great Christian writer (known by his pseudonym, Tristão [Tristan] de Athayde) brought Christian social thought to Brazil and developed it further, under the influence of Jacques Maritain (whose *Humanisme intégral* was published in 1937). From that point onward, there were two opposed tendencies vying with one another among the Catholic laity—an integralist and reactionary *Catholic nationalism,* whose leader was Gustavo Corção, and *social Christianity,* led by Alceu Amoroso Lima. The former served as the inspiration for ultra-rightwing integralist organizations in Brazil, which would flourish after the 1964 coup;[20] the latter was to be an inspiration for Catholic Action, especially between 1945 and 1960.

Before 1945 it was still *A Ordem* and the LEC that were the standard-bearers for populist New Christendom. The LEC began to decline in 1950, when it failed to block the election of João Café Filho as vice-president—even threatening excommunication—because he was a Presbyterian. When Vargas committed suicide (1954), Filho took office as the first Protestant president of Brazil. Nevertheless, the church-state alliance was so stable that it was under this Protestant president that the state shared the expenses of the Eucharistic Congress of 1955, in which the nation was dedicated to the Sacred Heart of Jesus.

Although there certainly was *structural continuity* between conservative New Christendom (1890-1930) and populist New Christendom (1930-1955), there was also a *basic difference:* during the populist phase the church came into contact with the political and social problems of the middle and popular strata, and, by the same token, those sectors made themselves felt *within* the church. In the populist dynamic the attitude of the church was one of paternalism and proselytism, an attitude that was foreign to the social and political interests of the popular and middle classes. The church manipulated its social base so as to increase the ecclesiastical power of Christendom, instead of taking a posture of service and disinterested evangelization vis-à-vis its social base. Populism was usually antipopular (this came out particularly in times of crisis) and in the case of "ecclesial populism" it was also antievangelizing.

Nevertheless, and running counter to populism itself, a deeper contact between the church and the middle and popular sectors in this case brought New Christendom into crisis, and opened the church to the interests of the middle and popular classes. This process was more marked during the phase following populism, the developmentalist phase (1956-1964). During the developmentalist period, populism entered into crisis and lost its base—that is, the social base of populism won its political independence from the bourgeoisie and began to look for a political program of its own, one that would serve its own class interests. Similarly the social base of populist Christendom won its independence and also struggled *within* the church *against* the structures and ideologies of Christendom and *for* the advent of a church that would be truly evangelizing, liberating, and popular in character.

1948: Birth of Specialized Catholic Action

The first significant development in the 1945-1964 period was the change within Catholic Action. Starting in 1948 there was a shift from the Italian model of Catholic Action, organized according to age and sex, to the French/Belgian model, organized by sectors or social classes. The first branch to be set up on the national level in Brazil was the JOC (*Juventude Operária Católica,* Catholic Worker Youth [equivalent, in English-speaking countries, to the Young Christian Workers]). In 1950 the JAC (*Juventude Agrícola Católica,* Catholic Rural Youth) was organized, followed by the JEC (*Juventude Estudantil Católica,* Catholic Student Youth), the JUC (*Juventude Universitária Católica,* Catholic University Youth), the JIC (*Juventude Independente Católica,* Catholic Independent Youth), and even more branches.

The JEC, JUC, and JIC roughly matched the sectors of the "middle strata" and of the petite bourgeoisie. This shift in Catholic Action Groups was a key development, and a sign that the church had a better grasp of social reality. In the long run, specialized Catholic Action groups (particulary JUC and JOC) were destined to be intermediary forces within the church leading to a line of Christian thought whose starting point was a "class" commitment and class social consciousness. The church did not change its New Christendom thought patterns, but whereas previously it defended its interests by relying essentially on the state, now it does so by relying on its active grassroots Christians, who lead the church to a deeper and more active participation in the life of the nation. The course taken by Catholic Action makes it possible to see, as in a microcosm, the course taken by they whole church, a point that will become clear further on.

1950: The Church and the Agrarian Question

Another significant development is the way the Brazilian church developed with regard to the agrarian problem, which in fact drew it into national political life. In 1950 there was a study week devoted to this issue in Campanha, Minas Gerais. Out of this meeting came a pastoral letter by Bishop Inocéncio Engelke, who hosted the conference. The title of the letter was very significant: "With Us, Without Us, or Against Us, There Will Be Rural Reform." In my opinion, there were three characteristics that clearly defined the point from which the church began its process of opening up to the social sphere.[21]

1. The church struggled for "a rural reform" from a *landholder's* viewpoint. It invited some sixty priests and two-hundred fifty landholders to the study week . . . but *not one campesino*. It was assumed that the ruling classes had the responsibility and obligation to carry out reforms. Episcopal letters never failed to appeal to those who had economic, political, or cultural power, because it was they who could and had to make changes. There was no place for the exploited population to be the *subject* of change. The "we" in Bishop Engelke's pastoral letter included the hierarchical church and the owners, but never the campesinos.[22]

2. The church, *on the defensive,* proposed a reform to head off, and protect itself from, a reform that might be carried out "without us" and "against us." Along with the owners, the church was afraid of the "agitation" and first stirrings of independent rural class-based organization beginning to appear in Brazil. What the church regarded with fear at this point, it will later see as a sign of hope.

3. In the eyes of the church, the socio-political field seemed to have about it a *dynamism of change* that was *inevitable.* It seemed that rural reform *would take place*—with, without, or against the church. That much was positive. But, why was there such a distinction between the church and the liberating dynamic force of history? What is the basis for saying that reform would certainly take place? The church knew it had a mission to carry out in the social sphere, but it did not know the historical mechanisms that could explain the social dynamism that made rural reform inevitable. There was a dualism between church and history. The church and Christians gave a meaning to history, but it was "others" who made that history. These "others" would carry out rural reform *in any case;* the bishops were concerned that they should do so "with us" and not "against us or without us."

What the church had not yet grasped was that *rural landholders* were part of the "we" and that behind the impersonal form—"there will be [land reform]"—there lurked its subject or agent—the campesinos. Hence the title of Bishop Engelke's pastoral letter could be rephrased: "With Us [Church and Owners], Without Us, or Against Us, the Campesinos Will Carry Out Rural Reform."

The church had a good grasp of the social problem, but because it did not have a social and political analysis of the overall situation, it was blind to the fact that it was tied up with those who held economic power. In other words, precisely because of this involvement, the church was incapable of working out a social and political analysis of matters that would reveal the class antagonism at the heart of things.

1956-1959: The Church and the Problem of Underdevelopment

Six years after Bishop Engelke's pastoral letter, another event revealed how quickly and how deeply the Brazilian church had been moving into the social sphere—the meeting of the bishops of the northeast held in Campina Grande, May 21-26, 1956. By then Brazil had moved into the developmentalist phase, with Juscelino Kubitschek as president (1956-1961). If on previous occasions, when it collaborated with the state with a view to solving social problems, the church had represented the interests of the ruling classes vis-à-vis the state, now the church was defending state reforms vis-à-vis the ruling classes.[23] Now identified with the governmental program for development, the church began to take some distance from the landholding oligarchies. By making it possible for church and state to work together, the previous populist phase (1930-1955) had carried out the mediation necessary for the church to move from conservatism (1890-1930) to developmentalism (1956-1964).

Government economists and Catholic experts worked together preparing the Campina Grande meeting. A development model for the northeast of Brazil was elaborated; the plan gave an important role to the state, something that ran counter to liberal postulates for economic growth. The hierarchical church, which had modernized its structures, starting with the establishment of the CNBB (*Conferência Nacional dos Bispos do Brasil*, National Conference of the Bishops of Brazil), which provided it with a powerful instrument for expressing itself politically on the national level, paid serious attention to the team that had prepared the Campina Grande meeting. At that meeting the church officially committed itself to the government's "Operation Northeast," which would give rise to SUDENE (*Superintendência de Desenvolvimento do Nordeste*, Superintendency of Development of the Northeast), headed by Celso Furtado. In May 1959, in Natal, the government organized a second meeting with the bishops of the northeast in order to put pressure on the national congress to pass the law that officially created SUDENE.

These two meetings, in 1956 and 1959, consolidated the alliance between the development-minded government and the church, and completely changed the image of the church in civil society. With developmentalism, the hierarchical church decisively turned toward social problems.

Although the SUDENE proposals basically favored the interests of the industrial bourgeoisie at the expense of landholders, the church came to interpret the developmentalist project in a wider social dimension, as the church became involved with the poor. The church acknowledged the situation in these terms:

> Within the economic and social structures that make up our political system and our system of private economy, there are terrible injustices, which lead the church to declare that it is utterly independent of those structures and not at all responsible for them. In view of its own evangelizing mission it states that it has no connection with these unjust situations, and that it takes its stand with the poor, cooperating with them in work of rescue and redemption.[24]

This change within the Catholic hierarchy, which must be regarded as positive, made it possible for the more dynamic sectors in the social base of the church to move from *social questions* to *political questions*. Various factors will be involved in this politicizing process among Christians, beginning around 1960. I shall examine those factors further on.

In order to understand the attitude of the church toward the Kubitschek government, it is useful to examine the president's thinking with regard to the church and Christianity.[25] The developmentalism associated with Juscelino Kubitschek took the "Christian character" of Brazil as the basis for its political options: "The solution to national problems is to be found in a political-legal blueprint suitable to our Christian character." In the same way Christianity was taken as a central reference point for ideological options: "We are under the banner of the West, and essentially that means defending the values that are proper to Christianity." Developmentalism found its justification and legitimation in Christianity. That is why Kubitschek used the social doctrine of the church, and based himself on Christian humanism:

> We are, and we want to continue to be, a Christian nation. . . . Being a Christian nation today means regarding social injustice for what it really is: a great sin against Christ. The nation that is indifferent to human misery and to underdevelopment, with all the horrors it entails, is not Christian. . . . Our policies, essentially inspired by Christianity, take their impulse from the human being, and see in the human being their end and purpose.

The developmental ideology, as we find it in Juscelino Kubitschek, was both *technical* and *moralist*. The technical view of economic and social problems was opposed to an ideological view. The moralist view was opposed to a political view. Hence, developmentalism was viewed neither ideologically nor politically. In passing over the ideological and political dimensions, developmentalism generally utilized Christian ideas. Developmentalist ideology thus acquired legitimacy within a Christian conception of humankind and society, and not by justifying itself ideologically and politically. This "Christian" character of developmentalism found a resounding echo among the bishops, who become identified with it. This paves the way for an alliance between the church and the developmentalist state, the basis and foundation of New Christendom.

The Christian Democratic Party (PDC) in Brazil provides another reference point for understanding New Christendom during the populist-developmentalist period.[26] Established in 1945 by Bishop Arruda Câmara, as a political party it was of little importance until 1953, when, in coalition with the Socialist Party, it won the municipal elections in São Paulo. In 1958 it won six congressional seats. It supported Jânio Quadros as a presidential candidate and took part in the Goulart government. By 1962 it had twenty deputies and one senator in the national congress. The party is made up primarily of an intellectual petite bourgeoisie.

As was the case with Christian Democracy all over Latin America, the party reflected two tendencies in Brazil: a right wing, led by the PDC president, Ney Braga, and Marshall Juarez Távora, and a left wing, whose best known leaders were Paulo de Tarso and Franco Montoro (ministers of education and labor, respectively, under João Goulart). Starting in 1960, when the mass movement became more important and the prevailing developmentalist approach entered into crisis, these two tendencies became violently opposed. In 1964 the rightwing current accepted the military coup and the leftwing current was forced to go underground or into exile. The PDC now had little influence on Brazilian national life. Leftwing Christian interest was reflected outside the PDC in *Acão Popular*, in grassroots movements, and in periodicals like *Brazil Urgente*, which had a much greater impact on Christian milieux than did the Brazilian PDC. The split within the PDC was nevertheless a significant event, and one quite typical of socio-Christian New Christendom.

Still another basic reference point for analyzing the Brazilian church was the direction taken by Catholic University Youth (JUC) and young Catholic workers (JOC-ACO [*Acão Católica Operária*]). These movements involved small minorities, but they reflected the overall complex of problems facing the Brazilian church. In effect, they amounted to "laboratories," where for more than ten years young Brazilians reflected on the connections between political practice and Christian life. The course taken by specialized Catholic Action after 1950 (I will not deal with the Italian model of Catholic Action that prevailed in Brazil from 1923 to 1948), and especially the way it became politically radicalized starting in 1960, will show quite clearly what the crisis of populist-nationalist New Christendom, and indeed of the Christendom model itself, was all about.

In the radicalization process within Catholic Action, there were two key events that marked a breaking point (a political breaking point with the New Christendom program, which did not necessarily entail a break with the church): July 1960 (the JUC tenth-anniversary congress) and June 1968 (the JOC-ACO national congress).[27]

It was no coincidence that the radicalization of the JUC took place before the 1964 coup, and that of the JOC afterward. All over Latin America the radicalization of the petite bourgeoisie (and of the "middle strata" in general) preceded the mobilization of the popular classes. The petite bourgeoisie became radicalized when the developmentalist model had reached its limits and was in crisis; the same thing happened to the popular classes when the capitalist system as a whole had gone into an overall crisis that was economic, political, and ideological. The latter situation was reflected within Catholic Action and it is from that socio-political perspective that one must interpret the process whereby it became radicalized.

From the time of its first congress in 1950 until around 1958, the JUC limited its activity to the "spiritual" realm: retreats, spiritual formation, pilgrimages, courses in church history, bringing religious services to state universities, and so forth. Then there came a change. JUC members became involved in *concrete social projects* and the *national reality* of Brazil became a topic of discussion. In 1959 Father Almery Bezerra proposed what was called the "historical ideal," popularized by the Instituto Superior de Estudos Brasileiros (Higher Institute of Brazilian Studies) and by intellectuals like Hélio Jaguaribe, Cândido Mendes, and others. At the "ten-year congress" held in 1960, discussion centered on the "historical ideal" and there was a *definitive break* from Catholic Action that was spiritual, apostolic, and social-Christian in focus. At bottom, what was going on here was the beginning of a much more radical and significant break from the New Christendom model. This incipient split, still confused and not yet mature, was one of the first that took place in Brazil on an institutional level, and among the first in Latin America as a whole.

The "historical ideal" was a response on the part of JUC activists to two discoveries they had made: that Brazilian society had to undergo a radical transformation, and that the social doctrine of the church was not an adequate instrument for carrying out such a transformation.[28] They did not deny that the Christian could find in the faith the *ultimate meaning of history*, but when it came to *concrete social and political action*, Christians did not find in their faith, or in the social doctrine of the church, the kind of mediation that would adequately meet their needs with regard to such action. As Father Almery said:

> If we want go get a kind of *Christian commitment* that will be effective in the temporal sphere, it is absolutely necessary to reflect extensively and seriously *in the light of reality* . . . and thus to come to certain intermediary principles that can express what I could call the "Christian historical ideal."[29]

The "historical ideal" was worked out *in the light of social reality*, not deduced from doctrinal principles provided by any social doctrine of the church. The theology underlying the "historical ideal" was that of the *distinction of planes, and it was different from, even opposed to, that of social Christianity*.[30] Political activism on the part of Christians needed not be excercised in "Christian" parties or organizations (such as Christian Democracy, a Christian labor movement, or other political institutions of New Christendom). The "historical ideal" opened up to Christians the possibility of being politically active in non-Christian parties and organizations, although that in no way meant giving up the faith as the "ultimate meaning of history." The JUC thus begans a process of breaking away from New Christendom, without breaking away from Christianity or the church.

The "historical ideal" set the tone for the "ten-year congress," and its position took form in a document entitled "Guidelines for a Historical Ideal for the Brazilian People." Students in the deparments of economics and sociology (especially those in Belo Horizonte), who had a better knowledge of the situation in Brazil, in both practical and theoretical terms, took charge of the congress. Maritain's influence was still present on the level of ideology (it was he who had coined the expression "historical ideal"), but they were making an effort to move beyond Maritain, looking too for support in Emmanuel Mounier, L.J. Lebret, and even in a kind of elementary and not well-assimilated Marxism. Also exercising an influence in the JUC at that period was the thinking of Thomas Cardonnel and Henrique de Lima Vaz. In the early 1960s there was no "liberation theology" that could have enabled anyone to come up with a theoretical critique of the way the faith was ideologized in the New Christendom model and a theoretical understanding of the convergence between radicalization in political commitment and radicalization in Christian commitment. Brazil was anticipating the excitement of the kind of "revolutionary Christianity" that Argentina, Uruguay, Colombia, and Chile would experience between 1968 and 1970.

For those involved in Catholic Action the JUC "ten-year congress" marked a shift from the "social field" to the "political field." In 1960 JUC members, together with other leaders and activists from the Marxist left, began to become politically involved in the student movement. At this point, Marxism was spreading throughout the universities. What led to the greatest tension with the hierarchy was not so much that JUC took ideological positions, but that it became engaged in political practice. In 1961 there was discussion of the question of JUC identity as as an apostolic movement, of the role of the laity in the church, of how JUC should obey the bishops in political matters, and so forth. There was no way to resolve these problems except by radically questioning *in theory* the New Christendom frame of reference. Such a *theoretical* questioning of New Christendom had not yet taken place in Brazil; activists were having an intensive experience of *political practice*, whose theoretical underpinnings were still quite intuitive and confused.

This impasse situation within the JUC led to huge conflicts and contradictions within the church, and led many activists not only out of New Christendom, but to leave the church itself. At the time, the impasse prompted the JUC to strive for a solution that would satisfy primarily the concrete demands of political practice, and provide them with an institutional framework that would be both effective and representative on the national level. All this is what led to the birth of *Ação Popular*, "popular action."

Ação Popular

Ação Popular (AP) made its first public appearance on June 1, 1962. Two general factors help explain its birth.

There was, first, the general political situation of the country: pressure on Christians from the popular movement and particularly the student movement, a political and ideological crisis, and the growing politicization of the petite bourgeoisie and the "middle strata" as a result of governmental reformist and "developmentalist" policies.

Then there was the situation of confusion and impasse, described above, that politically-involved Christians encountered in the JUC and in the church in general, closely tied as it was to the prevailing New Christendom framework. The AP was much more a political movement than a political *party*. It was made up essentially of former JUC and non-Christian activists. The AP emphatically insisted that it was not a Christian movement and it rejected any official relationship with JUC and the church. Nevertheless, in public opinion the AP continued to be seen as the political expression of revolutionary Christians.

In the AP there was a sharp split between political *practice* and political *consciousness* (a situation quite typical of political organizations throughout Latin America when their origins are Christian). The AP political practice, which it regarded as utterly essential, took its definition from Marxist class analysis and class struggle. At the same time, the political consciousness of AP activists took its inspiration from a historical and philosophical vision of humanity and society, which contained an original and coherent combination of theories taken from writers like Lebret, Mounier, Teilhard de Chardin, Hegel, and Marx. In the initial AP manifesto ("Documento de Base"), composed in 1963, one finds this split between political practice and political consciousness. On the one side, there were the conjunctural analyses done by Herbert José de Souza, and on the other, the historical and philosophical analyses of Father Henrique de Lima Vaz. This dualism was both cause and effect of the AP political limits. One manifestation was an exaggerated, overidealistic political optimism, where definitions of ends and means were not accompanied by sufficient reflection on the means and how long it would take to achieve the ends. Such dualism led the AP to fall into activism, pragmatism, idolization of the grass roots, and "workerism."

This dualism, combining *idealism* and *workerism*, was typical of the *first phase* of the radicalization of Christians almost everywhere in Latin America. They got beyond those weaknesses and limits in their political practice during a *second phase*, when the demands of that same political practice brought them into a better, more organic kind of political involvement in the popular movement, and from within that involvement they acquired a more adequate political theory.

Liberation theology also arose out of this growing maturation in political awareness, in depth of involvement, and in theoretical understanding. That theology would enable Christians to move beyond the easy path of dualism (between practice and awareness) or of a voluntarist, and therefore superficial, break with their Christian origins, and to start on the hard road that demanded both a critical assessment of their Christian past, which was ideologically and structurally distorted by the complexity of an alienating and oppressive system, and an elaboration of a new, liberative vision of the faith, the gospel, and the church.

Despite all its limits, the overall assessment of AP must be positive. It enabled many Christians to become involved in a revolutionary political practice, and hence to overcome the impasse and political frustration engendered by social Christianity and New Christendom. Beyond the circle of its own activists and its direct political activity and within the larger complex of civil society and the church, AP was at the starting point of a process of polarization, of politicization, and of a critique of how Christianity and the church were integrated into the prevailing ideology and system. It offered numerous Christians the chance to live a new vision of Christianity, and it created—socially and politically—the image of a revolutionary Christianity, the direct opposite of a Christianity manipulated by the ruling classes, and particularly by their nationalist and integralist sectors. Finally, it started a political discussion within the left on the general issues related to religion and Christianity, and specifically, on the revolutionary potentialities of the political practice of Christians. Thus AP opened the way and acquired a certain amount of experience on which other Christians in Brazil and other parts of Latin America would continue to build.

Worker Catholic Action, 1966-1970

The second key event in the evolution of specialized Catholic Action, one that was at the core of the process of breaking away from New Christendom, was the national conference of Worker Catholic Action (JOC-ACO) held in June 1968 in Recife. After the 1964 coup it was the JOC-ACO activists who occupied the place left by JUC in striving for a church in line with a revolutionary political practice. The JOC break from New Christendom—not from the church—took place in Brazil where military dictatorship, repression, and superexploitation of labor had undermined the basic legitimacy of the capitalist system. In view of the final crisis of the populist and developmentalist model, the labor movement began to move toward decisively breaking away from the state and from the industrial bourgeoisie. Despite the economic, political, and ideological repression, the labor movement had entered a process that would, over the long run, lead to maturity.

In the ecclesial and theological spheres, a number of important developments in the universal church had opened up, within the Brazilian hierarchical church, cracks and spaces that had not been present during the JUC period: the end of Vatican II (1965) and the publication of the encyclical *Populorum Progressio* (1967). All this was part of the socio-political and ecclesial context for interpreting the national congress of Worker Catholic Action in 1968.

There had been a shift in orientation on May 1, 1966, at the ACO conference in Recife. Thinking quickly matured and just a year later, May 1, 1967, the ACO published a manifesto in Recife, "The Northeast: Development without Justice." The discussion this document provoked throughout the Brazilian church made possible and stimulated the preparation of the final document of the JOC-ACO national congress in Recife in June 1968.

This text moved decidedly beyond the ideological ambiguities of the previous period and employed a historical analysis of the forms of production and of the dialectic of class struggle in Brazil. Its verdict on the prevailing system was categorical: "Capitalism is intrinsically perverse, because it prevents integral human development and the development in solidarity of the people as a whole."[31] Its rejection of a Christendom model and its affirmation of a liberating Christianity were consistent with the previous historical analysis. There was an explicit distinction between the *ecclesial* institution—the people become sign, the subject and bearer of Jesus Christ's redeeming will and of prophetic, critical consciousness—and the *ecclesiastical institution*, which may become an obstacle to the development of the ecclesial institution. Likewise, the document distinguished between faith and religon: Christianity is a faith, not a religion. Faith, however, should transform religion, the cultural expression of a people on its way toward liberation.

The hierarchical church reacted violently to the congress. But in contrast with the previous period (and especially with what the JUC experienced before 1964), Worker Catholic Action avoided a polarization between the movement and the hierarchy. Activists were aware that the main conflict was not intra-ecclesiastical but social and political. Reflecting considerable political and Christian maturity, the JOC-ACO executed a "tactical retreat" in order to avoid a clash with the hierarchy which could have led to a falsification of the political and prophetic orientation of the movement.

Thus something new emerged, something that will later spread throughout Latin America: confrontation with the ecclesiastical institution does not necessarily lead to an abandonment of one's ecclesial and Christian identity, an identity lived and expressed within a political practice of liberation. This new development implied a growing maturity in theoretical awareness of the part of Christians in Latin America, with regard to both politics and theology. Liberation theology will arise out of this new reality.

The course taken by JOC-ACO provoked a reaction on the part of the government's intelligence services. In 1970 the national leadership and two chaplains were jailed, tortured, and sentenced for the "crime of subversion." From that time onward, Christians active in the labor movement experienced ongoing repression in Brazil. That was a distinctive sign marking the popular church as it arose in the people's struggle, beyond any Christendom framework.

Movimento de Educação de Base

Some sectors of the Brazilian church in the countryside went through a process similar to what was experienced in university and labor specialized Catholic Action. A very significant case was that of the MEB (*Movimento de Educação de Base*, Movement for Grassroots Education). Started in 1961 in the northeast of Brazil, this movement used Paulo Freire's methodology for literacy and conscientization. The MEB arose as a *response of the church* to social and political needs in the uneducated rural population. This was the source of its revolutionary potential and this was what made it qualitatively different from the Christian rural unions, which arose as a *response of the New Christendom church* to the agrarian leagues (of Francisco Julião) and the rural unions (under communist influence).

The official MEB projects, with their developmentalist orientation, do not interest me as much as does its concrete practice, which was to lead the church to be involved in the social and political realm in a new way. I cannot carry out such an analysis here, but my study of the course taken by the MEB seems to me to confirm my interpretation of the Brazilian church.

Within the MEB, however, there was a gap between *strategy* and *practice*. The MEB strategy was defined in relation to developmentalist New Christendom, but its social and political practice led it to radically question the dominant system of New Christendom. When the practice of the church was in accordance with the popular movement, in the end it was always the movement that brought the church along with its strategy, freeing it from any suspicion of ideological or political complicity with the dominant system. The church created the MEB to raise the consciousness of campesinos, but in the end it was the campesinos who raised the consciousness of the church.[32]

The Zenith of New Christendom

In order to round out this examination of significant facts that reveal the thrust of where the Brazilian church was heading during the developmentalist period (particularly between 1956 and 1964), I must turn briefly to two basic texts issued by the hierarchical church: the "Emergency Plan for the Church in Brazil" approved by the fifth general assembly of the Brazilian Bishops' Conference (CNBB), April 25, 1962, and the statement made by the Central Commission of the CNBB, April 30, 1963, spelling out the 1962 Emergency Plan.

These two documents, which may be taken to represent the end-point of the evolution of the Brazilian church before the 1964 coup and the starting point for analyzing its subsequent evolution, manifest three basic characteristics of the developmentalist New Christendom church:

1. The church became conscious of the inhuman nature of the capitalist system. These documents exhibit a remarkable ability for analyzing the economic, social, and cultural misery of the people.

2. The church explicitly opted for the basic reforms that had to take place in order to change the inhuman nature of the capitalist system. Concretely, this support of the church for basic reforms meant supporting the government of João Goulart and its plans for reforms in land tenure, taxes, banking, the universities, elections, administration, and so forth.

3. At the same time that it was becoming aware of the inhuman nature of capitalism and opting for the radical reforms needed to change this situation, the church defined the limits of its social and political commitment. However, the definition of those limits was not expressed in *theological* terms consistent with its ecclesial nature, but in *political* terms proper to the project of New Christendom. These terms say more about the *political* identity of New Christendom than about the *theological* identity of the church. The basic limit that the church saw to its commitment against the inhuman nature of the capitalist system was the point at which that system might be replaced by another of a socialist or Marxist nature. Marxism seemed to be the main enemy, and as a solution, Marxist socialism seemed more inhuman than did capitalism. The church falsely felt that socialism was a threat to its own *theological* identity, when in fact what it really threatened was the *political* identity of New Christendom. That is why the church condemned Marxism in theological, not political, terms—that is, because it was "materialist" and "atheist."

The use of theological discourse vis-à-vis a political reality prevented the church from making a clear distinction between church and Christendom. In condemning Marxism in theological terms, the church became politicized: it defined its ecclesial identity by aligning itself with New Christendom. It reduced its ecclesial identity to the political identity of New Christendom.

When the oppressed classes embraced Marxism, it was not because of its "atheist" or "materialist" character. In opting for Marxism, the Latin American masses were not motivated by a moral or theological evaluation of atheism or materialism, but by the fact that they could use it as an instrument in their political and ideological struggle against the dominant capitalist system. The bishops could not oppose Marxism as an instrument for political and ideological struggle, and so they condemned it in moral and theological terms. The contradiction that the bishops saw between Christianity and Marxism led them to a political reduction of morality and theology, and consequently to a political reduction of the nature of the church. Implicitly, this political reduction of the church meant that it was identified with the New Christendom program. Thus the church set political limits to its option for radical reforms in the struggle against the inhuman nature of the capitalist system.

The same New Christendom mentality of the church that showed through in the 1962 and 1963 documents was also manifest in way the church regarded as "enemies" not only Marxism, but also Protestantism (especially in mass-based forms like Pentecostalism), Umbanda, and spiritism. The criterion used by the church for detecting and evaluating its "enemies" was not the alienating or liberating character of such movements, but their ability to compete with the church or replace it in particular sectors of society.

At that period Marxism was spreading rapidly among the "middle strata," especially among students and intellectuals. The church saw itself being replaced by Marxist-inspired movements in those sectors. The same was true of Protestantism, Umbanda, and spiritism, which were replacing it in the popular sectors, especially on the fringes of the big cities. These three movements were eclipsing the church in three vital functions: the function of "saving" (including physical cures), the function of "building community," and the function of "protection" against the system and the ruling classes.[33] The church is more interested in retaining its power in civil society than in adopting an evangelizing stance toward the aspirations of the people to be liberated from exploitation.

The attitude of the church shown in the 1962 "Emergency Plan" and in the 1963 CNBB Central Commission statement was largely shaped by the political situation of Brazil under the Goulart government (1961–1964). Goulart's developmentalism was presented as the only possible alternative vis-à-vis the debilitation and inchoative crisis of the capitalist system, and as the only model capable of channeling the growing mobilization of the popular classes. It was the lay Catholic movements within the church that mediated the pressure generated by the popular movement, and those lay movements were well on their way toward a political radicalization (especially the JUC, as sketched above). Furthermore, the church was more afraid of leftist solutions to the political impasse toward which the political situation of the country was heading than it was of rightist solutions. The New Christendom model found in developmentalism the only political expression that could resolve its own internal contradictions, particularly inasmuch as this developmentalism claimed to be of Christian inspiration. In the developmentalist project the church could take its distance from both capitalism and socialism.

This "third way" enabled the church to go quite far in its social and political commitment, as long as the developmentalist model remained in effect. When the model went into crisis, the negative character of this "third way" (defined in negative terms: neither capitalist nor socialist) led the church into a political vacuum and put its social doctrine in crisis.

Despite their limits and ambiguities, these documents of the Brazilian hierarchy in 1962 and 1963 were the most advanced of that period, and were an expression of the high-water mark of the evolution of developmentalist New Christendom. As such, they can be taken as a reference point for interpreting both the period that ended with the 1964 coup and the one that began at that point.

Interpretive Recapitulation

At the beginning of this section on Brazil, I stated that the main concern of my analysis of the Brazilian church from 1964 to the present would be the process of *crisis in New Christendom* and that of the *birth of a popular church*. In order to understand what is going on today, I first had to study the genesis and development of that New Christendom (1889–1964) after the period of crisis of the previous colonial Christendom (1808–1889). Analysis of that New Christendom could be expected to provide good insights into its period of crisis. That is why I should like to make a brief interpretive recapitulation of the preceding material before moving into the present period.

I have noted two stages in the devolution of New Christendom: one from 1889 to 1930, when a conservative New Christendom was in effect, and another from 1930 to 1964, when a New Christendom of a populist and nationalist, and later of a developmentalist, nature came to the fore. The year 1930 was a key date in Brazil, as it was throughout Latin America: the coffee boom ended for Brazil, the liberal state and the oligarchy plunged into crisis, a revolution ended the First Republic and led Getúlio Vargas to power, the populist era began, the church became reconciled to the newly emerging ruling classes, and a church-state alliance became the basis for populist and nationalist New Christendom.

Two phases can be distinguished in the period that began in 1930: first, a populist-nationalist phase extending from 1930 to 1955, and then a developmentalist transition from 1956 to 1964 (see the chronology, p. 111 above). At first, the Brazilian church evolved very slowly but change became undeniably visible from 1945 onward, and the pace quickened considerably after 1956, during the period of developmentalist governments.

I have made an overall interpretation of this evolution of the Brazilian church, starting from some particular events that I believe were the most significant: the birth of specialized Catholic Action, the stance of the church toward the agrarian problem and toward underdevelopment, the split of the Christian Democratic Party into two opposed tendencies, the direction taken by University Catholic Action and Worker Catholic Action, *Ação Popular*, the Grassroots Education Movement, and the documents of the Brazilian Bishops' Conference in 1962 and 1963.

The overall direction in which the church and New Christendom in Brazil moved was remarkable and my assessment of that movement has been positive. The church moved away from conservatism, from being a church on the defensive against liberalism, positivism, laicism, Freemasonry, and Protestantism, and became a church that took the offensive, struggling against underdevelopment; from being a church closed within the narrow circle of the oligarchical elites to being a church open to the middle strata and the popular classes; from being a church absorbed by issues of family, education, and devotional practices, to being a church concerned about social and political issues; from being a europeanized and romanized church, alien to the reality of Brazil and to the culture and religion of the people, to being a church that took the reality of the nation and of the popular masses as a starting point for seeking its own identity; from being a church of external and formal triumphalism, reflected in ecclesiastical organizations, massive public activities, and sacramentalism, to being a church that was pastoral, oriented to community, and educating involved Christians.

Nevertheless, when the church reached the high point of this evolution—in itself quite positive—it had already accumulated within itself all the contradictions that explain its subsequent crisis. The underlying reason for this crisis was the support it sought from political power in order to rebuild itself as church. And yet this crisis will be profoundly positive, for out of it and by its own dynamic there will arise the popular church in Brazil, that is, a church that does not seek support from the power structure and that affirms its specific identity as church as a sign of liberation, in faith and hope, within the popular and revolutionary movement opposing the dominant capitalist system.

1964-1978: Basic Chronology

I should like to introduce my analysis of the Brazilian church during the present period by situating it within a chronological frame of reference:

—March 31, 1964: military coup. Fall of João Goulart. Emergency period.
—April 11, 1964: president, General Castelo Branco.
—January 24, 1967: new constitution.
—March 13, 1967: national security law (decree no. 314).
—March 15, 1967: president, General Costa e Silva.
—January 8, 1968: creation of the National Security Council.
—December 13, 1968: second military coup. Institutional act no. 5, state of emergency (president given full powers).
—August 31, 1969: third military coup. Military junta. Institutional act no. 12.
—October 17, 1969: institutionalization of the dictatorship (reform of the 1967 constitution). State of emergency institutionalized.
—October 30, 1969: president, General Garrastazú Médici.
—1974-1978: president, General Ernesto Geisel.

In examining this period my primary aim is to interpret the *crisis of New Christendom* and the advent of a *popular church* in Brazil. These are not the only ecclesial processes during this period, but they are the basic lines along which the whole can be interpreted. The root causes of these two processes are the very same as those I have already highlighted for Latin America as a whole: an economic, political, and ideological crisis of the dominant system, the response of the popular movement, and the rise of a new model of domination. I here analyze how these three processes influenced the church, and the stages of their development in Brazil.

The Alternatives Facing the Church after the 1964 Coup

The two problems confronting the church after the 1964 coup were church-state relationships and the political radicalization of church activists and grassroots cadres. During the previous developmentalist period the church had been able to maintain control over its internal contradictions by collaborating with a progressive state that was taking the lead in social reforms, and, starting with its own openness to social and political problems, providing a channel for the aspirations for social and political change of the most alert and politicized lay persons and priests.

But when a military dictatorship that took its inspiration from the doctrine of national security replaced the developmentalist state, the hierarchy confronted the following alternatives: either to be utterly submissive to the military government and lose any possibility of relating to the popular social base and to the most politicized activists, or to identify with the social and political aspirations of the popular base and radically confront the dictatorship, in which case it risked suffering a sweeping systematic repression that could entail the destruction of the whole social and political institutionality of New Christendom and even the destruction of the ecclesiastical institution.

Faced with the 1964 coup, the church adopted a compromise position. In the statement of the Central Commission of the CNBB, May 27, 1964, the church legitimized the military coup but at the same time conditioned that legitimacy by making a number of moral demands. The church sought to combine its nonrupture with the state by legitimizing the military action that imposed *order*, and its nonrupture with its popular base by taking a stance in the struggle for social *justice*. Thus it was internally torn between the demand for *order* and the demand for *justice*. The church did not wish to give up the gospel demands for charity and justice, but it subordinated those demands to the order imposed by "legitimate" military authority.

Between 1964 and 1968 the posture of the Brazilian hierarchy was hesitant and contradictory. Sometimes the church challenged the government by defending the legitimacy of episcopal participation in social life (see, for example, the November 30, 1967, statement of the Central Commission of the CNBB after the conflict in the diocese of Volta Redonda and the stance taken by Bishop Waldyr Calheiros).[34] On other occasions the church defended the social rights of the people, popular participation in socio-political matters, grassroots education, or union organizing among the masses (see the document of the general assembly of the episcopate in July 1968, "The Mission of the Church in the Present Situation in Brazil"). Sometimes the church acted as a protector and "mediator" (for example, in 1968 student conflicts, when Auxiliary Bishop José de Castro Pinto of Rio and more than a hundred priests took part in a student march and defended the students in the face of government repression).

But on other occasions the church stepped back and submitted to the military dictatorship, avoiding any misunderstanding or conflict with the dictatorship, thus completely surrendering its right to speak out on social issues. When groups of integralist Catholics and the government itself criticized Christians and priests involved with the people and accused the church of being "infiltrated by communists" (particularly during the July-September

1968 antichurch campaign, when the press received Father Comblin's confidential memorandum, "Notes on the Preparatory Document for the Second General Conference at Medellín," or when some priests and Catholic Action movements became actively involved in the struggle against the dictatorship), the church hesitated, thus contradicting its other actions in favor of social justice.

Because of the confused and hesitant attitude of most of the bishops between 1964 and 1968, tugged back and forth between military order and social justice, the hierarchy lost its identity, could not provide guidance for its social base, and catalyzed political polarization in Catholic circles. Most of the hierarchy was under pressure either from the Catholic intergralist side or from Christians who were politically radicalized within the popular movement. There were not only lay persons and priests in the two political "extremes" but also bishops. This situation changed substantially, starting with the national political crisis of 1968–1969.

As far as the state was concerned, the fact that the hierarchical church had not taken a clear stand created a dangerous and explosive situation: the government feared that Catholic circles politically involved with the people might set the bulk of the church against it. Something along those lines had already happened in some instances, and it could spread in the future. Hence, starting in 1968, the military dictatorship elaborated a very clear political strategy for bringing the Catholic Church to heel. The fear of the military that the indecisiveness of the church might turn against it intensified in view of the overall evolution of the Latin American church, especially after the encyclical *Populorum Progressio* and the Medellín conference.[35]

The political aim of the strategic plan of the military was to incorporate the church as a whole into the national security state. I should first look at the traits of this episcopate that made possible such a tactic on the part of the military, and then at the two basic lines of the military strategy vis-à-vis the church. I leave out of this analysis of the episcopate those bishops who had already made a clear option for or against the state.

Characteristics of the Episcopacy Making It Vulnerable to State Manipulation

1. It was an episcopacy that was *hesitant, divided, torn between two contradictory tendencies*—a tendency to defend the autonomy of the church with regard to the state but to avoid any conflict or open break with it, and a tendency to take on the social and political problems of the oppressed classes but without identifying the church with political opposition groups, much less with groups in the Marxist opposition.

2. It was an episcopacy that was *confused*, lacking a distinct ecclesial identity. The church defined its identity by referring to its spiritual (supernatural) nature and to the universal and pastoral character of its mission. This way of defining its identity was theologically correct, but when the issue was

how to affirm the identity of the church in a civil and political society that was heavily polarized and highly conflictive, terms like "spiritual," "universal," and "pastoral" seem vague and not very operational. In addition, the church defined itself negatively, it affirmed its identity by *negation:* "spiritual," "universal," and "pastoral" were quasi synonyms for "nonpolitical," "nonpartisan," "nonconflictive." Often the term "ecclesial" had a connotation of "not connected with the state" and "nonpolitical." In one type of episcopal discourse the term "Christian" was even synonymous with "non-Marxist." In general, most bishops defined the structural identity of the church by negating extreme systems: the church was neither liberal nor Marxist, neither capitalist nor socialist, and so forth. This identification of the church, defined positively in theological terms and negatively in social and political terms, in the end will lead to a *political reduction* of the nature and mission of the church and will make it more vulnerable to being manipulated by the state.

3. It was an episcopacy with no political analysis. During the developmentalist period the church made use of a rather advanced sociological analysis of the situation in Brazil, but after 1964 it became obvious that the bishops had no political analysis. There were two consequences: it was difficult for the hierachy to grasp the strategy of the military vis-à-vis the church, and there was confusion, both political and moral.[36] That was especially clear when priests and activists were put on trial for subversion: if they were accused of a political offense (taking part in underground or illegal contestation) the bishops interpreted it in a moral sense and broke ecclesial solidarity with the accused, leaving it up to them to prove their innocence or accept their punishment.[37]

Strategy of the Military Regime

It was this majority of the bishops, confused and lacking in political savoir faire, that the military regime would seek to hold in subjection and integrate into the national security state. The two guidelines of its strategic plan vis-à-vis the church were (1) to avoid any conflict that could impede good relationships or a possible church-state alliance, and (2) to isolate or even suppress the sector of the church that was committed to the liberation of the poor and had taken a stand against the military regime.

The governmental strategy vis-à-vis the church was very intelligent and coherent. It reflected a clear grasp of the two processes that were moving the bulk of the episcopacy toward political radicalization: the break between church and state, and the pressure exercised within the church by minority groups of Christians involved in the popular movement. With the downfall of populism and developmentalism, the process of crisis and disintegration in New Christendom gathered momentum. Tied as it was to this New Christendom in crisis, the church could take one of two ways out: either rebuild a New Christendom project, this time allied with the national security state (as some bishops and groups of integralist Catholics had already done) or try—for the first time in the history of the Latin American church—to rebuild the church beyond any sort of Christendom project, a course that would involve a decisive break with the dominant political power (an option already being lived out by a minority sector in the church committed to the poor).

The two processes leading the church toward this second option were (1) the disaccord (and indeed incompatibility) between the church and the national security state, and (2) the pressure that prophetic minorities, operating out of the situation of oppression suffered by the bulk of the people, were bringing to bear on the church. By deflecting these two processes, the military regime took direct aim at the causes leading most of the church toward a confrontation with the national security state.

It was not in terms of the national security ideology that the bishops became aware of their collaboration with the strategic plan of the government; rather they saw it in "ecclesial" and "pastoral" terms. The basic stance of the hierarchy, one that made it vulnerable to being manipulated by the dictatorship, was its perennial objective of being allied with political power, or at least not breaking away from it and not being persecuted by it. The political or confessional character of the state was of little concern to the bishops, so much so that some of them looked to the church-state relationship in socialist countries as a model for how that relationship should be maintained in a country run by a military dictatorship (a proposal usually called the "Polish thesis"). This proposal—that the church should seek the mediation of *political society* in order to ensure its ecclesial and pastoral presence in *civil society*—is the quintessence of the Christendom model.[38]

I now examine briefly how the military dictatorship carried out its strategic plan against the church, especially after the crisis of 1968, what contradictions this plan occasioned, and what was the outcome.

The Church and the National Security State

In part 4, chapter 8, I provide a systematic analysis of church-state relationships. Here I propose only some reflections of the specific situation in Brazil. I am especially interested in analyzing the practice of the majority sector of the hierarchical church, which gave the military regime a conditional legitimacy (as can be seen in the statements of the Central Commission of the CNBB made on May 27, 1964, and February 19, 1969, after the military coups of March 31, 1964, and December 13, 1968).

In providing legitimacy for the military regime, the hierarchical church also clearly laid down the boundaries for arriving at positive solutions in church-state conflicts. If conflict were to go beyond those bounds, it would become a contradiction and would mean that the church would delegitimize the regime and break with it. The conditions for negotiating conflicts, and thus avoiding a church-state rupture were as follows:

1. The Brazilian church and state believed in the possibility and usefulness of

dialogue and negotiation. There would be no break between church and state so long as each side believed that conflict could be settled by dialogue and negotiation, that conflict was only a "misunderstanding" or an "abuse" of those in power, and that any break in dialogue would prevent the church from carrying out its mediating role vis-à-vis the state.[39]

2. Neither church nor state would cast doubt on whether its own identity was shared by the other party (that is, that the church would not question the Christian identity or character of the military regime, and that, by the same token, the state would not question the church's professed love for the country, and its loyalty to national goals and objectives). In this mutual recognition of orthodoxy there was usually a twofold assumption: that anyone who hated the country was probably an atheist, and anyone who hated religion was probably unpatriotic. With Marxism as the common enemy, being patriotic and being Christian came together under the heading "non-Marxist."

3. Church and state could define common objectives and interests. There was a conviction that there had to be common interests and objectives, because they would have the same basis in an order of values and a vision of humanity and of the world that both institutions shared. This presumed "common ground" was defined by such values as peace, liberty, democracy, homeland, unity, brotherhood, family order, and so forth.

4. Both church and state would make a clear distinction between an individual involved in conflict and the *institution* as such. The church would not confuse a member of the military who violated human rights with the army; the state would not confuse a subversive Christian with the church.

5. Church and state would recognize the legality or morality established by the other side: The church would regard as morally blameworthy those whom military courts declared subversive; the state would regard as juridically suspect those whom the church declared morally at fault, such as rebellious Christians or Christians who broke with the church.

In the history of Brazil from 1964 to 1978, there were many examples of conflict between the hierarchical church and the state settled positively within the limits set down by the two parties. Conflicts did not lead to either a basic contradiction or a break between church and state.[40] Nevertheless, I shall not make a purely descriptive or static analysis of these facts, much less draw from them any conclusion or definitive judgment on the hierarchical church in Brazil. It is more important to analyze the course of events, particularly from 1968 onward, and to ask what were the effects and the contradictions that arose within the church while it kept its resolve not to break with the state—that is, when it kept within the limits it had imposed on itself to negotiate conflicts with a state it regarded as legitimate.

These effects and contradictions became sharper as the national security state became more and more incapable of resolving the structural crisis of the dominant capitalist system and responded with greater oppression, exploitation, marginalization, and repression of the people. Rather than looking at isolated facts, I must examine the tendencies that stand out over the course of the ten years of church-state relationships in Brazil from 1968 to 1978.

In general terms, I find that negotiating church-state conflicts led, dialectically and over the long run, to the breaking of the church with the state. This break passed through stages and degrees: it could go from breaking with a particular *president* to breaking with a *government*, with one or other *sector of the state*, with one or another *government policy*, with the *military regime*, with a *state of emergency*, with the *political model of domination*, all the way to breaking with the *capitalist system* as such (a break that also went through stages: option for a noncapitalist path, option for socialism in general, or for a particular model of socialism).

The fact that the church recognized the legitimacy of the military government often meant that it was the only independent nongovernmental institution recognized by the state that could dialogue or be a mediator vis-à-vis the state in a given conflict (for example, the mediation of the church in a labor conflict where human rights were being violated). In fulfilling this role the church found itself subjected to a contradiction.

On the one hand, oppressed individuals or groups appealed to the church and pressured it to defend their cause, to really be the "voice of the voiceless" as they confronted the state. Of necessity this meant that the church had to get to know the problems of the oppressed and show solidarity with them.

On the other hand, in exercising its mediating role toward the military authority that it regarded as legitimate, the church found itself forced to believe in the "good will" and ability of the government to solve the conflict. That necessarily meant that the church had to accept the legal framework set up by the government, reaffirm the Christian character it had already recognized in the state, and accept the basic principles and objectives of the regime within an order of values that the church also shared.

The sharper the conflict between the military state and the oppressed, the more the mediation effort of the church would be confronted with this contradiction, and each time the incompatibility increased.

There were only two ways out of this contradiction:

1. The church could opt for the oppressed and hence find itself forced to radically question the legality of the government, its Christian character, and the values that sustained it.

2. The church could remain subject to the state and hence find itself forced to radically question the legality, the Christian character, and the values implicit in the cause of the oppressed.

Whichever option the church made, it took on a specific kind of political practice, which it interpreted and reflected, not in political categories, but in its own specific and proper categories (the church worked out its political practice within the relative autonomy of its social consciousness).

In the first case, the church affirmed its solidarity with the cause of the oppressed in terms of a liberating evangelization. It discovered the close relationship between evangelization and liberation, without confusing them. This liberating evangelization necessarily entailed direct confrontation with the legal framework and the values that the state considered legitimate and Christian. Evangelization thus took on a "subversive" content, which undermined the legal and religious foundations of the system of domination.

In the second case, the church expressed its political practice in moral and Christian terms that reinforced the legitimacy of the military government and delegitimized the cause of the liberation of the oppressed. The church disconnected itself from liberation struggles, arguing that their political and non-Christian character was opposed to the values found in the Christian vision of humanity and society, which it saw realized in the Christian policies of the state.

In either case, the solution to the contradiction brought about by the mediating role of the church did not take place in a single act or with the clarity of the theoretical framework presented here, but normally in the course of a long and difficult process, beset with contradictions.

If maintaining a good relationship between church and state meant that the church recognize the Christian character of the state and the state recognize the patriotic character of the church, then the result was a twofold process in which *the state is reconfessionalized* and *the church is politicized*. Legitimized by the church as Christian, the state exercised the right to decide which kind of Christian dogma and morality was compatible with the doctrine and practice of national security. Thus the military state played the role of a "parallel magisterium;" If the church disavowed this magisterium, it would be questioning the Christian character of the state and thereby its legitimacy. In order to avoid breaking with the state, the church would have to respect the limits imposed by this parallel magisterium; and by doing so, it would politicize its specifically religious activity. With the state reconfessionalized and the church politicized, the church could not remain uninvolved in any conflict between the state and the oppressed majority in the nation. The affirmation or denial by the church of its own identity and autonomy had to take place through its political option for or against the state. If the church stood in solidarity with the poor against the state, it was thereby affirming its own identity and denying the Christian character of the state and its parallel magisterium. If the church stood in solidarity with the state against the poor and oppressed, it was thereby denying its identity insofar as it subordinated itself to a definition of Christianity not set down by itself but by the parallel magisterium of the state. As long as there is a church-state alliance, the identity of the church was at stake in each and every social and political clash between the state and the oppressed majority. The church-state alliance itself forced the church to define its specific identity within social and political conflicts. The church either lost its identity by legitimizing the Christian character of the state, or it affirmed its own identity within a liberation process by denying that the state was Christian.

Isolation and Repression of the Popular Church

The second prong of the governmental strategy against the church was to isolate and repress the sector of the church that had made an option against the system of domination and the national security state. Even though only a minority in the church had taken this course, the military regarded it as very dangerous: its presence and activity within the church and society was both a constant reference point toward which the confused and hesitant majority might turn, and a permanent denunciation of any real or potential alliance between church and state, or between the church and any system of domination. This minority sector was considered dangerous, especially after 1968, because from that time onward it was no longer a marginal group, and it would not allow itself to be marginalized from either the church (because in both theory and practice it maintained its identity as church) or society (by its involvement at the heart of the popular classes and sectors). The military was not dealing with a sect or an elite, but with a church being built up from within the struggles of the people. The aim of the military with regard to this group was to isolate it from both the church and the popular sectors where it was to be found.

Two stages can be traced in the repression of this popular church: denunciation and direct repression.[41]

The aim of denunciation was to psychologically prepare the ground for direct repression and provide an ideological justification for it. Two lines of argumentation were used at this point, those connected with Christian doctrine and morality and those connected with the doctrine of national security. On the one hand, the political involvement of those Christians was presented as sundering the unity of the church, corrupting Catholic doctrine, threatening human and Christian values, and breaking down morality; on the other hand, those Christians were accused of collaborating with communism, or of being utilized by Marxist political groups. There was talk that the church was being infiltrated by communism and that those Christians were making the whole church suspect in the eyes of state security agencies.

This kind of denunciation and ideological campaign was all the more powerful insofar as theological reasoning was given a political dimension, and political reasoning was given a theological dimension. Thus, an offense against morality or against the church was considered to be an offense against the moral and Christian foundations of the state, and hence a threat to national security. Similarly, an offense regarded by the state as subversive was also seen as entailing moral guilt.

The second stage moved from verbal attack to direct repression. There were two kinds of repression, and they were complementary: repression by the church, serving state security, and repression by the state, serving to purify the church. The former took place when the church expelled, either from their ministry or from the country, priests who had been politically committed, or when the church dissolved a Catholic Action movement because of its political involvement, or simply when the church was silent or denied its solidarity with those Christians whom the state said were guilty of breaking the law, and whom the church then regarded as morally guilty and thus cut off from the ecclesial community.

The second kind of repression, that by the state, took place when the church did not carry out its own repression or did so only feebly. The state then intervened directly in the life of the church, arresting, torturing, or deporting priests and Christian leaders. As in the case of verbal attacks, theological arguments were mixed with political and national security arguments to give them greater force, and the church severed its affiliation with politically committed Christians because it feared that the military would use their membership as a pretext for directing repression against the church as a whole.[42] For its part, the internal state security apparatus considered very important the unity and integrity of the church—a guarantee against infiltration of the church by leftist or Marxist forces.

Evolution of the Brazilian Church, 1968-1978

My overall interpretation of the Brazilian church covering the 1968-1978 period is the result of an examination of the life of the church during that period. I do not believe it worthwhile to summarize here all the events that I have analyzed and that serve as the basis for my interpretation. I believe it more useful to ground my interpretation on a select few events that I believe can serve as a reference point for interpreting the period. My overall hypothesis is that during the 1968-1978 period there were two moments in the evolution of the church, one *negative*, when most of the hierarchical church submitted to the national security state, and the other *positive*, when the popular church gradually asserted its hegemony (from 1973 to the present).

This shift in the direction of the Brazilian church cannot be dated precisely. I have chosen 1973 as the pivotal year because it was then that there was an ecclesial event that expressed, summed up, and interpreted, symbolically and significantly, a deeper process pointing history in a new direction. That event was the simultaneous publication, on May 6, 1973, of two documents of the hierarchical church in Brazil, "I Have Heard the Cry of My People" (signed by eighteen bishops and religious superiors in the northeast), and "The Marginalization of a People: the Cry of the Churches" (signed by six bishops of the center-west region).[43]

In the course of 1968 and 1969 (especially on December 13, 1968, August 31, 1969, and October 17, 1968) the military dictatorship replaced the legal framework imposed by democratic consensus with another kind of "legality," imposed by means of violence and repression. It has already been noted that the crisis of developmentalist New Christendom (1964-1968) ended with the hierarchical church for the most part confused and hesitant, and with a Catholic environment polarized around two positions held by well-defined minorities: a "rightwing" position (that sought to impose an ecclesiastico-military New Christendom) and a "leftwing" position (that sought to build up a church committed to the poor). This situation peaked in 1968 and 1969, and from then on the bulk of the hierarchy seemed to drift more and more along with the national security state. One might say that the strategic plan of the military to neutralize and bring the church into subjection was more and more successful each day. In its statements on February 19 and September 20, 1969, the Central Committee of the CNBB was moving in that direction. It seemed that the state had arrived at a point where it found it easier and easier to negotiate all its conflicts with the church, and the sector of the church that was committed to the oppressed seemed to have been definitively isolated and eliminated.[44] The Eucharistic Congress in Brasília in 1979 seemed a triumphal symbol of excellent relationships between church and state.

One characteristic of this period was that the Brazilian church was isolated from the rest of Latin America, which, in general, was witnessing a period of rising popular struggle, and liberation theology was likewise on the rise, whereas Brazil was experiencing a period of setback and retreat. In effect, Brazil, during the 1968-1973 period, was anticipating in its own experience what the rest of Latin America was to experience between 1973 and 1975.

Although it is quite true that that between 1968 and 1973 the hierarchical Brazilian church was under the subjection of the state, it is just as true that same process of subjection gradually sharpened contradictions, and in resolving those contradictions, the church came to a better self-awareness.

I have already analyzed how those contradictions worked. The more the church was subjected to the military government, the more clearly did the contradictory nature of the situation bring out the liberating and subversive character of the gospel. Given the social and political clash between the state and the popular classes, the alliance between church and state continually raised as an issue the very meaning of the church and the gospel. After 1973, the gradually mounting social, moral and political force found its public and ecclesial expression in the church that I have called the popular church—that is, a church that was a sign of liberation, built up out of the struggle of the oppressed. Out of the internal contradictions experienced in social and political confrontation, there arose a church close to the vital needs of the people: land, work, shelter, socio-political awareness, grassroots community. There arose a church where members spoke without an intermediary, a church that turned away from dependence and itself assumed responsibility, a church that liberated all the revolutionary potentialities found in a people's culture and religion, a church that consciously assumed the risks and uncertainty of commitment, a church that was universal because it had broken with the system of oppression, a church that sought salvation in the struggle for justice.

In the document mentioned just above, "The Marginalization of a People," one can find the historical *project* and the basic *structure* of this popular church. This document—a founding act of the popular church—began with a statement by a peasant:

> When you're a peasant, it's hard just to get enough to live on. We know that in this world things are like they are in the river: big fish eat the little fish. The big people aren't content with just getting our sweat—they want our blood. That's why we're dying out there.

At that point the document went into a rigorous scientific analysis of the situation in Brazil: how rural Brazilians lived, how the production structure in the countryside was organized, what the overall situation in the rural areas was, and finally what the socio-economic system in Brazil was. The analysis was scientific, not in an academic sense, but because it was directly linked to action; the analysis was accurate and true because it grasped the issues from the side of the people.

An image repeated throughout the document, and one that served as a guide for action, was that of the fruit tree: if it does not bear fruit or bears bad fruit, you take certain steps. If those do not produce any results and you see that the whole tree is bad, then you pull it up, and plant another one in its place. In the document this tree that has to be replaced was, explicitly, the capitalist system:

> Capitalism must be overcome. It is the great evil, accumulated sin, the decaying root, the tree that produces the fruits we know well: poverty, hunger, sickness, and death. That is why we must go beyond private ownership of the means of production—factories, land, businesses, banks, credit agencies. Only a few persons are the owners of workplaces and of the means of production, whereas the vast majority are simply used, and their life is without hope. They work in order to enrich a small minority, and this minority gets rich at their expense.

The document clearly stated that it was the poor, as a people, who were the *subject* of revolutionary change in society:

> So little are their needs met that at the least spark [signaling a possible change] they can open their eyes, understanding how things are, and desirous of another kind of society. So why not strike the spark that will get them going? . . . Up to the present, in this world of money and profit, in this world of machines for producing outcasts, the masses have been nothing but an abandoned seed, a building block thrown aside. But they are due to become the seed, the building block, for the world of tomorrow. . . . We have to overcome the "fear of change." We must not retreat before the threats of the wealthy or let ourselves be sidetracked in the evasive tactics of our associates who are frightened by threats: *we must believe in the power of the people*, believe that we are capable of building a tomorrow that will dance for joy.

It was within this situation that the document analyzed the church: starting from the contradictions within society and political struggle, it reread the gospel and the documents of the magisterium, and thus became conscious of its mission *as church* within the process of the liberation of the oppressed.

Many other ecclesial developments along the lines of the two 1973 documents could be cited. One could get an immediate overall view of this "church rising from the people" in the series of national conferences of grassroots Christian communities that took place starting in 1975 in Vitória.[45] Another meaningful expression on the national level was the "Pastoral Communication to the People of God" by the Representative Commission of the CNBB, dated October 25, 1976.[46] No one of these documents encompasses all the wealth and depth of the process of change in the Brazilian church in recent years.[47] The process of crisis of New Christendom and the rise of a popular church in Brazil came at such a stage of accelerated maturity as to make it irreversible. It was and is a sign of hope for the whole of the Latin American church.

CHAPTER 7

Latin American Theology, 1960-1985

An effort to understand the history of Latin American theology is closely connected to, and intrinsically bound up with, everything that has been discussed up to this point. Our theology is but the "last word," uttered in the light of faith, within historical, political, and economic processes. We have experienced the Second Vatican Council, the activity of CELAM, the conferences of the Latin American bishops at Medellín and Puebla from within the Latin American social and political context, and we have worked out our theology while moving along this path. Moreover, the way Latin American theology is rooted in history and politics accounts for its ecumenical nature. Catholics and Protestants have discovered one another while engaged in the same political practice of liberation. Finally, Latin American theology has matured in the face of the oppressive and repressive violence of political and military systems.

Thus, writing the history of Latin American theology between 1960 and 1985 entails taking up *on a theological level* everything that has been said in the previous chapters. Our theology is only a "moment" or a "dimension" of the broad political and ecclesial movement taking place in Latin America. That is the source of its own particular identity.

For this discussion I shall be utilizing especially three works on the topic: Enrique Dussel, "Sobre la historia de la teología en América latina,"[1] Gustavo Gutiérrez, *Telogía desde el reverso de la historia*,[2] and Roberto Oliveros, *Liberación y teología: Génesis y crecimiento de una reflexión (1966-1976)*.

FIRST STAGES OF A LATIN AMERICAN LIBERATION THEOLOGY, 1960-1968

This period was bounded by two great events in the history of the Catholic Church: the Second Vatican Council (1962-1965) and the second general conference of the Latin American Bishops in Medellín, Colombia (1968). The spirit of the council took form and burst forth at two particularly important moments: November 21, 1964, the promulgation of the Dogmatic Constitution on the church (*Lumen Gentium*), and December 7, 1965, the promulgation of the pastoral constitution on the Church in the Modern World (*Gaudium et Spes*). Moreover, three great encyclicals, *Mater et Magistra* (May 15, 1961), *Pacem in Terris* (April 30, 1963), and especially *Populorum Progressio* (March 26, 1967), marked significant milestones in the life of the universal church and the Latin American church. The publication of the "Message of Third World Bishops," August 15, 1967, was also destined to leave a profound imprint on the Latin American mind.

Within Latin America itself there were four meetings, organized by various CELAM departments, that clearly defined the thinking of the church during this period: Baños, Ecuador, in June 1966, on collaborative pastoral ministry *(pastoral de conjunto)*; Buga, Colombia, in February 1967, on Catholic universities; Melgar, Colombia, in April 1968 on the missions; and Itapuâ, Brazil, in May 1968, on the church and social change. These meetings were more influential than were the regular CELAM assemblies during this same period.

This is not the place to describe or interpret each of these events (for that purpose one may consult the texts mentioned above). My concern is rather to delineate the evolution of theology within the Latin American church that experienced these events, and within that evolution to show its thrust or direction—that is, where theological development in Latin America *started from* and where it was *heading* during this period.

January 1959 witnessed two events that were a sign and promise of what was to take place in Latin America within the next decade: the victory of the Cuban revolution on January 1, and Pope John XXIII's announcement of the Second Vatican Council on January 25. These were seemingly disparate events, but they announced to us Latin Americans in a remarkable way the direction of our future Christian and theological evolution: from revolution to council. We experienced a Latin American revolution before the council. Throughout this whole period the *experience* of events continually preceded the *reading* of official texts. Learning about the great events in the universal church was thus but the final moment of a process of thinking that had already taken place, the *terminus ad quem* of a road already traveled, the ecclesial confirmation of a certitude already grasped. One already had the interpretation of the text through experience, before beginning to read it.

Texts or events in the life of the church had the nature of a "sign" insofar as they pointed to a commitment that had already been made or a stage that had already been passed. Latin American Christians were preconciliar or postconciliar, for or against *Populorum Progressio*, and the like, not on the basis of a deep analysis of a text but on the basis of a lived experience, which found symbolic expression in one text or another. This was a "hermeneutic inversion," a path taken in the opposite direction, and it was to provide theology with an unexpected vitality.

Some writers believe that Vatican II was a "violent earthquake" for the Latin American church, "because it had to assimilate passively and in a few months what the church in Western Europe had been preparing actively for more than eighty years."[3] That is not completely true. It could be said that to some extent the Latin American church—not the church as a whole but the most significant grassroots sectors—experienced the postconcilar stage before and during the council.

The European church found itself challenged by a modern world that had come of age economically, politically, culturally, and humanly. That fact pressured it to come to terms with its *past*, when it had resisted the modern bourgeois revolution. In Latin America, by contrast, the church was challenged by a world that was already being called into question and was in crisis, a world reeling and falling apart. This situation was pressuring the Latin American church not to come to terms with its past but to face its *future*, where already one could make out a new world that would constitute an alternative to the capitalist world.

It could be said that the European church experienced the council under the sign of the modern bourgeois revolution (typified in the French revolution of 1789), whereas the Latin American church experienced it under the sign of the revolution of those who were exploited by this same modern bourgeoisie (typified in the Cuban revolution of 1959). The European chuch was confronted with the problem of "faith and science" and entered a process of secularization, declericalization, and demythologization. The Latin American church faced the problem of "faith and revolution" and entered a process of liberation.

In Europe the theological challenge to the church was the structural *atheism* of modern society and its proclamation of the *death of God*. In Latin America the theological challenge was *exploitation* and *underdevelopment* which was causing the *death of the human being*. As it dealt with the modern world, the European church came to feel how far away it was from that world and sought to bring about a reconciliation. The Latin American church, by contrast, felt too *identified* with the modern world and thus sought to *break away* from it. In Latin America the conciliar opening to the modern world had the effect of hastening awareness of that world as oppressive. The "earthquake" for the Latin American church did not take place in Rome during the council, but in Latin America, and in the economic, political, and social spheres.

The great ecclesial and theological events affecting the universal church from 1962 to 1968 were received and interpreted in Latin America on the basis of a *social and political practice* that was *different* from that of the European churches. The texts of the magisterium were not "applied" to Latin America, but rather "reinterpreted" from within Latin America. This reversal is obvious at the second general conference of the Latin American bishops at Medellín (1968). The original intention of the conference was expressed in its official title, "The Church in the Present Transformation of Latin America in the Light of the Council." What actually took place was the opposite and its title could have been, "The Church of the Council in the Light of the Present Transformation of Latin America." Although the third synod of Mexico and the fourth synod of Lima in the sixteenth century were the application of the Council of Trent to Latin America, and the First Plenary Latin American Council in 1899 was the application of the First Vatican Council, the Medellín conference was not the application of Vatican II, but its reinterpretation in the light of the process Latin America was undergoing.

Liberation Theology before Medellín

In taking up the history of Latin American theology it is important to leave no doubt that liberation theology was well underway before the bishops' meeting at Medellín. The same was true of the processes of liberation in Latin America and of the experience of Christians within these processes, both of which antedated liberation theology. By uncovering the true order of these three events—liberation→liberation theology→Medellín conference—the key for interpreting them can be uncovered. The Medellín conference provided official expression and an ecclesial dimension to historical processes already underway.

One could object that only a small number of Christians were engaged in a revolutionary social and political practice and had elaborated a theology of liberation. This does not affect my argument at all: the processes that created a revolutionary situation in Latin America (economic, political and ideological crisis of the system of domination, popular movements, and the arrival of repressive dominant regimes) affected not only minorities but Latin America as a whole. Attentive Christian minorities were those who had the prophetic ability to interpret this overall historical situation and to communicate it widely among the churches. Those who try to disqualify these prophetic minorities because of how few they were, and label them pejoratively "elites," are ignoring the overall reality of the Latin America whence these minorities arose.

An elite is always a small group but not every small group is necessarily an elite. To disqualify a minority because of its restrictive membership amounts to a sociological reduction of reality. Such a procedure is completely foreign to the way theology argues from faith and is able to recognize in a minority the prophetic power of the Lord of history. Those prophetic minorities were able to play a mediating role between the overall situation of Latin America and the bulk of Christians in the churches. The Spirit who gave life to the Medellín conference sprang out of that prophetic mediation.

Roberto Oliveros provides a good summary of how liberation theology developed *before* Medellín.[4] A key point in this development was Gustavo Gutiérrez' conference in Chimbote, Peru, in July 1968, "Hacia una teología de liberación."[5] This conference marked the explicit break, the qualitative leap, from a worldvision tied to a "developmentalist" kind of practice to one tied to a practice of "liberation."

"Liberation" is not an abstract or academic term. It emerged in fact out of a very specific political practice, in Peru as well as in the rest of Latin America. During this period Peru was experiencing the failure of President Belaúnde's "developmentalism" (1963-1968), as well as that of the guerrilla movement, which came to sharpest focus around 1965-1966 (the Peruvian MIR movement in which Luís de la Puente and Lobaton were killed). In Latin America the word for "development" (in Spanish, *desarrollo*; in Portuguese, *desenvolvimento*) had to do with a specific overall economic, political, and ideological model: ECLA (Economic Commission for Latin America), the Alliance for Progress (1961-1969), governments like those of Juscelino Kubitschek (1956-1961) and João Goulart (1961-1964) in Brazil, or of the Christian Democrats in Chile (after 1964), and so forth. It also became clear that "developmentalism" was the final stage of the previous populist and nationalist period (Lázaro Cárdenas, Perón, Getúlio Vargas, Paz Estenssoro, Rómulo Betancourt, José María Velasco Ibarra). This whole "development world," however, rapidly began to break down and enter a crisis. "Dependence theory" was the theoretical expression of the recognition that the "developmentalist" model had failed.

By the same token, the word "liberation" referred to very concrete situations throughout Latin America: the Cuban revolution (1959) especially as seen against the background of the Bolivian revolution (1952), the Guatemalan revolution (1945), the Mexican revolution (1911), and the long Latin American revolutionary tradition. In 1968 the heroic resistance to the U.S. invasion of Santo Domingo (April 1965) was still a vivid memory. The word "liberation" in Latin America was also connected to the guerrilla movement, and especially to two figures who had a great impact on the whole of Latin America—Camilo Torres (killed February 15, 1966) and Ernesto "Che" Guevara (killed October 8, 1967). The term "liberation" also referred to the practice of many Christians who resisted and struggled against the dictatorship of Lt. Col Onganía in Argentina (1966) or, in Brazil, the dictatorship of Castelo Branco (starting in 1964) or of Costa da Silva (starting in 1967).

"Liberation" thus implied a *revolutionary option* and a clear *political and ideological break* from nationalist-developmentalist reformism and from the new military regimes. It is within this *specific* historical context that we must understand the shift from a theology of *development* to a theology of *liberation*, such as was expressed in Gustavo Gutiérrez's conference in Chimbote.

The bishops' conference at Medellín took place in this same historical context. It was a difficult context, one of harsh confrontations, and had nothing of euphoria or triumphalism about it, as some writers nevertheless maintain. Through the church as it met in Medellín, the prophetic minorities that had already taken a new direction politically, ideologically, and theologically, moving from a development practice to a liberation practice, were able to communicate the meaning of this historical shift in Latin America.

From Pastoral Practice to Political Practice

The theological revolution that crystalized in the July 1968 conference in Chimbote (among many other expressions) and best expressed the experience of Christians between 1960 and 1968, revolved around the concept of "practice." This pivotal concept in theology went through three stages.

At first it referred to the *pastoral practice of the church*. Gustavo Gutiérrez's study, *Líneas pastorales de la Iglesia en América latina* ("pastoral guidelines of the church in Latin America") belonged to this stage of development. This booklet was the product of a series of conferences given in 1964, subsequently reworked and presented in February 1967 to a group of Catholic university leaders in Montevideo in a MIEC seminar, and then published in 1968.[6] This work examined four forms or types of *pastoral practice*, those proper to Christendom, to New Christendom, to a pastoral practice of maturity in faith, and to a prophetic pastoral practice. Theology was regarded as a critical reflection on these types of pastoral practice.

At a second stage, the focal point of theological reflection was not so much the *pastoral practice of the church* as the *political practice of Christians* (not a Christian political practice but the political practice of Christians). The challenge to theology was militant involvement by Christians—often by priests and religious—in the popular movement, in leftist parties, and even in guerrilla movements during this period. Theology was done out of the pressing need to reply to deep and urgent questions raised by committed Christians. Theologians moved out of theology departments and seminaries and went to grassroots movements; a theological renewal began in a direct and ongoing dialogue with Christians who were well on their way to being politically radicalized.

At a third stage, theological reflection focused not only on the political practice of Christians but also on the *political practice* in which the agent or subject was simply the popular classes. Class analysis and class struggle were still not clearly present but this radical recognition that political practice was the starting point for theological reflection situated theology unequivocably as "second act" with regard to political practice, which was "first act."[7] This was the point at which *theological method* was turned upside-down. What changed throughout this whole evolution was not the *object* of theological reflection, but theological method itself—that is, the way theology is done. Political practice was not a new object for critical and theological reflection, but its starting point.

I must emphasize that this methodological reversal was not the "intellectual discovery" of any particular theologian, but that it arose out of a political practice that made it clear that the poor and exploited were the agents of liberation in history. It was this political practice that unveiled the shift in theology and made it necessary. This did not happen spontaneously and mechanically; its theological reflection was the result of the political practice of Christians. Taking as their starting point the poor and exploited as the real agents of liberation, Christians began to express, communicate, celebrate, and reflect on their faith in a different fashion.

Out of the experience of this process was to arise a new way of conceiving evangelization, pastoral activity, the building up of the church, and the task of theology. This gradual movement—starting from the pastoral practice of the church, moving toward the political practice of Christians, and finally toward class-based political practice—entailed a simultaneous political radicalization of theological activity and a theological radicalization of political activity. It was the radical nature of political commitment that enabled theology to find its identity as *theological* reflection.

SPREAD OF LIBERATION THEOLOGY IN LATIN AMERICA, 1968–1973

In order to show how Latin American theology evolved during this stage, I must briefly examine what was going on during these years. The ecclesial event that closed the previous period and opened the new period was the second general conference of the Latin American bishops at Medellín (1968). However, this ecclesial event takes on its full significance only if situated in the two basic historical processes surrounding it:

1. *The crisis of the system of domination.* Almost all writers (Theotonio dos Santos, Fernando Danel Janet) date the beginning of the structural crisis of the capitalist system in Latin America to 1967. Once the populist, nationalist, and —especially during these years—the developmentalist models reached their limits, the crisis of the system became obvious everywhere. The crisis was not simply economic, political, and cultural, but ideological as well.

2. *The rise of the popular movement.* During the period leading up to 1968, it was primarily the Latin American intellectual petite bourgeoisie that was becoming active. The most visible manifestations were student rebellions, university reforms, the birth of a generation of revolutionary intellectuals, the appearance of new left or leftist revolutionary parties, and the guerrilla movement. Around 1968, however, the popular classes as a whole began to make themselves felt: proletariat, subproletariat, peasants, and Indians.

It is on the basis of these two movements that the "Christian movement" of the 1968–1973 period can best be understood. The Medellín documents and the theology produced before 1968 were widely circulated and underwent a good deal of development and maturation within the "Christian movement," which was rooted in these two processes.

The end-point for the period begun in 1968 can be seen in the coups that established throughout Latin America a kind of military rule based on the doctrine or ideology of national security:

—*Brazil: March 31, 1964*, overthrow of the nationalist and popularly supported government of João Goulart. On April 11, General Castelo Branco took power. On December 13, 1968, with Institutional Act no. 5, the dictatorship became radicalized.

—*Bolivia: August 21, 1971*, overthrow of the nationalist and popularly supported government of General Juan José Torres. Colonel Hugo Banzer took over. The institutionalization of the dictatorship can be dated to November 9, 1974.

—*Uruguay: June 27, 1973,* President Bordaberry disbanded congress, assumed all powers, and provided a civilian cover for a military national security state.

—*Chile: September 11, 1973*, overthrow of the elected socialist government of Salvador Allende. A military junta, headed by General Augusto Pinochet came to power.

—*Peru: August 29, 1975,* overthrow of the nationalist military government of General Juan Velasco Alvarado. The prime minister, Francisco Morales Bermúdez, took power. The consolidation of a national security state can be dated to July 16, 1976.

—*Ecuador: January 13, 1976*, overthrow of the nationalistic military government of General Guillermo Rodríguez Lara. A junta headed by Vice-Admiral Alfredo Poveda Burbano took power and began to set up a national security state.

—*Argentina: March 24, 1976*, overthrow of the government of Isabel Perón. General Videla came to power.

Other Latin American countries, such as Paraguay and Nicaragua, remained under military regimes or else moved rapidly toward civilian regimes that were highly authoritarian and repressive.

Among all these dates September 1973 can be taken as a reference point, because it was in Chile that the contradiction between the previous popular movement and the coup and subsequent repressive violence was greatest. My concern here, however, is not so much an exact date as the economic, political, and social change set in motion by these military coups. This shift began in Brazil. What took place there between 1960 and 1964 (or 1968) was repeated to some extent in most of the other countries between 1968 and 1973 (or 1976). The dates vary but the historical processes were similar.

Latin American theology during the 1968-1973 period was closely connected to the "Christian movement," which was set in the historical context of the two processes mentioned above—the crisis of the system of domination and the rise of the popular movement. These two processes must be the starting point for studying the "Christian movement" during this period, and that movement must be the starting point for analyzing the theology to which it gave birth.

An important aspect of the crisis of the system of domination, and one that was to have a very direct influence on the "Christian movement" and on its theology, was the crisis of the model of New Christendom, which was linked to the system of domination. This crisis of the system, particularly in the ideological realm, had a profound effect on the Latin American church, especially when nationalist, populist, and developmentalist ideologies underwent crisis.

One of the elements of this crisis was the final crisis of "social Christianity" or of the "social teaching of the church." When the system was in crisis and the mass movement was on the rise, when all Latin America was undergoing an intense and widespread process of politicization, the hierarchical church was left without any clear *political doctrine*. Vatican II did not fill this vacuum: the European church had written the conciliar documents in a context of economic prosperity and political stability. Euphoria over the modern European world prevented the conciliar fathers from dealing with the political and economic problems of the Third World. At the Medellín conference the Latin American church turned its attention to the political problems of Latin America and searched for solutions from the viewpoint of the poor and of the process of liberation. But they did not work out any "political project" that could serve as an alternative to "social Christianity" or the "social teaching of the church."

It was in this situation, when the hierarchy had no clear teaching and the mass movement was putting pressure on the Christian conscience, that the "Christian movement" of the 1968–1973 period developed. The first manifestation came in the form of movements of priests which emerged on their own out of the grass roots of the Latin American church. The "Priests for the Third World" (Argentina), ONIS (Peru), and the Golconda movement (Colombia) all made their appearance around 1968. Given the silence of the hierarchy, the lack of effective social and political alternatives, and pressure from the popular movement, priests made public statements and acted *as church* within the Latin American political process. Thus began an "ecclesial practice" that was completely original, previously unheard of. During this period groups of priests made numerous statements on political developments, wrote open letters to the hierarchy on the urgent need for radical changes, and organized seminars outside official channels.

Immediately, in almost all Latin American countries, church movements arose out of grassroots experience in the popular movement and spontaneously tried to respond to the revolutionary moment Latin America was experiencing. In Chile the group called "the Eighty" took a public stand (statement of April 1971), as well as a group called "the Two Hundred" (priests organized to prepare for the 1971 synod on the theme of justice, with the Chilean political context as a starting point). "Priests for the People" took shape in Mexico; in Colombia it was a group called SAL (Priests for Latin America); in Ecuador, MNCL (National Christian Movement for Liberation); in Costa Rica, the Exodus movement; in Bolivia, ISAL (Church and Society in Latin America), and so forth. One of the strongest expressions of this whole process was that of the first Latin American conference of Christians for Socialism, in April 1972, in Santiago, Chile.[8]

The period following Medellín was inscribed within this same historical context. It is very important to note that it was the "Christian movement" that interpreted and diffused the Medellín teachings to the Latin American masses. It is true that some episcopates tried to publicize and elaborate on Medellín. There was the Peruvian episcopal document on justice in the world (August 1971) and the meeting of the Argentine bishops in San Miguel (April 21–26). One of the best interpretations of Medellín was the work of some regional groups of the Brazilian bishops' conference, such as the document of the bishops of the center-west, "Marginalization of a People: Cry of the Churches" and that of the bishops of the northeast, "I Have Heard the Cry of My People."[9] The Uruguayan bishops provided similar examples. The spirit of Medellín also spread to some bishops in Mexico, Ecuador, and Central America. However, groups of priests and grassroots Christians did the most important work of interpreting and publicizing the Medellín documents. That was why Medellín became "dangerous": the power of the Spirit broke through with unheard-of ecclesial and prophetic practices, things that had never been seen before. This happened apart from any planning or programing by the hierarchy.

It is in this historical and political context, more specifically within the "Christian movement" after Medellín, that the theological advance made during the 1968-1973 period must be studied. The year 1970 saw a profusion of theological meetings: in March a symposium on liberation theology in Colombia ("Liberation: Option for the Church in the Decade of the 70s"); a little later in Bogotá, a "Second Conference on Liberation Theology"; in August, in Buenos Aires, ISAL organized another conference on the same topic; in October, in Ciudad Juárez, Mexico, there was a "Seminar on Liberation Theology"; in Oruro in Bolivia, two months later, a pastoral course on liberation theology. On October 8, 1970, Néstor Paz Zamora, "Francisco," died in the Teoponte guerrilla struggle in Bolivia. His diary and letters are one of the best testimonies to Christian commitment and theological searching during these years.

At this point, as a result of all the pastoral and intellectual ferment, liberation theology attained a rather high level of theoretical expression. Gustavo Gutiérrez's *Teología de la Liberación: Perspectivas* (English translation: *A Theology of Liberation*) was published in December 1971. Hugo Assmann's *Opresión-liberación: Desafío a los Cristianos* (English translation: *Theology for a Nomad Church*) had already appeared in May of that same year. These two works pointed liberation theology in the direction it would take. José Míguez Bonino,[10] Rubem Alves,[11] Leonardo Boff,[12] Enrique Dussel,[13] José Porfirio Miranda,[14] and others were representative of the theological efforts being made during this period. During these years liberation theology became the theology of Christian groups committed to the Latin American liberation process. Later on it spread throughout the whole church. The meeting in San Lorenzo del Escorial, Spain (July 8-16, 1972), on the topic of "Christian Faith and Social Change" was a prelude to this burgeoning.[15]

Opposition to the "Christian movement" and to the liberation theology it originated—which was indeed the ecclesial interpretation most in line with the Medellín conference—began to be organized at a high level during this period. One example was the meeting of the CELAM Department of Social Action held in Rio de Janeiro (June 23-25, 1972). Out of this meeting came a "police-state-type" circular letter sent to the social action committees of the national episcopal conferences.[16] More serious yet was the increasingly anti-Medellín direction taken by CELAM, starting with its sixteenth ordinary assembly, in

Sucre, Bolivia (November 15-23, 1972). During this meeting Archbishop Alfonso López Trujillo became secretary general of CELAM.[17]

MATURATION AND GROWTH OF LIBERATION THEOLOGY, 1973-1978

The basic process that characterized this period was the imposition of a *new model of domination* throughout Latin America. The most visible aspect of this new model was the rapid series of coups and the establishment of military national security regimes. I have taken the year 1973 as a reference point, when the process of state militarization reached its high point with the coup in Chile. Even in countries where, strictly speaking, no coup took place, something similar happened as governments became authoritarian and the repressive apparatus of the state was strengthened. Nothing that the dominant classes or imperialism proposed as an alternative to this political model of domination differed essentially from already existent models. The political proposals of Jimmy Carter or of the Trilateral Commission or of "democrats" who spoke approvingly of "restricted democracy" did not change the situation: political projects almost always reflected the economic interests imposed by transnational corporations or by the new international division of labor.

Many writers believe that the fact that since 1973 a new model of domination (whether national security state or authoritarian state) had been set up throughout Latin America means that the previous period was decisively closed and an entirely new period begun. This radical shift in history would also demand a radical shift in theology. These writers characterize the two previous periods as "developmentalist" (up to 1968) and "liberationist" (up to 1973). According to them we would now be living in a completely *new* and *different* period, one that demands that we get beyond the "liberationist" vision of the previous period. Inasmuch as the "liberationist" period (1968-1973) would be over, the period of liberation theology would also be finished. It would now be time to work out a theology that could be an alternative to liberation theology, one apt for the present period of military dictatorships and authoritarian governments.

This vision of history is radically false: it looks at the new model of domination in isolation, disconnected from the economic and political crises of the capitalist system and unrelated to the popular movement and the historical dialectic of class struggle.[18] This falsifying of history inevitably leads to a false picture of Latin American theology during the present period.

There was a basic and intrinsic connection between the new model of domination spreading throughout almost the whole of Latin America around 1973 and the historical processes that began during the 1960s, as I have noted. The new model of domination was connected to previous processes and radicalized them. The historical context in which liberation theology arose not only remained present but was reinforced and deepened. The deeper and sharper the oppression, the greater was and is the urgency of liberation and the need to keep pursuing liberation theology. Any "alternative" to liberation theology inevitably risks being an ideological retreat. The birth of liberation theology was not tied to a "liberationist" period (a period distorted by being presented as triumphalistic and full of euphoria). From the viewpoint of the poor and of the exploited classes, there never has been any liberationist, triumphalistic, and euphoric period. Liberation theology is situated precisely in this perspective of the poor and it does not change its basic options. Indeed, now more than ever it deepens and strengthens those options, because oppression and repression have increased. The worse the situation of captivity of the popular classes becomes—and that captivity is now centuries old—the greater will be the need to deepen a prophetic theology of liberation and hope.

Liberation Theology and Other Theologies

One of the tasks of liberation theology since 1973 has been that of challenging the Latin American currents of thought that have retreated in the face of sharpened repression and that propose false alternatives. Among the theological currents I could cite are the populist current that is unwilling to allow the popular movement to be an independent class-based movement. I may also mention those defeatist currents of thought that make repression an object of theological reflection or a framework for such reflection. Finally, I may mention the theological current that challenges the military doctrine and ideology of national security, and seeks to develop theology by focusing on human rights and the process of redemocratization. This theology situates itself *above* economic and political processes and *outside* the popular movement. That is its weakness, although it has some valid elements.

Another area of confrontation for liberation theology during this period was that of liberal theology. Against this "progressive" theology, liberation theology has had to defend what has been called the "interlocutor" of theology. This interlocutor was not the secularized "modern world" whose agent in history was the bourgeoisie. The interlocutor of theology was the underdeveloped world, and its exploited classes were the subject of liberation. Liberation theology succeeded in pulling theology away from an exaggerated polarization over such axes as "faith-and-atheism" or "church-and-world," in order to reorient matters around "oppression-and-liberation."[19]

Positive Gains

1. Liberation theology spread to the whole of the popular church in Latin America. Theology was communicated not only through books, journals, and conferences, but primarily through the life of Christian base communities. Theology thus took on a popular character and spread far beyond small circles of activist Christians and prophetic minorities.

2. Liberation theology spread throughout the whole church. Liberation theology is not an exclusively Latin American theology, but rather a theological dimension of the universal church. In this sense, the meeting of Third World theologians in Dar es Salaam, Tanzania (August 5-12, 1976),[20] and the Pan-African Conference of Third World theologians in Accra, Ghana (December 17-24, 1977),[21] were important events. In these two conferences the perspective of liberation theology was accepted and worked out from a universal Third World viewpoint. Other important moments in the spread of liberation theology were the publication of the special issue of *Concilium* (no. 96), in June 1974, completely devoted to this theology, and the "Theology in the Americas" meeting held in Detroit (August 17-24, 1975).[22]

3. Liberation theology penetrated all theological fields and disciplines, while retaining its method and original inspiration. There was a liberation thrust in the areas of biblical studies, pastoral theology, and spiritual life. Liberation theology has also been a theology of the renewal of the religious life in Latin America (see the works of CLAR and A. Cussianovich). Liberation theology also underwent development in the areas of ecclesiology and christology (see the works of Leonardo Boff and Jon Sobrino). Liberation theology also established a serious dialogue with Latin American sociology and political economy. There were theological studies on the problem of death and life in capitalist societies, on the problem of the relationship between the church and civil and political society, and so forth. Here I may mention the meeting between theologians and social scientists held in Costa Rica in February 1978. Finally, and this may have been one of the most important efforts, there was a renewal of Latin American church history from a liberation theology perspective. In this area I should single out the writings of Enrique Dussel and work done by CEHILA (*Comisión de Estudio para la Historia de la Iglesia Latinoamericana* [Study Commission for Latin American Church History]).

WORLDWIDE RECOGNITION AND SPREAD OF LIBERATION THEOLOGY, 1979-1985

The third general conference of Latin American bishops was held in Puebla, Mexico, from January 28 to February 13, 1979.[23] The preparatory documents drawn up by CELAM led to fears that liberation theology would be condemned or at least that a Latin American alternative to liberation theology might be introduced. Nothing like that took place. On the contrary, in the Puebla Final Document we can find basic elements of liberation theology. This Final Document was not a consensus statement, and in fact contained different opinions in juxtaposition. What is important is that liberation theology was present in the Final Document. All the liberation theologians were kept out of the CELAM conference itself, but this kind of thinking had such deep roots in the church that it could not be excluded.

Let me briefly survey the sections in the Puebla Final Document where liberation theology is present or where its decisive influence can be detected:

Nos. 3-14: historical overview of Latin America
Nos. 28-30: Latin American poverty and its causes
Nos. 31-39: presence of Christ among the poor
Nos. 87-89: the cry of the poor for justice
Nos. 90: poverty and evangelization
Nos. 96-97: positive assessment of Christian base communities
No. 263: positive definition of the "popular church"
Nos. 385-96: evangelization of culture
Nos. 444-69: evangelization and popular religiosity
Nos. 470-506: liberating evangelization
Nos. 507-62: evangelization, ideologies, and politics
Nos. 1134-65: preferential option for the poor
Nos. 1166-1205: preferential option for the young
Nos. 1207-20: collaboration of the church with the builders of a pluralistic society in Latin America
No. 1308: the new person
No. 1309: signs of hope and joy

Many other texts spread throughout the Puebla Final Document also reflect liberation theology; I have singled out only the most important ones. Moreover, these texts provide an overall interpretation of the Puebla conference; the remaining texts, which do not reflect liberation theology, do not constitute a homogeneous and coherent body that could represent a theology that would be different from, and an alternative to, liberation theology. Those other texts constitute rather a collection of nuances and precautions, and point to possible deviations and risks threatening the church, or simply repeat previous theological positions, usually imported from Europe. After Puebla, liberation theology continued to be the only coherent theological current with its own specificity within Latin American theology. That is why since its appearance the Puebla Document has been interpreted through the perspective of liberation theology.

Central America

On July 19, 1979, the Sandinista revolution in Nicaragua achieved victory. From that point onward, Central America became the most important region in Latin America from both a political and an ecclesial viewpoint. From the theological viewpoint a new element was the participation of Christians in this process. Christians took part in the revolution at different levels: at a *popular level*, inasmuch as the vast majority of Nicaraguans were Christians and Christian inspiration was continually at work in the process on a wide scale; at an *ecclesial level*, inasmuch as Christian communities and pastoral ministers (priests, sisters, and delegates of the word) were present in the revolution in a way that was strictly pastoral; and finally, on the level of *Christian activists*, inasmuch as a significant number of Christians (explicitly motivated by liberation theology) participated in the FSLN (Sandinista National Liberation

Front). This same kind of diversified participation can be seen in the revolutionary process in Guatemala, and much more intensely in the Salvadoran process. All this created a new climate in liberation theology in Latin America. Liberation theology received a sweeping validation from the people within a concrete liberation process.

Basic challenges to liberation theology arose in three fields:

1. The field of *spirituality*. Christian participation in revolution posed the problem of God in a new perspective: the problem was not basically that of knowing whether or not God exists, but of knowing where and how God is revealed in the history of a people. There was a new experience of God, as the God of life, the God of the poor, within revolutionary processes. This experience was not limited to small groups in the church, but was widely shared among the masses. There was an experience of faith from within the general population, because God became present in a new and different manner when the liberation of the poor came into play. This new experience of God was expressed in songs, poetry, symbols, and especially in the witness of martyrs; many have given their lives, making an explicit confession of their faith in the God of Jesus Christ. This expression of faith had nothing to do with atheism but with idolatry: the God of the campesinos, of the Amerindians, of the poor and oppressed, was not the "God" of the oppressive system, the "God" created by the West to support the domination of another people. The point was not to "prove" the existence of God, but to *recognize* God's presence among the poorest. A widespread popular spirituality came into being, one destined to explode in a true "evangelical insurrection" (the term explicitly applied to the religious-popular movement that Father Miguel D'Escoto's fast in August 1985 set in motion in Nicaragua).

2. The field of *ecclesiology*. The massive transformation of popular religious consciousness, the massive education of faith on the level of popular religiosity, took place in Central America through the creation of Christian base communities (CBCs). The CBCs were the basic reference point for this massive transformation of the religious consciousness of the people. The CBCs were the visible tip of an iceberg. They were what could be seen publicly, but the invisible bulk of the iceberg was forming within the mass of ordinary persons through the evangelization work of the CBCs. What is called the church of the poor, a new model of church that has appeared with vigor in Central America, was not simply the sum total of CBCs but rather the whole process of the transformation of religious consciousness within the population. Liberation theology assumed as an important challenge the task of defining and defending the full ecclesial nature of these CBCs and the entire church of the poor. It can be said that liberation theology became the theoretical space in which the church of the poor was legitimized, withstanding the threat of both political or theological reductionism, both of which, from different angles, denied its full nature as church. The church of the poor must define and defend its *specific and independent identity* within the political processes of liberation and must also define and defend its *ecclesial legitimacy*, as a

renewal movement within the church whose basic unity it constitutes.

3. The field of *theological reflection* in the strict sense. Here the great challenge was the same as it has been throughout Latin America since the beginning of liberation theology: the education of the faith of militant Christians. Those who continued to live and explicitly confess their Christian and ecclesial faith from within a revolutionary process found themselves faced with all the political, organizational, and theoretical demands of revolutionary practice. Faith had to be expressed, celebrated, and pondered within a new rationality, the rationality demanded by the revolutionary process. This education of the faith did not take place spontaneously or mechanically; it called for a demanding, ongoing work of theological reflection alongside active Christians and with their collaboration. This work has become especially dynamic in groups of young persons and among Christian rural leaders.

Liberation Theology throughout the Third World

I mentioned above the meetings of Third World theologians in Dar es Salaam in 1976 and in Accra in 1977. In 1976 the Ecumenical Association of Third World Theologians (EATWOT) was set up. It met in Sri Lanka in 1979, primarily in order to help Asian theologians organize.[24] EATWOT also met in 1980 in São Paulo, to organize Latin American theologians on a regional level.[25] This meeting was very important in that it took place after Puebla and it was there that the Puebla Final Document was correctly interpreted. The theme of the meeting was "The Ecclesiology of Popular Christian Communities" and the Final Document of the meeting is the best summation of ecclesiology we have and the one that best reflects the situation of the church of the poor in Latin America.

In New Delhi (August 17–29, 1981) EATWOT organized and held an assembly of all its member theologians, who were now organized on each continent.[26] The Final Document represented a consensus reflecting all the wealth of the theological thinking and systematization taking place in the Third World. In this meeting there was a convergence between the three major issue areas that each continent had been working on separately. Latin Americans had focused on *liberation*, Africa on indigenous *culture*, and Asians on *traditional religions*. At this point these three themes were mutually enriched and the participants came to a consensus on a Third World theology, including the interests of ethnic minorities and oppressed groups in the First World.

The conference document recognized that the majority of humankind lives in the Third World and that the basic contradiction that the whole world is experiencing today is the North-South contradiction—that is, the contradiction between the poor peoples of the Third World and the oppressed among all peoples, on the one hand, and the centers of power located in the developed world, on the other. The contradiction is not with the *peoples* of the First World, but with the *centers* of economic, financial, technological, military, political, cultural, and religious power, which are located primarily in the First

World. We see these centers of power as centers of death, and hence the Third World option is the option for life. Hence the life-death contradiction is the basic contradiction in a Third World theology.

Christians also began to think of the church from this angle. They began to build a church that could be the spiritual power of the poor in the Third World as they struggle against the centers of death. They rejected a church conceived of basically as a Western spiritual power, struggling against so-called non-Christian countries. It was the North-South contradiction—not the East-West contradiction—that provided the basic criterion for the church of the future. We are rediscovering all the cultural and religious treasure of the Third World and we see that the future of Christianity lies in its ability to dialogue with the great cultures and religions of the Third World. More and more Third World persons are becoming aware of the Western pattern of colonialism and domination, and they seek to rebuild church and theology from the "periphery of the world"—which for us is now the center.

At the 1981 meeting in New Delhi a decision was made not to meet again for another five years. In the meantime two working commissions were set up in order to deepen a Third World theology. The first commission was made up of historians. A good number of church historians from Asia, Africa, and Latin America met to write the history of the universal church from the viewpoint of the Third World. A commission of women theologians from Asia, Africa, and Latin America was also set up to reflect on church and theology from the perspective of the situation of women in the Third World.

In Geneva, Switzerland (January 5-13, 1983), there was a dialogue between EATWOT and First World theologians.[27] The meeting was not very successful: the First World theologians were not well organized among themselves and they were not ready for this kind of dialogue. Soon, however, First World theologians showed their solidarity with Third World theologians, increasingly threatened by persecution.

Between 1980 and 1985 liberation theology became stronger and came to a much clearer understanding of things in Latin America. There were several pan-Latin American meetings. In particular there was a deepening of what we have called the "rootage" of Latin American theology: it became more deeply rooted in Amerindian and Afro-American culture, and Latin America opened up to Africa and Asia, seeking non-Western Third World roots. In addition, this period saw the beginning of a very large project, that of writing a compendium of liberation theology, which would be both a point of arrival for the journey covered thus far, and also a point of departure for further development.

Opposition to Liberation Theology

In March 1983 the Peruvian episcopate received from the Sacred Congregation for the Doctrine of the Faith ten observations on the theology of Gustavo Gutiérrez. At the same time a worldwide campaign against Gutiérrez and liberation theology was set in motion in both church and political bodies.

Institutions were set up and magazines launched for the express purpose of attacking this school of theology.

In 1980 an important group of President Reagan's advisors had prepared a lengthy document on U.S. political strategy toward Latin America. In speaking of "internal subversion" this "Santa Fe Document" proposed that U.S. policy "must begin to counter liberation theology as it is utilized in Latin America by the 'liberation theology' clergy." Various institutions, such as the Institute on Religion and Democracy, in Washington, D.C., have taken up the call to do battle with liberation theology, and throughout Latin America there was unleashed a media campaign against this kind of theology. Behind the ideological campaign was political repression, aimed particularly at those pastoral ministers who work among the poor and outcast. The aim was to confuse and intimidate the poor, Christian masses of Latin America and thus to take away the social base of liberation theology.

On August 6, 1984, the Sacred Congregation for the Doctrine of the Faith released its well-known "Instruction on Certain Aspects of Liberation Theology." It was a document of discernment and did not condemn liberation theology. Hence it was a disappointment to all those who expected the church to issue a sharp condemnation of liberation theology. The Vatican document evidenced a serious ignorance of this Latin American theology. In particular it was unaware of the spiritual and ecclesial source where this theology finds its deepest root. Nevertheless, the document was not a condemnation, but rather a call for discernment in liberation theology. The net result was that the theology of liberation became more widely known and studied.

On September 7, 1984, the Brazilian theologian Leonardo Boff was summoned to Rome to appear before the Sacred Congregation of the Doctrine of the Faith to clarify some points in his book *Church: Charism and Power*. Two Brazilian cardinals accompanied him to Rome. The decision against Boff prompted an impressive worldwide show of solidarity with him personally and with liberation theology.

The strength of this theological current, its deep spirituality and ecclesial character, its roots in the poor and believing masses, and the international solidarity it receives, again stood in the way of a condemnation of liberation theology. Liberation theologians themselves decided to submit their theology to a deep process of discernment in order to purify and strengthen it and to root it as much as possible in the life of the church and in the deep faith of the poor and believing masses of Latin America. Liberation theology emerged from this crisis rejuvenated and purified. But there were no grounds for triumphalism or false hope, as long as the definitive liberation of the poor and oppressed has not taken place.

PART THREE—CONCLUSION

I have come to the end of this analysis and interpretation of the crisis of New Christendom and the emergence of a church that is outside (and in contradiction to) any existing or possible Christendom model—namely, the "popular church." I believe that my initial hypothesis, set out in the introduction to part 3, on the *character and significance* of the crisis of Christendom in Latin America, has been confirmed. The characteristics of this crisis justify the way I have divided the history of Christendom into three long cycles: one beginning in 1492, another in 1808, and a third in the 1960s. The beginning of this third broad historical cycle does not necessarily mean that Latin American Christendom is in its final crisis or about to disappear, but it undoubtedly means that New Christendom is confronting the alternatives of either an overall restructuring process that will enable it to survive or a total destruction leading to its utter disappearance.

My analysis leads me to conclude that the crisis of New Christendom that began in the 1960s is leading irreversibly to its complete breakdown. The factors directly making this crisis an irreversible process are not only those of an economic, political, social, or ideological nature. These very same factors have made possible the rise of a church that stands in direct contradiction to the New Christendom model. The crisis of colonial Christendom during the first half of the nineteenth century provides a historical analogy. The great difference, however, is that at that time there was no defined and structured church project, with significant sociological and theological weight behind it, that could stand opposed to colonial Christendom. In the present crisis, in addition to socio-political contradictions, there is the contradiction between Chistendom and church. This contradiction, given the historical background sketched above, is what makes irreversible the crisis of the New Christendom prevailing before 1960 (approximately).

No doubt it is possible that New Christendom may be radically and totally restructured. That could occur on the basis of a new alliance with Latin American authoritarian states and with the new hegemonic sector of the dominant classes. I have shown how one sector of the hierarchical church has clearly opted for a new version of New Christendom, one radically different from the populist, nationalist, or developmentalist model, and which I have called "ecclesiastico-military New Christendom." In this New Christendom Christianity is even regarded as compatible with national security ideology. Such a restructuring of New Christendom, however, will have to deal not only with opposition from all sectors or classes that are oppressed, repressed, or shunted aside by new forms of domination, but also with the contradictions between the New Christendom model and a church that rejects any possible Christendom model.

PART FOUR

Church, Authoritarian State, and Social Classes in Latin America

In this section I shall attempt to work out an analytical model or theoretical framework that will enable me to reorganize or reinterpret the previous chapters within an overall vision. This overall vision will inevitably be schematic, abstract, and more synchronic than diachronic. This final section may also serve as a springboard for further research.

The pivotal reference points I haven chosen for a theoretical framework are the relationships between church and state and between church and social classes. These two relationships are the basic structures of the Christendom pattern: the church strives to guarantee and extend its presence in civil society using political society as its mediator. There is a mutual determination between the kind of church-state relationship in effect and the social or political engagement of the church with particular sectors, classes, or blocs of classes. I believe it is not enough to analyze church-state relationships and neglect social classes and civil society. Similarly, a social or "class" analysis of the church that leaves aside the church-state relationship is also incomplete.

When I speak of the "church" I refer directly to ecclesiastical structures, whether of the hierarchy or the base (that is bishops, episcopal conferences, priests, religious, religious orders, parishes, Catholic action movements, etc.). Indirectly, I am also referring to mixed ecclesiastical structures: ecclesiastico-economic structures (e.g., church properties), ecclesiastico-political structures (e.g., a concordat), ecclesiastico-social structures (e.g., Catholic social work) and ecclesiastico-educational works (e.g., a Catholic school, or publishing house, or radio station). I refer primarily to the Catholic Church, inasmuch as, sociologically speaking, it is the majority church in Latin America. I have other churches in mind to the extent that their dynamic is similar to that of the Catholic Church on the social and political level.

The concept of *"authoritarian state"* is a general concept, one standing in opposition to the democratic state in the classic liberal sense (a state built on the consent of the majority and thereby legitimized). Under the heading "authoritarian state" come different types of states, such as emergency states and highly repressive, restricted-democracy states.

The terms "conservative church," "social-Christian church," and "popular church" do not designate formally organized churches. *They are different ways of conceiving of church and living as church. These different forms or types of church usually exist side-by-side in a contradictory fashion within the same formally established ecclesiastical unit.* The three terms designate opposed tendencies or contradictory proposals for how the church should be, proposals that run through the same ecclesiastical structures. It is in this sense that I speak of the "ecclesial practices" of one or another type of church. The concept of "ecclesial practice" points directly to the way the church acts with regard to the state and with regard to the interests, projects, values, and strategies of different social classes and the political institutions that represent them. *"Ecclesial practice" is not a purely external or formal concept: it includes a historical project, an ecclesial strategy, or a theoretical reflection that has been worked out as an integral part of this practice.*

The three kinds of ecclesial practice should not be regarded as constituting a rigid or structurally stable typology. *Reality is much more complex, fluid, and dynamic. My classification is intended to be an analytical model for interpreting reality, not a static, unchanging structuration.* As things are at present in Latin America, the factors involved in a particular kind of practice can change very quickly. There are gaps between theory and practice, between a particular project and the concrete form it takes. Hence there is no room for any static, abstract, or unhistorical typology. That does not mean, however, that it is futile to work out an analytical model or theoretical framework that can enable one to interpret a given historical reality.

Finally, I should like to recall here two methodological principles explained in the Introduction. *These two principles* seem *to be contradictory, but they are* dialectically *interconnected.*

The first principle views the church as a real entity in history that does not stand outside the reality of social classes and class struggle.

The second principle points to the relative autonomy of the church within economic, political, and social processes. The effect of this relative autonomy of the church is that, although classes and class struggle are certainly present in the churches, they are there in a manner that is different *and* specific. *No one can carry out a class analysis of a church by* mechanically *applying frameworks taken from the analysis of economic or political matters.*

CHAPTER 8

Differing Ecclesial Practices

ECCLESIAL PRACTICE OF THE CONSERVATIVE CHURCH

This church has historical ties to the old oligarchy, specifically to the large landholding oligarchy. It has maintained a direct and explicit alliance with conservative political parties and with others that are confessionally Catholic. Today it agrees ideologically with the hegemonic sector of the bourgeoisie, which is allied to military regimes and in partnership with imperialism and transnational corporations.

The conservative church model prevailed in Latin America from 1870 to 1930, with variations from country to country. The point here is not to determine exact dates but situate this period of the church between two other processes, the crisis of colonial Christendom (1808–1870) and the rise of the social-Christian church (1930–1960). As soon as this latter form became the dominant form, the conservative church, already in crisis, had to withdraw into silence. After the series of coups and the hardening of authoritarian regimes, this church enjoyed a resurgence and recaptured some of its lost social and political space.

In general this church has minority status among Latin American bishops, especially in Brazil, Peru, Chile, Uruguay, and Bolivia. Most of the bishops in Argentina, Colombia, and Mexico are conservative. The base of the conservative church is quite narrow, among both clergy and laity. I can situate in this church the many integralist and far-right movements in Latin America, from the Cursillos de Cristiandad to paramilitary organizations. Although it is true that this church has minority status, it enjoys considerable social and political power. Military regimes tend to make it the dominant church, it has media at its disposal, and its integralist organizations enjoy the protection and support of police and intelligence agencies.

This church provides totalitarian and military regimes with *unconditional legitimation*. Thus it plays the classic political role of *the church as ideological apparatus of the state*. The church carries out this role in its explicit public discourse, in official religious acts (with the participation of important state figures), in symbolic acts (blessing churches or monuments that have a religious-military significance), or by the fact that military chaplains have official status and that Catholic colleges and universities and other Catholic institutions have juridical protection.

Internally the conservative church is an authoritarian and dogmatic church, closed to any social, political, or religious change. It is a church focused on the past, one that repeats the past, one that is basically concerned about moral problems at the personal and familial level (sex, abortion, divorce, education of children). There is no social concern, and little emphasis on the social teaching of the church. This a formal, ritualistic, sacramentalistic church, a church that has not accepted Vatican II reforms or has applied only superficial and secondary reforms. In its public discourse (sermons, pastoral letters and documents) there is almost a total absence of defense of human rights or a critique of the development model of authoritarian regimes. Military governments are legitimized (both in their origins and their workings) because they can impose "order" and discipline, and "depoliticize" matters, and because they are determined to battle "Marxism" on all fronts. This church experiences social and political conflict as a clash of values between good and evil, truth and error, light and darkness. Thus it endows anti-Marxism with a dogmatic content and a religious mystique typical of crusades. Not only is this church against the people; it is opposed to any democratic participation and development among the people.[1]

ECCLESIAL PRACTICE OF THE SOCIAL-CHRISTIAN CHURCH

Historically, this church is close to antioligarchical sectors of the bourgeoisie, to the "nationalist-developmentalist" bourgeoisie, and is linked to the process of industrialization or to "representative democracy" in government. It is also a church that is influential among what may be called the middle classses (essentially a bourgeoisie of small and moderate income) and among the more backward popular sectors. This church has close connections with Christian Democratic political parties and with other social or cultural institutions with a Christian label. During the period of populist, nationalist, or "developmentalist" regimes during the 1950s and 1960s, this church broadened its alliance with the social and political base of these regimes. Today, after the military coups, when the populist and "developmentalist" movements have disappeared, the social-Christian church is associated with nonhegemonic sectors of the bourgeoisie—that is, those bourgeois sectors that military dictatorships have pushed aside.

I can fix 1930-1960 as the period when this church reached its high point. Afterward it went into a deep structural crisis, a crisis that is still unresolved. Between 1930 and 1960 the Latin American church went from an oligarchical-conservative Christendom model, which was extremely antiliberal, to a New

Christendom model, one that was liberal-bourgeois, progressive, modern, reformist, and profoundly antisocialist as well. This process enabled the church to expand its social base considerably and also to reshape its internal structure. In those countries where the church had moved furthest in this direction and where consequently the Vatican II reforms were deeper, and also where the Christian Democratic Party was stronger, even taking power in some cases, the crisis of the social-Christian church began later, but it was all the more shattering. In Chile, for example, the year 1967 marked a violent and deep crisis for the Christian-democratic church.

The 1960s and 1970s were years of crisis for liberal-reformist Christendom and the church linked to it. This crisis occurred after a period of expansion of the church tied to the development and expansion of "nationalist-developmentalist" or "populist" bourgeoisie, especially between 1945 and 1960. When military regimes appeared on the scene, the social-Christian church became clearly linked to the bourgeois or democratic opposition to such regimes. This church, which had turned inward during the crisis of the "developmentalist" and "populist" regimes, again became extremely prominent and became immeasurably important politically. Although the church seemed to have recovered from its structural crisis, in fact that crisis was still there and becoming deeper.

Like the conservative church, the social-Christian church provides explicit legitimation for authoritarian regimes, but now that legitimation is *conditional*, subject to the defense of human rights, to critique of the development model, and to the demand for a return to institutional order or redemocratization. The legitimation given to coups and military regimes is based on the need to use force to deal with "economic chaos," a "power vacuum," or the "Marxist threat." Military intervention is regarded as a "lesser evil" in comparison with the greater evil represented by the establishment of a "Marxist dictatorship." There is also recognition of the ability of a military government to restore "order," halt mass movements, depoliticize the country, and above all to stand up to "Marxism."[2]

Despite its own structural crisis, the social-Christian church is presently the majority church and the most representative one in Latin America, particularly among the bishops, but this church is rapidly approaching minority status at its base—clergy and laity. Military regimes try to silence this social-Christian church when it radicalizes its conditions for accepting them. This church loses its social and political space to the degree that military dictatorships fail to meet the conditions demanded by the church or the nonhegemonic bourgeoisie is unable to set up a democratic regime representing an alternative to military regimes.

In order to characterize the social and political role of this church one must distinguish within it three tendencies—right, center, and left. This dispersal is a result of the multiclass nature of this church and of the structural crisis it is undergoing.

Rightwing Social-Christian Tendency

The *conditional* legitimation the church provides military dictatorships and authoritarian regimes makes its role that of being a *critical ideological apparatus of the state*. In the case of the rightist sector of the social-Christian church, the critique that puts conditions on legitimacy comes down to an abstract repetition of the social teaching of the church and an unhistorical moralizing in a humanistic kind of language. A central theme in this discourse is reconciliation, peace, and national unity. This critique—ambiguous, abstract, and moralistic—is *dysfunctional* for the kind of politicization carried out by military governments and for the ideology of the hegemonic bloc of the bourgeoisie. Military discourse is about punishment, war, the annihilation of the left and of all sectors branded "Marxist." The limits to the critique that this sector of the church directs against authoritarian states are marked by the legitimation it provides. The conditions it attaches to its support or the critique it makes do not question the legitimacy of the military state.

Centrist Social-Christian Tendency

Inasmuch as the church never at any point questions the legitimacy of the authoritarian state, ultimately it finds itself mocked and manipulated by military regimes. The church believes in the "good will" of governments and in the "promises" they make when the bishops criticize them. The promises are not kept and the church withdraws into itself in silent impotence. The military dictatorships seem to be playing with the bishops and ridiculing them. Usually this situation cannot continue for long, and the centrist social-Christian church begins to distance itself from the government. This distancing changes the role of the church with regard to the state, although it does not terminate its basic legitimizing function. The church gradually ceases to be a critical ideological apparatus of the state and begins to carry out a different role, that of a "mediating" church, or a church that is a "court of appeals" vis-à-vis the state, an "intercessor" church for all those who are "persecuted" or "repressed" by the state. The church regards itself as the "voice of the voiceless"; it intercedes, defends, accuses, and makes denunciations in the name of those who are persecuted by the regime. Although it is true that this role is dysfunctional with regard to military domination and sometimes leads to serious church-state conflicts, it still does not mean that the church declares the regime illegitimate. Even when the church is exercising this role, both church and state acknowledge one another.[3]

To the extent that the church ceases to play the role of ideological apparatus of the state and assumes the "mediating" or "court of appeals" role, military dictatorships begin to build or reinforce their own state ideological agencies. The "lay state" of the liberal-democratic tradition begins to become reconfessionalized. There arises a kind of "parallel military magisterium," which decrees doctrinal or moral issues *outside* the official churches. Hence, there arises a "state religion" contrary to Christian faith and independent of it. In this effort the military "manipulates" the conservative church, integralist Catholic groups, and in some cases Protestant churches and sects that are glad to replace the Catholic Church in its role as ideological apparatus of the state.[4] This reconfessionalization of the military state outside the churches and against them leads to a weakening and breakdown of the churches. The church experiences the contradiction of legitimizing a state that administers religion parallel to and independent of the churches.

As opposed to the rightist social-Christian tendency, the centrist social-Christian church does not limit itself to repeating the social teaching of the church in an abstract and moralistic manner. It comes to the point of speaking *concretely* about human rights and about the economic program of military governments. The church protects the living standard of the masses, does not accept the so-called social cost, and specifically denounces the lack of participation and freedom. Nevertheless, the language of the church is plainly liberal-populist. There is simply no political analysis of the class nature of the state or the political role of the armed forces in an authoritarian state. The church begins to use a nationalistic political discourse to defend democracy that it did not use prior to the military coups. The alliance between Christianity and nationalistic liberalism becomes clearest and most legitimized in the context of standing up to military dictatorships. The church becomes more politicized than ever before in its history, but this politicization fits within the framework of nationalistic liberalism.[5]

Leftwing Social-Christian Tendency

When the church follows this tendency, it takes on a political role that goes considerably beyond being a critical ideological agency of the state or of "mediator" or "court of appeals." Today the church is playing a *"suprapartisan"* political role worked out within bourgeois opposition to military dictatorships. To the extent that the conditions demanded for legitimizing military dictatorships are not met, the church begins to establish direct ties with the nonhegemonic bourgeois parties (whether they are tolerated or illegal). The conditions for legitimation, which previously revolved around defending human rights or on critiquing the development model of military regimes, now takes on a more political content. The church begins to challenge national security ideology and doctrine, and it begins to press for a normalization of the authoritarian state (also called the "emergency" state) and for a liberalization or redemocratization of the military regime.

These new conditions do not mean that the church ceases to legitimize the authoritarian state, in terms of either its origins (a military coup) or its workings. The church shares the consensus uniting all fractions of the bourgeoisie (hegemonic and nonhegemonic) that an authoritarian state is legitimate and necessary in order to rebuild the political system of bourgeois domination. The church does not reject the authoritarian state because it is a form of bourgeois domination, but because of the way this domination is carried out. It is around this point that the church raises conditions regarding the normalization, redemocratization, liberalization, or humanization of the state.

In this moral and legal framework the church comes to question not the authoritarian state but the *dictatorship*, the *government*, or the military *regime*. The aim is a state that will be more "human," less repressive, less arbitrary, more normalized institutionally, with more participation, freedom, and so forth. At no point, however, is the system of capitalist domination, the capitalist mode of accumulation, the rule of the bourgeoisie over all the exploited classes, and so forth, called into question. Hence the conditions the leftwing social-Christian church lays down for legitimization do not mean that it is open to a noncapitalist path toward development, let alone an alternate socialist project. That is why this social-Christian church is so radically anti-Marxist and antisocialist. The anti-Marxism of this church tends to become deeper to the extent that military governments make no distinction between the democratic-bourgeois opposition and revolutionary-socialist opposition. The more radically the church stands up to the regime, the greater need it has to distinguish itself from the left, and thus its language must become even more anti-Marxist.

What is the "suprapartisan" political role that the leftwing social-Christian church plays within the bourgeois-democratic opposition? To begin with there is *economic support* for economic and political institutions belonging to this opposition force and to the bourgeois parties that represent it. The church often puts up the money for, or invests in, small or medium-sized industries, subsidizes cooperatives, channels international economic aid, and backs up projects or lines of credit that give economic support to the infrastructure of the nonhegemonic opposition bourgeoisie.

More important, however, is the *political support* the church provides for social or political institutions of the democratic opposition. In countries with a military dictatorship, the church is often the only legal institution independent of the state that the state tolerates. The church uses the legal and independent space it has to promote the interests and objectives of the democratic opposition to dictatorship. The church also serves as an intermediary for obtaining international political support on behalf of opposition forces.

Another role exercised by the social-Christian church has to do with creating a *democratic consensus* against military dictatorships and gaining popular support for that consensus. This role is especially important in countries where bourgeois opposition parties are illegal or do not have access to public opinion. The church is the only nongovernmental institution that can speak publicly and exercise considerable social and political power. Because of its "apolitical" nature and distance from any kind of political party interest, the church plays an irreplaceable role in creating a democratic consensus against military dictatorship.

In creating this consensus the church can even go so far as to propose a *political program*. In order to unify the bourgeois opposition, the church promotes a program in which the most usual demands are that there be an independent judiciary, that the army act in a professional manner, that there be free elections, that there be a national political life with democratic parties, that opposition be legitimate, that there be greater participation in decision-making, that democratic freedoms be established, that the state of siege be ended, that the economic model be changed.[6]

The church plays a political role in not only creating a consensus within the nonhegemonic bourgeoisie, but it plays a mediating role in channeling the *popular support* needed to legitimize a bourgeois-democratic consensus. If political parties have been suspended or made illegal, their ability to maintain a social base of support is curtailed and tends to disappear. The overall depoliticization carried out by military regimes also tends to make this task difficult. In such a situation the church is seen as the privileged institution for channeling the social suppport that a bourgeois-democratic opposition needs. Moreover, the church has an ideological influence over significant sectors of the middle classes of the petite bourgeoisie and even over popular sectors, especially among rural populations and the subproletariat. Some leftist parties that indirectly support the democratic opposition of the bourgeoisie accept and pursue this political role, which consists in mediating a popular social base in support of bourgeois opposition. When they play this role they tend to divide the left and to impede a process of accumulating force and of organizing popular resistance to military dictatorships, so that the working class may have hegemony over all the antidictatorial classes or class sectors.

By associating with the bourgeois opposition to military dictatorships, the leftwing social-Christian church substantially modifies the political role of "mediation" or of a "court of appeals" played by the centrist social-Christian tendency. The distance between church and state is much greater in this case, particularly in the case of military governments. Although it legitimizes the authoritarian state, it has now come to a quasi-break with military *governments*.

The church associated with the bourgeois-democratic opposition modifies its "mediation" role in two ways. On the one hand the church defends not only *persons*, but *institutions*. These are basically economic, political, social, and cultural institutions controlled by the democratic opposition or potentially organizable within this democratic opposition. Hence the church defends small and medium-sized enterprises, cooperatives, small or medium-sized agricultural holdings, schools, universities, trade unions (especially those that are not "class" unions and are controlled by the bourgeoisie) the media, and so forth, against the dictatorship. The church "mediates" the interests of these insitutions vis-à-vis the government, it provides protection for them as well as moral and juridical legitimacy, it defends their legal representatives, and so forth.

The church previously stood up against the government in favor of the *person* who was persecuted or a victim of repression. These persons were generally activists on the left. Defending them did not compromise the church ideologically, because it was acting out of purely humanitarian motivation and thus it did not cease to provide legitimation for the military dictatorship. When the church acted on behalf of the left or defended it, it was always acting on behalf of *individual persons* and its motives were *humanitarian, not political*. Now, however, when the church shifts its "mediating" role and becomes involved with the bourgeois opposition, it is defending not only persons, but also institutions. When it acts in this fashion the church substantially *politicizes* its "mediating" role. The function of the church is no longer *humanitarian* but *political*.

Moreover, and as a consequence of what was said just above, when the church incorporates its "mediating" or "court of appeals" role within its own structures, the church changes that role. The more politicized the role of the church toward the government and the state becomes, the more it tends to internalize this role—that is, to make it an internal function of the church, an ecclesial function institutionalized within the hierarchical structure of the church.

A good example of this politicization and incorporation is shown by what happened when the Chilean church dissolved the Committee for Peace and created the Vicariate of Solidarity. The committee was relatively independent of the Catholic Church: it was both ecumenical and national. Through it the church played its "mediating" role with regard to the military dictatorship. When this mediation became politicized and entered into conflict with the dictatorship, the church disbanded it and created the Vicariate of Solidarity, which was then an institution of the church. Mediation then became an *internal function* of the church.[7]

Generally speaking, the church incorporates within itself its mediating role vis-à-vis military dictatorships in order to meet two needs: to protect its own role from repression and to avoid exposing that role to excessive pressure from the popular sectors on whose behalf the church is acting. That it has to do so is a consequence of the inevitable politicizing of the role of the church under a dictatorship. This politicization increases to the extent that dictatorships intensify repression and disregard the church's efforts to mediate and defend the people. If the church draws its mediating function into itself, it can protect that function from repression: from then on, any repression of an *act of defense* on the part of the church or of a mediating *institution* of the church (such as the Vicariate of Solidarity in Chile) becomes direct repression against *the church itself*.

At the same time, however, the church protects itself from uncontrollable pressure from those on whose behalf it is interceding. Such pressure tends to increase to the extent that repression increases. Inevitably this pressure becomes political, and the church usually interprets it as a "political utilization" of the church by leftist political parties. In order to control this politicization and to prevent any "infiltration" into its mediation with a military regime, the church tends to incorporate this role into its own institutional framework, because then it can control it and direct it in accordance with its own interests and aims.

The Church Politicized as a Result of Repression

The church is politicized as a result of the dynamic of oppression and repression of military dictatorships. The church cannot escape this *spiral of politicization* and particularly the politicizing of its mediating role toward dictatorships. If, in order to avoid such politicization, the church stopped carrying out this mediating role, it would face an emphatic rejection from its popular base of support, and would also be cut off from any connection with the bourgeois democratic opposition and the social and political sectors that make up and represent it. The church would lose all influence and would isolate itself from the political process of the nation. The church must deal with this intensifying spiral of politicization and it does so by making it part of its own structure. In doing so, however, the church takes on the process of politicization, entailed in this mediation, and it becomes internally politicized—that is, it politicizes its specifically hierarchical and ecclesial structures. This process then produces new contradictions within the church. Experiencing a sharpened crisis of its own structures, it experiences a positive development toward new forms, which will be examined below.

Political Discourse Turned into Pastoral Discourse

One particular way to incorporate within itself this "mediating" political role of the social-Christian church toward military dictatorships is to give it a "pastoral" dimension. Inasmuch as this church regards such military governments and military leaders as "Christian," it can relate to them in pastoral, rather than political, terms. That is, the church relates to the military as members of the church, who thus fall under its pastoral authority and are subject to church law. The church-government relationship takes on an intraecclesial character, and political discourse shifts to pastoral discourse. If repression sharpens and if the mediating activity of the church must become politicized, this "pastoral" relationship becomes critical and conflictive.

For the church to break this pastoral relationship and challenge the government in political terms would imply denying the confessional nature of the state, denying that it is inspired by Christianity, and denying that military leaders are Christians. The upshot would be that the church would no longer be legitimizing the authoritarian state. Confronting this type of situation, which is strictly *political*, the church finds itself forced to acknowledge the confessional nature of the state—that is, to recognize that it is inspired by Christianity and that military leaders are themselves Christian. For its part, the military dictatorship, if it is to retain the legitimation of the church, finds that it must declare that it is Christian and the military must show in some fashion that they accept

Christianity and the church. Obviously, this christianization, under pressure of *political* circumstances, brings yet another contradiction into the church. The result is a radicalization of the internal crisis of the church, leading toward the limit-point of an ecclesial and political break. Out of this break will issue a new kind of church, as will be seen below.

ECCLESIAL PRACTICE OF THE POPULAR CHURCH OR THE CHURCH OF THE POOR

The term "popular church" reflects a political or sociological analysis, whereas the thinking behind the expression "church of the poor" is more theological. Both expressions are legitimate and point to a new model of church, one that stands in opposition to Christendom. This is not "another" church but a renewal movement that remains within the unity of the church.

In the following pages I examine the ecclesial practice of the popular church, first primarily from a sociological angle and then taking the theological dimension into account.

When the church engages in its practice under an authoritarian state two kinds of practice can be distinguished, one that is *socially* committed and another that is *politically* committed to the popular movement. I shall now add some observations on the popular church under "restricted-democracy" regimes, or in regimes where there is a "democratic opening" (as is the case since 1984 in Brazil, Argentina, Uruguay, Peru, and elsewhere). I shall also add something about the practice of the popular church under revolutionary governments (such as Cuba and Nicaragua).

This third form of church is sharply distinguished from the social-Christian church in the sense that it does not provide legitimation for military dictatorships or authoritarian regimes. It does not regard the authoritarian state or military governments as legitimate forms of governance. Nevertheless, this form of church has not made a political option for an alternative, class-based, socialist project. This church is ambiguous, fluctuating, and hard to define.

This church rejects the political roles taken by the social-Christian church in relation to the dominant classes. Thus it clearly rejects the successive roles of being an ideological apparatus for criticizing the state, of providing "mediation" or of serving as a "court of appeals" with regard to the state, or the role of being "suprapartisan" in connection with the bourgeois-democratic opposition. Hence it refuses to incorporate these roles into the ecclesial and hierarchical structures of the church, and thus rejects the resulting internal politicization of the church. This church wants to be *genuinely* apolitical precisely to express this rejection. This is an *antibourgeois*, apolitical stand, a refusal of the church to become allied with the dominant classes. This rejection of politics is a rejection of a *particular kind* of politics: the politics of the social-Christianity kind of alliance—and a refusal of the kind of church bound up with that kind of alliance. When adherents say that the church "should not be involved in politics" they mean that it should not be involved in the kind of politicization that characterizes the dominant social-Christian church.

Thus far I have been underscoring how this church is different from the social-Christian church. Let me now examine in a positive sense how this socially committed church understands and defines its own identity. It does so on two levels: that of practice and that of theology.

On the level of *practice*, the church defines its identity by limiting its activity to the popular sectors of the national population. This is a church present and working among campesinos, among the subproletariat (in shantytowns called *favelas, poblaciones, villas misera, barriadas*, etc.), with Amerindians, and also with impoverished sectors of the middle strata in society. The practice of this church is a popular practice. The church knows the problems of the popular world through experience; it is involved in its organizations and struggles. It also experiences social conflict and the oppression/repression the state unleashes against the people. It perceives class struggle in terms of an opposition between "rich" and "poor," "exploiters" and "exploited," "oppressors" and "oppressed."

On a *theological or theoretical level* this church strives to find its identity by "going back to its origins," identifying with "primitive, apostolic Christianity." This is a church that takes on a gospel identity, a prophetic identity. Its primary activity is evangelization carried out as part of its practice of liberation along with the people. This church emerges and becomes organized from the ground up, by rereading the gospel within the context of oppression, and of the struggle against the ruling classes and military or authoritarian regimes.

When this kind of church defines itself as "popular" and "evangelical," the adjective "popular" carries a clear connotation that it has split away from the ruling classes, from the state, and from the bourgeois democratic opposition and the political parties that represent it. And the adjective "evangelical" also has a precise connotation. In the way this church lives and in its theology there is an essential linkage that runs: gospel; evangelization; the oppressed; the struggle of the oppressed for their liberation.

In the effort of this church to establish its "gospel" identity, there is a secondary connotation: this church sets itself off from the popular movement insofar as that movement is politically organized and politically orientated, in particular with regard to leftist parties, and especially with regard to "Marxism." Contrary to the social-Christian church, this church is not utterly "anti-Marxist" and indeed has no need to be so. Nevertheless, it is a church that explicitly intends to be "non-Marxist." This church never uses anti-Marxist discourse, but it does defend its own independent identity as "evangelical" and hence "non-Marxist." The theological idea of the "distinction of planes" is reworked from within a commitment to the popular classes. This church, contrary to all the preceding forms, is not only familiar with Marxism, but it knows Marxists as well. It lives with them, it meets them in a common practice, and many of them are actively involved in Christian base communities.

Nevertheless, this church does not make a class or socialist political option *as church*. It consciously keeps its distance from any kind of politicization, whether theoretical, practical, or organizational, within the popular movement. This church, as church, does not employ any political analysis of class and class struggle.

The "popular" and "evangelical" identity of this church means that it *fluctuates* between the bourgeois democratic opposition to the military regime and the conscious and organized popular movement. This church swings back and forth between "right" and "left." How it shifts depends largely on the way forces line up in each country. In general one can say that the stronger the bourgeois democratic opposition becomes and the more accentuated the contradictions between the social-Christian church and the government, the more will the socially committed church become aligned with the social-Christian church. On the other hand, the more powerful the resistance and the popular movement, and the more the social-Christian church capitulates to authoritarian governments, the more will the socially engaged church break with the bourgeois opposition and become aligned with the resistance and the popular movement.

This church plays various political roles within the popular movement, particularly under highly repressive military regimes. This political role is the same as that of political parties in situations where the political organizations of the left have been broken up or where repression leaves them a very limited margin for political activity within the masses. Here I shall limit myself to enumerating the different political roles this church fulfills.

First there are functions of information and communication. The church disseminates a great deal of information, at the local, national, and international levels, and it becomes an irreplaceable source of information for those who want to know about the mass movement. Secondly, there are activities of linking, regrouping, politicizing, and conscientization. These activities become vitally important when the popular movement has been dispersed, and when the ideological repression of military dictatorships becomes heavier.

Those Christians who are most articulate carry out a higher level of political action, that of keeping alive a kind of "awareness or memory of history" within the popular movement. In situations of sharp repression this "recall" of the history of the working class movement plays an important conscientization role. Present within that movement, the church also transmits a kind of political ethic of survival, of nonresignation, of hope, of struggle and resistance, of physical, moral, and spiritual resistance to military dictatorships. Other more organizational activities include leadership training among grassroots urban and rural workers, and promoting grassroots popular organizations (such as youth clubs, neighborhood organizations, soup kitchens, employment agencies, production cooperatives, health care services, and so forth). Some of the more advanced sectors of this church, together with leftist activists, take part in beginning to work out political programs within the mass movement. This activity both precedes and goes along with the rise and expansion of the worker and campesino movement.

It should be noted that the church does not carry out these political tasks as a "parallel" activity, one that complements its specific activity as church. These tasks arise from its own specific activity; they are not "added on." When carrying out these social and political roles, the church keeps its identity as church, along the lines described above. What is going on here is that the church is internalizing or integrating political activities into its own essence. Contrary to the process that takes place in the social-Christian church, *this process of integration is coherent with the particular identity the church has taken on*. The process of internalizing the political dimension is not contradictory to, but consistent with, the popular identity of this church, and particularly its evangelical identity. Politicization is consistent with its activity of liberative evangelization.[8] Consequently this politicization does not provoke a process of crisis as happens with the social-Christian church. The church that is socially committed to the popular movement in Latin America is thus not a church in crisis, even though it often undergoes repression and disarticulation.

This form or type of church explicitly embraces a political project, one that stands as an alternative to the dominant capitalist system, while maintaining its own identity and relative autonomy as church within that option. Opting for an alternative revolutionary project also means consciously opting for theoretical elaborations of praxis and for the organizational and political character of this practice. The political theory and organization connected with praxis are taken on in themselves, for their own intrinsic worth, and not for reasons foreign to praxis. This eliminates the possibility of any kind of "clericalism of the left" or any "political religious messianism," or any "political third way" or any "social Christianity." Hence the popular church is not some kind of "Christian left"—I am not referring to any particular political party but rather to a theoretical concept—or a struggle for some "Christian socialism" or some "Christian revolution." That there is a working-class movement and a left, and that the revolution stands on its own, is taken for granted. However, on the basis of this praxis, those Christians who make up the popular church seek to redefine how they practice their faith and experience the church. The result is a deep and radical transformation of the way the faith is expressed and the concrete ways the church is built up. These Christians experience a convergence between the radical depth of their political commitment and the radical depth of what faith demands.

The so-called popular church, or politically committed church, takes up the same political tasks as the social-Christianity church, but it does so not from an ecclesial, but from a political perspective. In this sense, the political process that previously politicized an apolitical church, now "de-politicizes" a church that expressly intends to be political. The basis for this depoliticization is the need of the popular movement to be independent. The church does not constitute an autonomous *power* within the popular movement, but keeps its specific character as a *sacramental* community and community of faith. If the church were to lose its specific character and become a political power, it would betray the class-based autonomy of the popular movement. Hence it is that within this church the demands of the political situation become a demand for continual conversion to its own specific character as church.[9]

This church, or this kind of ecclesial practice, plays an important role, not within the working-class movement, but rather within the churches as a whole and within the "Catholic movement." Although it is indeed usually small in numbers, in qualitative terms this church has a decisive influence. By its very existence it polarizes the church as a whole and forces it to take a stand. This church is a continual standard of comparison for the socially engaged church. It represents an ongoing denunciation of the alliance of the social-Christian church with the ruling classes and the legitimation it provides for authoritarian regimes.

Today the popular church in Latin America is something real, not merely an idea. To state that this popular church exists is to state both that the social-Christian church is undergoing a structural crisis and that there is a popular movement. If there were no popular movement in Latin America and there were no Christians participating in that movement, there would be no such thing as the kind of church I have called "popular church" or "politically engaged" church.

Ecclesial Practice of the Popular Church under a "Democratic Opening"

In some Latin American countries—Brazil, Uruguay, Peru, Argentina—there has been a process of democratic opening or a return to democracy since 1984, after the fall of national security military dictatorships. The popular church regards this change as positive, but it also sees it as a new challenge to its own ecclesial practice. This challenge can be briefly described in relation to the state and in relation to the popular movement.

The popular church takes up a vigilant stand toward the state and defends the people's right to participate. This vigilance, and sometimes critical opposition, is necessary: "democratization" may mean a mere change of regime or government, with the social and political structure of the system of domination remaining unchanged. The church regards a return to democracy as something positive but it does not want it to mean that citizens are once more deceived and frustrated, and that the popular movement once more loses momentum. That is why, as part of its vigilant attitude, the church of the poor takes up a strategy of defending the people's right to participate. The church is no longer simply defending the human and social rights of the people, but the people's fundamental right to be the agent of its own destiny. The church encourages popular participation in the economic, social, political, ideological, cultural, and religious realms. Popular mobilization in all spheres is regarded as the main force in a genuine return to democracy, a force that can end the danger of a new dictatorship once and for all.

In both Brazil and Argentina sectors of the church have published a book on the violation of human rights during the previous military dictatorship. It is significant that in both cases the book was entitled "never again"—that is, there must never be a return to the terror imposed by national security states. The only thing that can prevent such a return is popular awareness and organization. One concrete example of this attitude took place in 1985 in the archdiocese of São Paulo, Brazil, where the cardinal called the people to the cathedral to promote an active and real participation in the discussion leading to a constitution for the new republic.

With regard to the popular movement, the church of the poor must take up the challenge of redefining its own identity as church. During the period of military dictatorship, the church was almost the only space for social and political expression and almost the only organization tolerated by the military regimes. As noted before, this gave the church a great deal of social power. With the return to democracy, political parties and many other social and cultural organizations reappeared at the popular level, and they contested the quasi monopoly on organization and public expression that the church enjoyed during the dictatorship. At first this created confusion in the church: many Christians felt that the new organizations were shoving them aside. Subsequently, however, they overcome this initial confusion by redefining the identity of the church within the people. The church found itself challenged to rediscover its space and its own way of being part of the popular movement, by redefining its own identity and its specific, prophetic mission: to educate in the faith, to celebrate the liturgy, to accompany the people pastorally, and to reflect theologically.

In a process of democratization the popular movement does not push the church aside, but it demands that the church redefine its role so that it can be a public reference point, in both theory and organizational potential, for faith and the popular practice of religion in the new political situation.

Ecclesial Practice of the Popular Church within Revolutionary Processes

In countries like Cuba and Nicaragua, where the revolutionary process has achieved victory, and in countries where it is making rapid strides, the popular church has to respond to challenges that are utterly new. Christendom begins to fall apart very quickly and a new model of church begins to be built up. The new political power that emerges from the revolution does not expect the church to serve as a force for political legitimation. The revolution seeks its legitimacy in the revolution itself—that is, in its ability to provide the people with work, health care, education, participation, and so forth. In this sense, the revolutionary process goes beyond Christendom, which from colonial times onward revolved around a relationship in which church and state legitimized one another. Now the revolutionary state does not need the church as a force for ideological legitimation.

Nevertheless, inasmuch as Latin Americans are essentially religious and indeed Christian, and inasmuch as recently there has been a strong Christian participation in revolution, a new possibility is opening up for the church to be present in society. The only valid model in the new revolutionary situation, however, is the model of the popular church or the church of the poor. Although there is no room for Christendom, there is plenty of room for a popular church. Political revolution spurs ecclesial revolution—that is, the shift from Christendom to the church of the poor, with all the theological, pastoral, and spiritual demands that this ecclesial revolution entails. Hence, in a revolutionary process, the contradiction between Christendom and the church of the poor becomes much sharper. This process, which was slow and not very clear in Cuba, is rapid and very obvious in Nicaragua. In countries like El Salvador, where the revolutionary process has not yet attained victory, the popular church has already gone beyond the ecclesial process that took place in Nicaragua.

The church of the poor within revolutionary processes exists and expresses itself on three levels:

1. The general level of a poor and believing people. Here the church of the poor takes up the challenge of transforming a people's religious awareness. If such a change does not take place, there is a danger of a gap between the revolutionary process and religious awareness, a split that affects the very roots of a church of the poor and seriously damages the possibility of a genuinely liberative evangelization.

2. The level of Christian base communities (CBCs): a poor and believing people organized as institutional church. The whole people of God cannot be organized into CBCs, but CBCs provide a way for the whole people of God to find expression. The CBC brings to ecclesial expression a people believing but not organized.

3. The level of Christian activists and pastoral ministers. Here the basic challenge is that of education in the faith and of theological reflection on a properly theoretical level. A revolution brings with it the demand for a new way of looking at the world, a new way of thinking. The faith must be thought through, communicated, and celebrated with this new way of thinking. This does not happen by itself or through some mechanical process. There must be a commitment of the popular church and it must work directly at this level.

The church of the poor takes up its place on these three levels. A fourth level—that of the nonorganized Christian people as a whole—is the most diffuse level of all, and it is almost invisible; the expression it finds in CBCs is not so much quantitative as qualitative. The church of the poor grows within the wider believing population, not so much through the number of CBCs (of which there should be as many as possible) as through its ability to give public expression to a new way of being Christians and of living and celebrating the Christian faith within the revolutionary process. This nonorganized body of persons which nevertheless finds interpretation and expression in the CBCs, is like the bulk of an iceberg, which is below the surface and cannot be seen; its presence can be made out only through the tiny part visible that reveals that it is there. The mission of Christian activists and pastoral ministers is to provide leadership for the CBCs and to provide a new theological legitimacy for the church of the poor, both within the universal church and within the revolutionary process. It is very important that the popular church not be reduced to pastoral ministers or CBCs. They certainly are the church, but the important thing is their influence on the whole body of the poor and believing Christians and their influence on the social classes and sectors that are the foundation and the strength of the revolutionary process. The church of the poor has power and it has a future in proportion to its ability to evangelize the whole body of believers. Most of them are not yet organized although they are becoming increasingly organized into CBCs.

Theological Analysis of the Ecclesial Practice of the Church of the Poor

In order to define the nature and identity of the church of the poor within the popular movement, it will help to reflect on the three constitutive dimensions of the church: priestly, prophetic, and pastoral. These are not tasks of the church but simply what makes the church the church. I want to show how each of these three ecclesial dimensions takes shape in general and specific terms within the popular movement today.

Priestly Dimension

The priestly dimension of the church can be defined on the basis of three elements: the process of history, the kingdom of God, and the church. The kingdom of God is something greater and more important than the church. It is an absolute; the church is something relative. Moreover, the kingdom of God in this present phase appears within our history, within the process of our own history. There is only one history, and God's presence, God's liberating and saving action, is revealed within this single history. However, this presence of the kingdom of God in the movement of our history is not something obvious; a discernment of faith is required. It is the function of the church to enable us to make this discernment of God in history. Without the church we could scarcely discover, announce, and celebrate this presence of the kingdom of God in the ongoing history of Latin America. The priestly dimension of the church is not that of celebrating itself, for its own sake, but of celebrating the presence of God's liberating action in history for the sake of all humankind.

A theology built on the three aspects mentioned above (kingdom, history, and church) is reflected in the living spiritual experience of the CBCs within the popular movement. The popular movement is not simply a social and political space: it is also a place for encountering God. The communities discern and celebrate this presence of God within the history of the people's liberation, just as Israel did in the history of the exodus. The church is built up around this basic and absolute experience. The church fulfills its priestly dimension to the extent that it can discover and celebrate this liberating presence of God in history.

Prophetic Dimension

It is particularly in evangelization that the church fulfills its prophetic dimension. To evangelize means to announce the God of Jesus. One of the most basic experiences of the CBCs is the discovery of this God of Jesus in the history of the liberation of the poor. Persons discover that this God of Jesus is not the God everyone talks about and in whom everyone believes. The God of the poor is not the God created by oppressors or the God the dominant system manipulates. At the very center of the whole complex of issues surrounding the popular church stands the problem of God, and that problem creates contradictions for society and for the church as well. The greatest achievement of liberation theology is to have made possible this discovery of God in the political practice of liberation.

In order to provide a better and more systematic expression of this prophetic dimension of the church of the poor, I want to describe briefly a concrete method for evangelization that has been created in the practice of our communities. There are three moments to this methodology: it begins as *spirituality,* continues as *biblical discernment,* and ends in *theological reflection.* These are not three chronological stages, but three logical moments that show us the thinking process underlying evangelization, the concrete path it takes in our communities.

1. *Spiritual experience within the political practice of liberation.* The root of all evangelization is the experience of God in the history of the oppressed. The poor evangelize us when, from within their liberation struggles, they communicate to us the "secrets of the kingdom" that have been revealed to them alone (Matt. 11:25). This spirituality is not a matter of mere individual feeling; it comes to bodily and community expression in innumerable signs, celebrations, songs, and prayers, in which believers express their faith and announce what kind of God it is in whom they believe. One expression of this evangelizing spirituality is the celebration of the martyrs. Here we have the most intense and dramatic *bodily* expression of the *transcendent* and *spiritual* dimension of liberation struggles. In this kind of celebration there is not only a recalling of the past, but also an expression of the absolute sense of God in the practice of justice for which martyrs have surrendered their lives.

There is precondition for this spirituality, without which this spirituality will not take shape and will not be true or genuine. This precondition is the kind of knowledge of the reality of ongoing history that is acquired through militant practice within the popular movement. In political terms all those who struggle for justice must have this kind of knowledge, but this same political demand, when it is assumed as part of a process of evangelization, takes on a spiritual dimension in addition to its political dimension. The history of the poor is the place for meeting God, and one who is not in this place cannot discover and announce the God of the poor. Such knowledge of reality does not lead us to experience God by any sort of mechanical necessity, but it is the proviso that makes it possible for us to receive the gift and grace of that experience. That is why the practice of evangelization in our communities always starts with political commitment and the analysis of the de facto situation as something demanded by faith, which then opens us to God's revelation in history. Ignorance of the way things are renders us spiritually incapable of evangelizing the God of Jesus.

2. *Biblical discernment.* Evangelization begins as spiritual experience in the liberating practice of the oppressed, but that experience must be communicated to others if evangelization is to take place. We must move from the *practice* of faith to the *witness* of faith, which is what enables faith to be communicated and spread within the popular movement. This communication of faith normally takes place through a *rereading of the Bible.* The biblical text is not the direct revelation of God but an *instrument of discernment* of the revelation of the living word of God in our ongoing history. It is this discernment of God that we communicate in a rereading of the Bible. This is not a mere commentary on the Bible, but the experience of God in the history of the oppressed, discerned through the criteria present in Bible reading and *communicated through the instrumentation of a rereading of the Bible.*

3. *Theological reflection.* All that I have been saying should lead to a theoretical treatment of the overall reasoning process guiding the liberation of the oppressed. The experience of God in history should not only be lived, celebrated, and communicated: it should also be reflected on, "theologized." This theology, as a part, and an extension, of an evangelization process carried out by the CBCs within the popular movement is what enables us to provide a "reason *(logos)* for our hope" (1 Pet. 3:15). This is the theology that enables evangelization to reach down into popular consciousness. The church of the poor lives its faith with the thought categories that the poor take on, understand, and spread in their liberation struggles.

Evangelization is thus a *conflictive activity* within society and within the church as well. It is quite important to clarify the nature of the conflict created by evangelization. It has usually been said that evangelization stands opposed to atheism, but this is not so much the case in Latin American, where evangelization must primarily challenge *idolatry.* Idolatry means not only bringing in other gods; it also means manipulating or distorting God.

CBCs very often reflect on the present-day idolatry of the system in which we live, and especially on the *idolatrous roots of oppression.* Behind every ruling-class agent there is another abstract and universal agent, with which the ruling-class agent identifies. Those who oppress never do so in their own name, but in the name of a "supernatural" agent who comes with "divine" features. The fact that oppressors refer back to and identify with this "divine" subject in this fashion empowers them to act without restraint. When oppressive agents become "divinized," they become dangerous: they oppress and repress in the name of a "god" and anything is allowed. One of the causes of the widespread savage repression of the peoples in Central America today is the fact that political power has been made an idol. Evangelization denounces this repressive idolatry and clearly distinguishes the God of the poor from the god in whose name Central Americans are being killed. Evangelization within the popular movement exorcises all the mechanisms of domination; destroys all the untouchable fetishes of the system. Evangelization creates a spiritual climate within the popular climate that stands at the opposite pole from the "spiritual" climate of the dominant system. Hence evangelization unleashes the "battle of the gods": a radical confrontation between the God of the poor and the idols of oppression.[10] By living at this spiritual depth within liberation struggles, the church of the poor fulfills its prophetic dimension.

Pastoral Dimension

Not every Latin American is a member of a CBC. The challenge for the CBCs is to have a spiritual and liberating impact on the people as a whole. This is where the question of pastoral work is posed, not only as a problem for the hierarchy, but as a dimension of the whole church as church. A CBC is a presence of the church in a barrio or a town. The church is born in a barrio or a town when a CBC emerges out of that bottom level. The CBC is the church at the bottom or in a local area. The CBC therefore has the pastoral responsibility of providing spiritual leadership for that area.

There are two requisites for a CBC to have a pastoral influence among the people. The first is that the CBC be an integral part of the people, that it be a space within the popular movement, a slice of the populace become a church. The second requisite is that the CBC have an identity as church and retain its own independence. Although it might seem contradictory, the CBC takes its place within the people and the popular movement only when it has a clearly defined ecclesial, spiritual, prophetic, and pastoral identity. If the church loses its identity, it cannot really take its place within the popular movement, because it will enter into competition with other cultural or political institutions. However, it is also true that unless the church becomes fully a part of the popular movement, it will not be able to achieve its priestly, prophetic, and pastoral identity: that identity can be achieved only from within the poor and their liberation struggle.

Future Challenges to the Identity of the Church of the Poor

In the future the church of the poor will have to face a twofold challenge. On the one hand, it will have to strengthen its nature and specific mission by becoming ever more a part of the popular movement. On the other hand, it will have to extend its own experience of ecclesial renewal to the church as a whole. This is very difficult: it means putting up with contradictions both within the popular movement and within the church. I say "putting up with" because many of these contradictions will not be solved in the short run. Such contradictions will be solved only in the long run but they must be accepted in order for the church to continue to mature as a sign of the kingdom of God in Latin America.

The church of the poor will be able to grow to the extent that it accepts this twofold challenge in the popular movement and in the church. It must avoid breaking off from either the church or the popular movement if it is to live up to its priestly, prophetic, and pastoral nature and calling, both in the whole church and in the popular movement.

In order for the church of the poor to respond to this twofold challenge it must be as *theologically creative* as possible. The contradictions the church finds in the popular movement and in the church as a whole must be thought through with all the theological rigor they require. Theology must respond to the challenge of clarifying and deepening the identity of the church of the poor: it will be necessary to continually affirm that the church of the poor *is really church* within both the popular movement and the institutional church. Political or ecclesiastical reductionism (seeking to reduce the church of the poor to a purely political movement or to a mere renewal within the church with no significance for ongoing history) could lead to a denial that the church of the poor really is church.

By way of example, we may recall all of Saint Paul's theological activity in order to defend the possibility of salvation through faith, outside the law (that is, the legitimacy of a Christanity and church outside Judaism with all its legal and cultural demands). Today liberation theology must defend the ecclesial legitimacy of CBCs set in the midst of the world of the poor. In previous decades theology made it possible for Christians committed to the popular movement to maintain their claim to be Christians, and the result was what have been called "prophetic minorities." Today theology must defend and provide a basis for the claim of the church of the poor to be fully church.

The Historical Project of the Church of the Poor in the Popular Movement

The historical project of the church of the poor arises out of its own identity within the popular movement. In Latin America this identity is not simply an idea, but something real that arises out of many years of genuine practice. The evangelizing *prophetic* dimension of the popular church, which is the work of the CBCs in the heart of the popular movement, has revealed a great capacity for educating the religious consciousness of the people, and that in turn has unleashed the liberating potential of the social consciousness of the poor. Evangelization has proven that it has a liberating power within popular consciousness. The *priestly* dimension of the popular church within the popular movement has also been awakening all the spirituality that is latent in revolutionary processes. The church, present in the people through the CBCs, becomes a space for affirming the transcendent, spiritual, and utopian dimension of liberation. Finally, the *pastoral* dimension of the church of the poor has meant that a people has really been accompanied in the midst of the political and military processes of recent years. This pastoral accompaniment has not only provided ordinary persons with consolation and spiritual strength, but has also been decisive in helping them to resist and struggle to the end. The definition of the historical project of the church of the poor should start from this specific experience in the processes taking place in Central America.

By "historical project" I do not mean a group of tasks or an action program. It is rather a concrete theoretical framework for organizing and guiding the activity of the church within society. Here I shall simply make an outline sketch of this historical project for the church of the poor in Latin America.

First, the church should concentrate its prophetic, priestly and pastoral work where its greatest force and strength lie—in the exploited and believing mass of the people. The power of the popular church is in the spiritual experience of the people; that is the soil in which the church must sink its roots. The church must arise out of the "liberating potential of the poor"—that is, out of the power of the faith of the poor to discover and announce the true God, who is the liberating God of the Bible, and also out of the power of the faith of the poor to destroy the idolatry and the fetishism of the system of domination. Hence the challenge to the church of the poor is to develop a "popular" kind of pastoral work, a pastoral activity that will reflect the "logic of the majority" and likewise to be a church that is built up as the people of God through its ability to provide pastoral leadership for the people, those who are the majority. Through CBCs the church must grow throughout the whole body of the people, not in order to dominate it as a "people of the church" but to serve it as the "people of God."

Secondly, the church of the poor is not a political project and should never use political power as a means for expanding or defending itself. It is true that Christians live their faith within the popular movement whose political aim is to take power and build a new society. In this sense there is no "apoliticism" within the church of the poor. However, it is one thing to live, confess, celebrate, and reflect on faith within the popular movement, and it is quite another thing to make use of this popular movement as a political force at the service of the popular church. It would be even worse if the popular church were to use such political power in order to resolve its conflicts and contradictions within the church. The church of the poor must not make use of political power in order to deal with the other model of church—namely, Christendom. The popular church must take its support only from the power of the gospel, the power of its faith, hope, and love. This might seem like a weakness of the popular church, but its strength is to be found precisely in that weakness.

Thirdly, the final element of this project in history is ecumenism. This ecumenism is not something accidental to the popular church but basic and intrinsic to it. Nothing is more damaging to the mission of the church than religious sectarianism and proselytism. Ecumenism asserts that human beings are not the private property of any church but that they belong *to God*. Ecumenism is a basic requirement if the church is to be discovered and affirmed as people of God. Ecumenism demands that we be available not to serve the churches politically, but to serve the people spiritually. What gives scandal is not so much that we Christians are divided, but that we regard each other as enemies in our desire to "conquer" or "rule" the people ecclesiastically. All the churches, coming from their different religious and Christian traditions, must serve the people as the people of God.

Conclusion

Having concluded my analysis and interpretation of the process of formation and of crisis of both Christendom and New Christendom in Latin America, it can be seen that my general hypothesis on the nature and structure of the Christendom model and my specific hypothesis on the character and meaning of the present crisis of New Christendom, which began around 1960, have been confirmed. It can also be seen that my hypothesis on how the history of Christendom and of the church in Latin America should be divided into periods has been confirmed. This periodization into three large cycles, beginning approximately in 1492, 1808, and 1960, fits with my interpretation of the present crisis of New Christendom. The depth and newness of this crisis justifies my assertion that the historical cycle that began in 1808 closed around 1960, and there has begun a new cycle, whose characteristics are becoming plain in the present period of crisis. My periodization also enables us to make a comparison or analogy between the process of formation and crisis of the former colonial Christendom and the process of formation and crisis of New Christendom. It is particularly meaningful to compare the crisis of Christendom between 1808 and 1870 and the crisis of New Christendom starting in 1960, showing both similarities and differences.

An examination of history has revealed the nature and basic structure of the project of Christendom espoused by the hierarchical church, a project it never critiqued. During both colonial and neocolonial periods, the Latin American church always sought the mediation of *political society* in order to guarantee its presence in *civil society*. I have had to seek the origins of Christendom in the three centuries of the colonial period, and especially in the institution of the *patronato regio*. The way the church fit into colonial society was not merely superstructural, as is commonly believed. The *patronato* was superstructural in nature but its function was to give the church a mediating and integrating role in colonial society as a whole. In examining the colonial period I was particularly interested in studying social and political contradictions because they provide the basis for interpreting the integrating role of the relationship between the hierarchical church and colonial power-holders.

The crisis of independence showed how integrated the church and colonial society were. All the social and political contradictions that shattered colonial society also became manifest in Christendom, producing an internal crisis that was structural and final. Nevertheless, the crisis of colonial Christendom did not lead the church to question the Christendom model in itself. For three centuries the church had sought to impose itself on colonial society and to be an integral part of that society by using the force and power it had through its connection with colonial political power. Nor did the new national states that arose out of the wars of independence question the Christendom model: if the church could use colonial political power to make certain that it was an integral part of colonial civil society, henceforth the new republican states felt quite justified in using the church to impose their political rule over the nations. The "republican regalism" of the first half of the nineteenth century fitted with the Christendom model the church itself had been defending.

With the consolidation of the liberal-oligarchical state (approximately 1870–1930) and the ideological power of positivism, the crisis of the Christendom model reached its deepest level. The church, however did not question the Christendom model but rather struggled throughout this period to rebuild that model. Generally finding political power closed and indeed hostile, and prevented from using state aid in order to assure its presence in civil society, the church chose to shore up its power in civil society directly, apart from the state, but always aiming at rebuilding the Christendom model. The church did not question the model itself but simply reversed the normal model that it had always followed in building Christendom. Instead of first seeking an alliance with political power, and then, by means of that alliance, acquiring greater power in civil society, the church went in the other direction: it sought to expand its influence and power in civil society so it could thereby make an alliance with political power and the state in order to have their support. The church worked directly in civil society outside the liberal state, even suffering repression from that state, but the aim of its work was always to reconquer political power in order to rebuild a New Christendom. The crisis in church-state relationships during the liberal-positivist period did not question the Christendom model. The church was looking for new paths but the objective always remained the same.

This aim of rebuilding Christendom began to have some success around 1930 when the liberal-oligarchical state entered into crisis and a new model of state appeared, one that was populist, nationalist, and developmentalist. The church now had enough social power to force the state to acknowledge its political and social "rights." For its part the state needed the church for its own legitimacy and to expand its social base. From that point onward, the project of New Christendom returned to the normal and traditional way of functioning.

The success of the church in building New Christendom, especially between 1945 and 1968, legitimized and fortified the Christendom model. Nevertheless with the bankruptcy of populist, nationalist, and developmentalist models, with the structural crisis of the capitalist system, with the process of political radicalization among those who provided the social base for previous models and with the advance of the popular movement starting in the 1960s, New Christendom entered a crisis.

My historical analysis of Christendom in Latin America, from its origins to the present, confirms my general hypothesis on the nature and structure of Christendom. Successive restructuring of political power and the social and political contradictions throughout history have not changed the underlying structure of Christendom in Latin America. It is against this historical background that my specific hypothesis on the present crisis of New Christendom is borne out.

In the present crisis of New Christendom the church/state/civil society relationship begins to break down. That relationship is structural and is what constitutes New Christendom. Hence I can speak of a *structural crisis*. It is not simply a crisis of the church, or a merely superstructural crisis of the church-state relationship, but a crisis of Christendom—that is, a crisis of a particular way the church has been present, and exercised power, and historical and structural hegemony, in civil society, based on and mediated through an alliance or relationship between church and state. The crisis of Christendom does not mean a crisis for the church considered abstractly and in itself, but the crisis for a particular type or historical form of the church—namely, the church linked to the New Christendom project.

If we compare the present crisis of New Christendom with previous crises, and particularly with the one that developed out of the wars of independence and the establishment of the new national states (approximately 1808-1870), or with the deepening of this crisis during the period of the liberal-oligarchical state (approximately 1870-1930), we can note a number of elements that are completely new and different in the present crisis.

The New Christendom that was now entering its structural crisis had a large social base and is rooted in the people. Never in its history had Christendom attained hegemony with such an extensive social base and with such a significant representation from the middle and popular sectors. The church achieved this hegemony over a large and popular sector in civil society particularly between the end of World War II and the 1960s. The social base that the church controlled and subjected to its own hegemony during colonial Christendom had been small and narrow. The same was true during the nineteenth century and the beginning of the twentieth century, when the social base of the church under New Christendom was restricted almost exclusively to the Creole oligarchical elites, although it is true that through these elites the church had an influence over civil society as a whole. The situation changed during the period of populist, nationalist, and developmentalist projects when the New Christendom church managed to win hegemony or direct influence over a large and popular sector of civil society.

In this situation the crisis of New Christendom took on particular characteristics. Most significant is the fact that the social and political contradictions that the large and popular social base was experiencing were drawn into the church and into Christendom. For the first time in their history, the church and Christendom were directly and internally affected by social and political problems.

The process of political radicalization now ran straight through the church and Christendom. In order not to lose hegemony over its social base, the church found itself forced to deal with social and political problems. Its social base prevented it from evading the "spiral of increasing politicization." The problems connected with the crisis of the Latin American capitalist, underdeveloped, and dependent system were very complex and related to violence; the hierarchical church was overwhelmed and unable to respond to them. Insofar as the church did not reach any adequate response, its hegemony over civil society entered into crisis. The crisis of New Christendom led to the crisis of a particular form of the relationship between the hierarchical church and civil society.

Another novel characteristic of the crisis of New Christendom was the political radicalization of front-line activists and leaders of the church, starting in the 1960s. Not only did these problems, conflicts, and social and political contradictions come into the church in a general way but there was a large-scale political radicalization of Christian activists—lay persons trained in Catholic Action, Christian intellectuals, base community leaders, and priests, brothers, and sisters involved in pastoral work among the poor.

The fact that many leaders of insurrectionary or popular movements were Christians was nothing new in Latin America. What was new was the active participation of a significant number of Christians in the popular movement and in leftwing political parties in Latin America. This active participation signified a political participation of Christians in liberation movements in a way consistent with and following from their responsible participation in church movements. Moreover, it was out of this active political participation that there has arisen a theology proper to these groups of Christians, and which today is called "liberation theology." This new phenomeonon made it possible for the church to internalize social and political contradictions, which accelerated the breakdown of New Christendom. During other periods in church history, the participation of Christians in popular movements or the rise of Christian social protest movements ("messianic movements," for example) was something apart from the church, often marginal to its internal life. These movements usually formed "sects" outside church structures. Today, because of the active participation of Christians in liberation movements, things have gone beyond any such kind of marginal or external relationship.

Another novel feature of the present crisis of New Christendom is the head-on contradiction between Christendom and church—that is, between New Christendom and the church that is being born today in Latin America outside any possible Christendom project, whether real or potential. The destructive impact of this new contradiction on New Christendom is even more important than that of the factors listed previously. In studying the Brazilian case I have paid particular attention to this contradiction. This phenomenon is still recent in Latin America, tending to spread around 1975. If this contradiction should become fully developed, the breakdown of New Christendom will be irreversible.

Yet another novel feature of the present crisis of New Christendom is the growing contradiction between the church and the new model of domination gradually forced upon Latin American during the 1960s and 1970s. Two developments especially underscore this contradiction today: the renewal of the Latin American hierarchical church during the 1960s (Vatican II and Medellín) and the extremely oppressive and repressive nature of the new states or governments that came on the scene, reflecting the new political situation and the new model of domination. What aggravated the situation was the fact that these governments took on a confessionally "Christian" character.

The points mentioned above fully confirm my initial hypothesis that the present crisis of New Christendom is structural in nature. The same facts also justify the way I have divided the history of the church and of Latin American Christendom.

As I bring this work to a close, I believe it is appropriate to mention some political and theological perspectives consistent with the central thesis I have sought to demonstrate. In all honesty, I must say that these are the perspectives that have motivated and sustained me in my work. My political activism and my Christian faith have not in the least lessened the scientific rigor I have striven to achieve in delineating the object of this study, in working out a methodology, and in probing my thesis; on the contrary they have strengthened it.

As activist and believer I view the central thesis of this study from the following perspectives:

My *political perspective* is that the final crisis of New Christendom and the rise of a church that is totally at odds with any Christendom project, whether real or potential, is, and will be, a basic and decisive element in the process whereby Latin America becomes free of the dominant capitalist and imperialist system.

My *theological perspective* is that it is only within this very process of finally getting beyond Christendom, within the framework of a broader process of political liberation, that the church will find its own proper identity and mission.

In theological terms, Christendom reduces the church to the "realm of law," which stands opposed to the "realm of faith and hope." The church identified with Christendom is not only a church politically tied to the state and to the ruling classes, but also a church that, theologically speaking, has lost its identity, a church without faith or hope. The church will not be able to reconstitute its own identity and become a believing and hoping church except insofar as it makes a radical break from New Christendom within a process of political liberation of the whole of Latin America. There is a convergence and consistency between the basic contradictions "oppression and liberation," "Christendom and church," "law and faith."

Looking toward the future, I can see that what is most impressive and what gives most reason for hope is the development of this model of church opposed to the Christendom model. This new model of church is not only a theological idea, but a reality in every country in Latin America. Christians experience the confrontation between the two models: Christendom and church of the poor. This confrontation is experienced within the overall unity of the church. The new model of church does not seek to destroy church unity but to renew the church by making it move from a Christendom model to another model. This new model is not opposed to the hierarchy or to the institutional church, but opposed rather to another modeling of church.

The church of the poor arises and develops in the heart of Christendom: hence we should not separate this new model from its "mother" institution prematurely. Little by little, however, it is becoming clear that the church of the poor is the only meaningful alternative for the future of the church. Perhaps old forms of Christendom will continue to exist long into the future. Nonetheless, I believe that the church of the poor will continue to gain ground as a credible and meaningful church, particularly in the eyes of the poor and the young.

Similarly the church of the poor is gaining ground as a model of church for the whole Third World. Christendom will continue to be a Western construct, increasingly irrelevant for the Third World. The church of the poor appears as the only future for the universal church, built up out of the perspective of the poor and oppressed of the Third World.

Notes

Works not accompanied by full bibliographical details are to be found in the Bibliography.

CHAPTER 1

1. I have taken this thesis from André Gunder Frank, but in some aspects I have corrected it in light of the research of Ernesto Laclau, Ciro Santana Cardoso, and others, as I shall point out in further discussion.
2. See Frank, *Lumpenbourgeosie,* where these theories are discussed and refuted.
3. See Gutiérrez, *Reverso,* pp. 35-36.
4. Dussel, *Caminhos,* p. 172.
5. Letter from Karl Marx to Paul Vasilievich Annenkov (Brussels, Dec. 28, 1846.)
6. On the importance of black slavery in Latin America and the challenge it poses to church history, see José Oscar Beozzo, "As Américas Negras e a historia da Igreja na América Latina," in *Religião e Sociedade,* São Paulo, no. 10, 1983.
7. See Dussel, *Historia,* pp. 226-32; Vicaria, *Chile.*
8. See Vicaria, *Chile,* pp. 7-30.
9. The *patronato regio* was established by Pope Alexander VI in the bulls *Intercetera* (1493) and *Eximia Devotionis Sinceritas* (1501). The legislation was revised by Pope Julius II in 1505 and Pope Paul IV between 1555 and 1558.
10. See Alba, *Mouvement,* p. 37.
11. See ibid., pp. 47-58; Rama, *Historia,* pp. 14-19; idem, *Mouvements,* pp. 25-72.
12. See Lewin, *Rebelión,* and Valcarcel, *Rebelión.*
13. Alba, *Mouvement,* p. 53.

CHAPTER 2

1. A junta was formed on Sept. 21, 1808, in Montevideo, and the authority of Liniers, the viceroy, was rejected. On May 25, 1809, the liberation movement began in Peru (Chuquisaca). It moved to La Paz, and then in 1810 as far as Argentina, Mexico, Colombia, Chile, and Venezuela. On Dec. 9, 1824, the Battle of Ayacucho ended Spanish rule in Peru and throughout Spanish America, except Cuba and Puerto Rico.
2. Some writers situate the crisis between 1870 and 1875; others extend it from 1873 to 1896. The dates I have chosen are approximate. The most important element is the profound change within the international capitalist system.
3. Many writers limit this subperiod to 1850. I find that to be too short. The period when the liberal ideas unleashed by the European revolutions of 1848 began to circulate in Latin America was a liberal period in an ideological sense, but it did not entail any significant break in terms of the economy and political life. For example, in Mexico

there was the liberal reform of Benito Júarez in 1857, but the liberal state really arose with Porfirio Díaz (1877–1880 and 1884–1911). In Argentina oligarchical rule began with General Roca (1880). In Venezuela there was the dictatorship of Guzmán Blanco (1870–1888). In Guatemala the liberal reform is dated 1871–1893. In Brazil slavery was abolished and a republic established in 1889. Then there was Eloy Alfaro in Ecuador (1895–1911), Lorenzo Latorre in Uruguay (1872–1876), Domingo Santa María in Chile (1881), and so forth.

4. Vitale, *Interpretación Marxista,* vol. 2, *La Colonia,* p. 156, quoted in Frank, *Lumpenbourgeoisie,* pp. 47–48. See also Sandoval, *Crísis Políticas,* pp. 47–75.

5. See Soler, *Clase y Nación.* Although I do not agree with this writer's central thesis, the information he provides on the question of social classes during the late eighteenth century and the early nineteenth century is very useful.

6. Frank, *Lumpenbourgeoisie,* pp. 51–62 (Frank quotes a report by Guizot to the French Chamber of Deputies).

7. See Soler, *Clase y Nación,* pp. 40–46. It is an error to regard the agrarian bourgeoisie as a whole as "conservative," and the merchant bourgeoisie as a whole as "liberal." A "liberal" merchant bourgeoisie (tied to the English market) can be distinguished from a "conservative" merchant bourgeoisie (tied to the Spanish market). Similarly, a "liberal" agrarian bourgeoisie (owning free lands) can be distinguished from a "conservative" agrarian aristocracy (owning lands in mortmain).

8. Statistics from Rama, *Mouvements,* pp. 63, 66, 79, and 82.

9. Soler, *Clase y Nación,* p. 43.

10. Vitale, *Interpretación,* pp. 171–72, quoted by Frank, *Lumpenbourgeoisie,* p. 49.

11. See Tormo and Gonzalbo, *Historia;* Dussel, *Historia;* Prien, "Die Krise der lateinamerikanischen Christenheit im Zeitalter von Aufkläring und politischer Emanzipation," in *Geschichte.*

12. The complete texts of the papal brief *Etsi longissimo,* and the Bull *Etsi iam diu* are found in Tormo and Gonzalbo, *Historia,* pp. 11–12 and 18–19.

13. Ibid., p. 46.

14. Ibid., p. 41.

15. *Lumpenbourgeoisie,* chap. 4, "Civil War: Nationalism Versus Free Trade," pp. 51–62.

16. Ibid., pp. 52–53.

17. See Prien, *Geschichte,* pp. 435–37.

CHAPTER 3

1. "Concretely, we propose the hypothesis that the liberal reform did not originate when the new wave of liberal ideas initiated by the European revolutions of 1848 reached Latin America, or because certain enlightened groups wanted reform for philosophical reasons. We maintain that the assumption of state power and the imposition of the new liberal policy occurred in each country only after an appreciable increase in the production [of coffee, sugar, etc.] . . . Such a development fortified the economic and political power of the liberals, enabling them to impose liberal policies" (Frank, *Lumpenburguesía,* pp. 72–73).

2. See Prien, *Geschichte,* chap. 42, "Kirche und Gesellschaft im Zeitalter von Spätliberalismus und Szientismus."

3. On the labor movement in Latin America, see Alba, *Mouvement;* Rama, *Mouvements;* idem, *Historia;* Sacchi, *Movimiento Obrero.*

4. See Rama, *Historia,* chap. 3, "América Latina y la Primera Internacional."
5. See Witker Velásquez, *Trabajos.*

CHAPTER 4

1. Frank, *Lumpenbourgeoisie,* pp. 76-77.
2. The study with the best summary and analysis of the issues, providing a typology of dependent development in the different Latin American countries, is that of Bambirra, *El capitalismo dependiente latinoamericano.*

CHAPTER 5

1. This is not the place to undertake an in-depth analysis of the contemporary crisis of capitalism; I take up here merely some major elements that give a general outline of the crisis. I take as a basic reference source the studies prepared for the meeting of Latin American sociologists and theologians held in Costa Rica, February 1978, and published in Tamez and Trinidad, *Capitalismo.* See also Frank, *Reflections;* Theotonio dos Santos, "La crísis capitalista: carácter y perspectivas," Mexico City, Seminario permanente sobre Latino-América, 1977 (mimeographed).
2. Fernando Danel proposes the following divisions for the history of capitalist production: first phase, from the rise of industrialization to 1873 (the classic phase of the capitalism of free competition); second phase (the development of capitalism at the world level): a) from the 1873-1896 crisis to 1914, the consolidation of imperialism; b) from the 1914-1939 crisis to 1967, the maturation of imperialism; c) from the crisis beginning in 1967 and still continuing (Danel, "Crísis y reconstitución," pp. 72-73).
3. The process of industrialization has not been homogeneous in Latin America. There was a form of industrialization prior to 1930 (in Brazil, Argentina, Mexico, Chile, Uruguay, and Colombia); there was another, later form when industrialization had become a product of world monopoly integration and of the transnationalization of capital; and there has been industrialization without diversification (Paraguay, Haiti, and Panama). See Bambirra, *Capitalismo.*
4. See Gorostiaga, "Notas."
5. On counterinsurgency, see Klare, *War Without End.* On the doctrine of national security, see Comblin, *The Church and the National Security State.*
6. The best collection of studies on this topic is found in Assmann, *Carter y la lógica del imperialismo.*
7. See G. Silva, *Geopolítica;* Gurgel, *Segurança;* Schooyans, *Destin du Brésil.*
8. See Gorostiaga, "Notas," pp. 53-57.
9. Cited in ibid., p. 54.
10. For the complete list of members of the Trilateral Commission, together with economico-political connections, see Assmann, *Carter,* vol. 1, pp. 153-60.
11. See the following articles in Assmann, *Carter:* Hugo Assmann, "Introducción: Los Trilateralistas nos sugieren una clave de lectura de este libro—El Tercer Mundo visto como amenaza," vol. 1, pp. 11-22; Franz Hinkelammert, "El credo económico de la Comisión Trilateral," vol. 1, pp. 203-32; J. Petras, "La nueva moralidad de Carter y la lógica del imperialismo," vol. 2, pp. 201-14; A. Sist and G. Iriarte, "De la suguridad nacional al trilateralismo (razones por las que el gobierno de Carter defiende la vigencia de los Derechos Humanos)," vol. 2, pp. 215-30; R. J. Barnet, "El diseño redentor de Carter," vol. 2, pp. 231-42.

12. "The passing of the crisis [the dissipation of the 1945-1966 model of accumulation] will not be possible until mechanisms and structured transformations are developed that can make possible a new mode of capital accumulation at the world level.... The processes of transition to a new model are already present within the course of the crisis" (Danel, "Crísis," p. 67).

CHAPTER 6

1. This was especially true of Archbishop Guilland of Paraná and Archbishop Caggiano of Rosario, who soon became a cardinal. I note that seminaries in these two dioceses were built by the state.

2. See my "La démocratie chrétienne."

3. Among works on Argentina in the Bibliography, I single out the following: CELADEC, *Iglesia Argentina;* Gera and Rodríguez, *Apuntes para una interpretación;* Mayol et al., *Los católicos postconciliares;* Bresci and Gera, *Sacerdotes;* Büntig, "La Iglesia Argentina"; Zorzin, "L'Eglise catholique en Argentine."

4. See Bresci and Gera, *Sacerdotes.* I have also interviewed many members of this movement.

5. Published in *Témoignage Chrétien* (Paris), Aug. 31, 1967, and also in *Between Honesty and Hope* (Maryknoll Publications, 1970), pp. 3-12.

6. From a meeting of regional and national coordinators, Nov. 9-10, 1968. See Bresci and Gera, *Sacerdotes.*

7. Ibid., document 27.

8. Ibid., document 48, "Peronismo-Nacionalismo," and document 49, "Declaración de Carlos Paz."

9. See Ianni, *Formación,* pp. 18-19.

10. See *Criterio* (Buenos Aires), 1705-6 (Dec. 1974).

11. See *La Opinión,* Sept. 21, 1975. In Tucumán, the nuncio, Bishop Pio Laghi, blessed the weapons of "Operation Independence" to be used against the guerrillas.

12. *La Opinión,* Sept. 24, 1975.

13. Quoted in CELADEC, *Iglesia Argentina,* pp. 23-24.

14. Ibid., pp. 68-69.

15. Adur, "Une Eglise," p. 19.

16. Quoted in Prien, *Geschichte,* p. 563.

17. For most of the historical data in this section, see Prien, *Geschichte,* pp. 562-73.

18. See Bernard et al., *Tableau des partis politiques en Amérique du Sud,* pp. 105ff.

19. See Prien, *Geschichte,* pp. 569-71.

20. See Antoine, *Intégrisme.*

21. For this section and what follows, see Alves, *L'Eglise et la politique au Brésil,* esp. chap. 6, "Les discours dissonants," and Bruneau, *The Political Transformation of the Brazilian Catholic Church,* esp. part 2, "The Church Faces the Modern World, 1950-1964."

22. In the document dated May 6, 1973, analyzed below, "Marginalization of a People," the *agent* of change is radically different. In that document the "we" refers to the campesinos themselves with whom the bishops have become identified. The campesinos do not act "along with," but "despite" or "against" the interests of the ruling classes.

23. See Alves, *Eglise,* pp. 166-70.

24. CNBB, "Declaration of the Bishops of the Northeast," Campina Grande, May 21-26, 1956, quoted by Alves, *Eglise,* pp. 167-68.

25. See M. Cardoso, *La ideología dominante*. This is a detailed study of the developmentalist ideology of Juscelino Kubitschek. See esp. the chapter on "Order as Christian Civilization," pp. 242-44. My quotations are from this book.

26. See Bernard, *Tableau,* pp. 141-42.

27. See de Kadt, "JUC and AP," and Alves, *Eglise,* pp. 114-54.

28. See Alves, *Eglise,* p. 120.

29. Cited by de Kadt, "JUC and AP," p. 199 (italics added).

30. See Gutiérrez, *Reverso,* pp. 26-28; idem, *Theology of Liberation,* pp. 63-72. Gutiérrez makes a distinction between the *social-Christian* current of thought and the *distinction of planes* current. The first was important especially in Argentina, southern Brazil, Chile, and Uruguay. For a longer time than was the case elsewhere, it served as the channel for the social and political concerns of Christians, thus slowing down their political radicalization. The second current was influential in Brazil, Peru, and Uruguay. The distinction of planes enabled Christians to take up a scientific analysis of social reality that need not be a "Christian analysis." The result was that Christians in these countries were radicalized more rapidly than was the case where social Christianity predominated.

31. Cited by Alves, *Eglise,* p. 159.

32. For the history of the MEB, see Alves, *O Cristo do povo,* and de Kadt, *Catholic Radicals*.

33. See Lalive d'Epinay, *El refugio de las masas,* and Willems, *Followers*.

34. See Antoine, *Eglise,* pp. 110ff.

35. The Rockefeller Report and the Rand Corporation Memorandum on the Church in Latin America, prepared for the United States State Department, are essential reading for understanding the attitude of the United States, and especially the State Department. See *The Rockefeller Report on the Americas,* Chicago, Quadrangle Books, 1969. The Rand Corp. Memorandum = Memorandum RM-6136-DOS, Oct. 1969, Rand Corporation, Santa Monica, Calif.

36. The study done by Bishop Cândido Padim in July 1968, "La doctrina de la Seguridad nacional a la luz de la doctrina de la Iglesia," is a remarkable and clear-sighted exception, which confirms what I have said of the majority of the episcopate.

37. This was the attitude of most of the hierarchical church in November 1969 when some Dominican priests were accused of being involved in the urban guerrilla activities of Carlos Marighela. See Antoine, *Eglise,* pp. 234-39: "The danger of confusing 'political guilt' with 'moral guilt' increases much more because the issue is that of clerics who have been repudiated by the hierarchy, which tends to think that resistance to established power is a sin before God" (p. 239).

38. The *ecclesiology* implicit in the Christendom model had its historical explanation: the *patronato regio,* republican regalism, the negative experience of the church with the liberal state, the church/populist state, the church/developmentalist state alliance, and so forth. A *theological explanation* is to be found in the direct clash between a model of church whose force is law (power) and another whose force is faith (hope). See Hinkelammert, *Armas*.

39. A cardinal expressed this attitude well with an image: "If I want to keep sheep out of the lion's claws, the most important thing is not to provoke the lion or make it angry, but to strive to become its friend." The same image was used for a long time by some German bishops to justify their collaboration with Hitler.

40. See Alves, *Eglise,* particularly chap. 7, "Le conflit Eglise-Etat." "What the press called a conflict between church and state was simply a misunderstanding" (p. 187). See also Antoine, *Eglise*.

41. See Antoine, *Eglise,* pp. 256-57.

42. The attitude of some bishops toward the popular church reminds me of a passage from St. John's Gospel (11:47-48): "The chief priests and the Pharisees called a meeting of the Sanhedrin. 'What are we to do,' they said, 'with this man performing all sorts of signs? If we let him go on like this, the whole world will believe in him. Then the Romans will come in and sweep away our sanctuary and our nation.' "

43. CEP, *La Iglesia en América Latina,* pp. 216-59 and 259-315, respectively.

44. The period between 1969 and 1975 entailed a serious setback for the Brazilian left, particularly after November 4, 1969, when Carlos Marighela was killed. Starting in 1976 there was a new upsurge of the popular movement.

45. See Mesters, "Una Iglesia que nace del Pueblo."

46. *Servir* (Mexico City), 13/68 (March-April 1977) 217-34.

47. An overall view of this development can be found in MIEC-JECI, "Iglesia y Estado. Documentos de obispos brasileños."

CHAPTER 7

1. In *Liberación y cautiverio,* pp. 19-68.

2. English text in Gutiérrez, *The Power of the Poor in History,* pp. 169-221.

3. This is the thinking of, for example, José Comblin; see his "La Iglesia latinoamericana desde el Vaticano II. Diez años que hacen historia."

4. See Oliveros, *Liberación,* pp. 101-16.

5. Published by *Documentos MIEC-JECI,* June 1969, Montevideo.

6. "La pastoral de la Iglesia en América latina," *Documentos MIEC-JECI,* Sept. 1968, Montevideo.

7. "Theology is a reflection, that is, a second act; it is a going back; reflection comes after action" (Gustavo Gutiérrez, conference in Chimbote, quoted by Oliveros, *Liberación,* p. 115). It should be emphasized that "first act" is this practice and not—as many mistakenly assert—social science or Marxism. There is also "second act."

8. See my study, *Cristianos por el Socialismo.*

9. See above, chap. 6, pp. 138-41.

10. "Teología de la liberación," *Actualidad Pastoral,* 3 (1970) 83-85.

11. *Religión, ¿opio o instrumento de liberación?* Montevideo: Tierra Nueva, 1969 (English translation: *A Theology of Human Hope* [Washington, D.C.: Corpus Books, 1969]).

12. *Jesus Christ Liberator* (Maryknoll, N.Y.: Orbis, 1978).

13. Among his numerous works I single out his *Historia de la Iglesia en América Latina.*

14. *Marx y la Biblia* (English translation: *Marx and the Bible: A Critique of the Philosophy of Oppression* [Maryknoll, N.Y.: Orbis, 1974]).

15. Conference papers published by the Instituto Fe y Secularidad, *Fe cristiana y cambio social en América Latina: Encuentro de El Escorial, 1972* (Salamanca: Sígueme, 1973).

16. See *NADOC,* Nov. 15, 1972, and the editorial commentary in *Contacto* (Mexico City), 10/1 (Feb. 1973).

17. Those so inclined may consult *Democrates Altee* by Juan Ginés de Sepúlveda. This sixteenth-century theologian was, by anticipation, the founder of antiliberation theology.

18. Regarding theological reversals in the political situation in Latin America, see my

article, "La théologie de la libération dans la situation politique actuelle en Amérique latine."

19. See my article, "L'Evangile entre la modernité et la libération," *Parole et Société*.

20. See Sergio Torres and Virginia Fabella, eds., *The Emergent Gospel: Theology from the Underside of History* (Maryknoll, N.Y./London: Orbis/Chapman, 1978).

21. See Kofi Appiah-Kubi and Sergio Torres, eds., *African Theology En Route* (Maryknoll, N.Y.: Orbis, 1979).

22. See Sergio Torres and John Eagleson, eds., *Theology in the Americas* (Maryknoll, N.Y.: Orbis, 1976).

23. See John Eagleson and Philip Scharper, eds., *Puebla and Beyond: Documentation and Commentary* (Maryknoll, N.Y.: Orbis, 1979).

24. See Virginia Fabella, ed., *Asia's Struggle for Full Humanity: Towards a Relevant Theology* (Maryknoll, N.Y.: Orbis, 1980).

25. See John Eagleson and Sergio Torres, eds., *The Challenge of Basic Christian Communities* (Maryknoll, N.Y.: Orbis, 1981).

26. See Virginia Fabella and Sergio Torres, eds., *Irruption of the Third World: Challenge to Theology* (Maryknoll, N.Y.: Orbis, 1983).

27. See Virginia Fabella and Sergio Torres, eds., *Doing Theology in a Divided World* (Maryknoll, N.Y.: Orbis, 1985).

CHAPTER 8

1. In some countries—Argentina, Brazil, Chile—one must make a distinction between two sectors within the conservative church. One of these is conservative out of inertia or because it prefers things the way they were before Vatican II and thus rejects any innovation, be it theological, pastoral, social, or political. The other tendency knowingly accepts the doctrine of national security espoused by military regimes. This sector is explicitly promilitary and is striving to build an "ecclesio-military New Christendom," which will be based on an alliance between the church and the armed forces. One can find an example of this promilitary trend in the section on Argentina in chap. 6, above. See also the homily given by Bishop Gillmore, the bishop in charge of the military vicariate of the Chilean armed forces on Sept. 11, 1974, in DIAL, no. 187.

2. See M. Duclercq, *L'Eglise face aux dictatures militaires*. In this book there is a distinction between legitimizing a coup with or without reservations. Villella ("Iglesia y democracia") studies particularly the tension between legitimizing an authoritarian state and making a corrective critique of how power is exercised.

3. See Hermet, *Les functions politiques,* and Alves, *Eglise,* chap. 7, "Le conflit Eglise-Etat." Alves states that in the Brazilian case there is not a genuine church-state conflict, but rather a misunderstanding, because a conflict demands that three conditions be present: (1) the parties must refuse to dialogue; (2) their objectives must be incompatible; and (3) their ideologies and interests must be opposed. As long as the church legitimizes the state, these three conditions cannot be met. Two factors prevent such a conflict from breaking out: (a) both church and state prove their orthodoxy to each other: the church gives assurance that it loves the nation and the military show that they regard themselves as Christians; (b) a small and nonintegrated minority is blamed for problems that arise between church and state: for the church it is always a "group" of military officers who are the problem (torturers, for example), but not the army itself; and the military say that the problem is "subversive priests" but not the church.

4. A typical example took place in Chile: when the Catholic Church refused to allow

a *Te Deum* to be sung in the cathedral on the anniversary of the coup, a group of Protestant churches offered their church building. See "Chili: le soutien des Eglises Evangéliques au gouvernement," DIAL, no. 208.

5. See Communauté "Pacem in Terris," "L'Eglise Catholique du Chili," and Hinkelammert, *El Dios mortal*.

6. For example, see the statement of the Permanent Council of the Chilean bishops (March 25, 1977), "Nuestra convivencia nacional," DIAL, no. 373 (April 21, 1977). In this program the Chilean hierarchy endorsed the political program of the democratic opposition to General Pinochet. In 1985 the church was the primary impulse behind what was called the "National Agreement," a program for returning to democracy, which demanded that General Pinochet be replaced and that the military dictatorship be brought to an end.

7. On the crisis of the Committee for Peace, see DIAL, nos. 255, 259, 262, 265, 266, 271.

8. See Comblin, "La nueva práctica."

9. See my *1959-1978: l'Eglise latino-américaine entre la peur et l'espérance* (esp. chap. 3, dealing with the rise of the popular church), and "Amérique latine: Une Eglise que naît des luttes du peuple."

10. See Pablo Richard et al., *The Idols of Death and the God of Life: A Theology* (Maryknoll, N.Y.: Orbis, 1983).

Bibliography

The titles of works that I have found to be of particular value are preceded by the symbol (•).

Abesamis, C. H., et al. *Thélogies du Tiers Monde. Du conformisme a l'indépendance. Le Colloque de Dar es-Salam et ses prolongements.* Paris: L'Harmattan, 1977. (For the same conference, see Sergio Torres and Virginia Fabella, eds. *The Emergent Gospel: Theology from the Underside of History.* Maryknoll, N.Y.: Orbis, 1978.)
Adur, J. "Une Eglise profondément divisée." *Témoignage Chrétien* (Paris), June 29, 1978.
Alba, Víctor. •*Le mouvement ouvrier en Amérique latine.* Paris: Ed. Ouvrières, 1953.
Alcantara M. Domingo. *Cien años de presencia protestante en Centro-América.* Santiago: Prensa Latina, 1973.
Allaz G., Tomás. *¿Hambre o revolución? La iglesia contra la pared.* Montevideo: Nuestro Tiempo, 1971.
Alves, Marcio M. *O Cristo do povo.* Rio de Janeiro, 1968.
———. *L'Eglise et la politique au Brésil.* Paris: Cerf, 1974.
———. *De la Iglesia y la sociedad.* Montevideo: Tierra Nueva, 1971.
Antoine, Charles. *L'Eglise et le pouvoir au Brésil. Naissance du militarisme.* Desclée de Brouwer, 1971. (English translation: *Church and Power in Brazil.* Maryknoll, N.Y.: Orbis, 1973.)
———. *L'Intégrisme brésilien.* Paris: Centre Lebret, 1973.
Antoncich, Ricardo. "A evangelização na América Latina e os Direitos Humanos." *Revista Eclesiástica Brasileira*, 38149 (March 1978) 103–17.
———. "El magisterio de la Iglesia y la propiedad privada. La Iglesia reconsidera el concepto de propiedad privada." *Estudios Indígenas*, 6/2 (Dec. 1976) 35–55.
Araya, Victorio. *Fe cristiana y marxismo. Una perspectiva latinoamericana.* San José, Costa Rica, 1974.
Arroyo, Gonzalo. "Represión a la Iglesia." *Diálogo Social* (Panama), 74 (1975).
———. "El Salvador: les risques de l'Evangile." *Etudes*, 3 (March 1978).
———. (Assmann, Hugo. "Cautiverio y liberación de nuestra fe. Etapas en la maduracíon crítca de la conciencia (esbozo de una charla)." *Pasos* (Santiago, Chile), 21 (Oct. 2, 1979).
———. "La función legitimadora de la religión para la dictadura brasileña," in *Teología desde la praxis de la liberación.* Salamanca: Sígueme, 1973. (English translation: *Theology for a Nomad Church.* Maryknoll, N.Y.: Orbis, 1976.)
———. *Opresión-Liberación. Desafío a los cristianos.* Montevideo: Tierra Nueva.
———. ed. *Carter y la lógica del imperialismo.* Costa Rica: Educa, 1978, 2 vols.
Baez, C. Gonzalo. "Los protestantes y la revolución mexicana."*Estudios Ecuménicos* (Mexico City), 11 (1971) 14–16.

Bambamarca, Pastoral Team of. *Vamos Caminando. Los campesinos buscamos con Cristo el camino de nuestra liberación.* Lima: CEP, 1977. (English translation: *Vamos Caminando: A Peruvian Catechism.* Maryknoll, N.Y.: Orbis, 1985.)

Bambirra, Vania. •*El capitalismo dependiente latinoamericano.* Mexico City: Siglo XXI, 2nd ed., 1975.

Barreiro, Alvaro. "Communidades eclesiales de base y evangelización de los pobres." *Servir,* 13/69-70 (1977).

Barreiro, Julio. "Iglesia y poder político. Amsterdam 1948—Nairobi 1975." *Cristianismo y Sociedad* (Buenos Aires), 45 (1975) 27-37.

Bastide, Roger. "Contribución a una sociología de las religiones en América latina." *Contacto* (Mexico City), 11/6 (1974) 12-27.

Belda, Rafael. "Los cristianos por el socialismo ante el ateismo marxista." *Servicio Colombiano de Comunicación Social* (Bogotá), 5/12 (Dec. 1975).

Bernard, J. P., et al. *Tableau des partis politiques en Amérique du Sud.* Paris: Beauchesne, 1981.

Beozzo, José Oscar. •"A reorganização da Igreja perante o Estado liberal (1850-1930)." Bogotá: *CEHILA, 9-10 (Feb. 1977) 13-17.*

Boff, Clodovis. *Comunidade eclesial e comunidade política.* Petrópolis: Vozes, 1978.

———. "A ilusão de uma Nova Cristandade. Crítica a tese central do Documento de Consulta para Puebla." *Revista Eclesiástica Brasileira,* 38149 (March 1978) 5-17.

Boff, Leonardo. *Eclesiogênese.* Petrópolis: Vozes, 1977. (English translation: *Ecclesiogenesis: The Base Communities Reinvent the Church.* Maryknoll, N.Y.: Orbis, 1986.)

———. *Igreja: carisma e poder.* Petrópolis: Vozes, 1977. (English Translation: *Church: Charism and Power—Liberation Theology and the Institutional Church.* New York: Continuum, 1985).

———. "Las imágenes de Jesús en el cristianismo liberal del Brasil." *Cristianismo y Sociedad* (Buenos Aires), 46 (1975) 31-50.

"Bolivia, los cristianos y la resistencia al fascimo." *Pasos* (Santiago, Chile), 36 (Feb. 5, 1973).

Borge, Tomás, *La revolución combate contra la Teología de la Muerte.* Bilbao: Desclée de Brouwer, 1983.

Borrat, H. "Ouverture ecclésiale et blocage politique. L'après-Concile en Amérique latine." *Foi et Développement* (Paris), 35 (March-April 1976).

———, and Büntig, A.J., eds. *El imperio y las Iglesias.* Buenos Aires, 1973.

Bravo, Carlos. *Apuntes para una eclesiología desde América Latina.* Mexico City: CRT, 1982.

Bresci, D., and Gera L. •*Sacerdotes para el tercer mundo. Crónica—Documentos—Reflexión.* Buenos Aires, 1972.

Broderick, Walter J. *Camilo Torres: A Biography of the Priest-Guerrillero.* Garden City, N.Y.: Doubleday, 1975.

Bruneau, Thomas C. •*The Political Transformation of the Brazilian Catholic Church.* London: Cambridge University Press, 1974.

Büntig, Aldo J. "El catolicismo popular y su aporte al proceso de liberación en América Latina." *Pasos,* 31 (Nov.-Dec. 1972).

———. "La Iglesia Argentina en las diversas etapas del proyecto neo-colonial," in Borrat and Büntig, *El imperio,* pp. 69-115.

———. "Las Iglesias latinoamericanas frente al Estado e ideología de Seguridad nacional (la realidad y sus causas)," in Tamez and Trinidad, *Capitalismo,* pp. 19-51.

Camargo, Procopio. "Essai de typologie du catholicisme brésilien." *Social Compass* (The Hague), 14/5-1 (1967) 399-422.
Cardoso, Fernando Henrique, and Faletto, Enzo. •*Dependencia y desarrollo en América Latina*. Mexico City: Siglo XXI, 13th ed., 1977. (English translation: *Dependency and Development in Latin America*. Berkeley: University of California Press, 1979.)
Cardoso, Miriam L. •*La ideología dominante. Brasil. América Latina*. Mexico City: Siglo XXI, 1975.
Castro, B. *La Iglesia, el subdesarrollo y la revolución*. Mexico City: Nuestro Tiempo, 1968.
CEAS *(Comisión Episcopal de Acción Social)*. •*Signos de renovación. Recopilación de documentos post-conciliares de la Iglesia en América Latina*. Lima: Ed. Universitaria, 1969. (English translation: Peruvian Bishops' Commission for Social Action. *Between Honesty and Hope*. Maryknoll, N.Y.: Maryknoll Publications, 1970.)
CEDETIM. "L'Eglise équatorienne traversée par la lutte de classes." *Equateur. Nouvelle Strátegie de l'imperialisme bourgeois et lutte des classes*, Bulletin de liaison du CEDETIM (Paris), 38 (June 1976) 53-55.
CEDIAL *(Centro de Estudios para el Desarrollo e Integración de América Latina)*. •*Cristianos latinoamericanos y socialismo*. Bogotá: CEDIAL, 1972.
CEE *(Centro de Estudios Ecuménicos)*. *Crísis capitalista e Iglesia en América Latina. La Iglesia en la hora de represión*. Mexico City CEE, 1977.
CEFRAL *(Centre France-Amérique Latine)*. *L'Eglise d'Amérique central et les Droits de l'Homme*. Paris: CEFRAL, July 1977.
CEHILA *(Comisión de Estudios para la Historia de la Iglesia en América Latina)*. *Para una historia de la Iglesia en América Latina*. Barcelona: Nova Terra, 1976.
CELADEC *(Comisión Evangélica Latinoamericana de Educación Cristiana)*. •"Iglesia Argentina: ¿Fidelidad al Evangelio? ¿Conquista del poder?" *Docet* (Lima), A, 5 and 6 (1977).
———. "Situación de la Iglesia de El Salvador." *Docet* (Lima), A, 6 (March 1978).
CELAM *(Consejo Episcopal Latinoamericano)*. •*III Conferencia general del episcopado latinoamericano: "La evangelización en el presente y en el futuro de América Latina." Preparación* [Puebla, Mexico, 1978]. *Documento de Consulta a las Conferencias episcopales*. Bogotá: CELAM, 1977.
———. *Liberación: diálogos en el CELAM*. Bogotá: CELAM, 1974.
———, Department of Missions. *Antropología y Evangelización. Un problema de la Iglesia en América Latina* (documents from the first continental conference on missions, held in Melgar, Colombia, April 1968). Bogotá: CELAM, 1969.
Centre Lebret. •*Marginalisation d'un peuple. Des évêques brésiliens prennent la parole*. Paris: Centre Lebret, 1974.
CEP *(Centro de Estudios y Publicaciones)*. •*Bolivia: 1971-1976—Pueblo—Estado—Iglesia*. Lima: CEP, 1976.
———. *La Iglesia en América Latina. Testimonios y Documentos (1969-1973)*. Lima: CEP, 1973.
———. *¿Una Izquierda cristiana? Debate*. Lima: CEP, 1972.
———. •*Sigmos de lucha y esperanza. Testimonios de la Iglesia en América Latina, 1973-1978*. Lima: CEP, 1978.
———. •*Signos de liberación Testimonios de la Iglesia en América Latina, 1969-1973*. Lima: CEP, 1973.
Churruca, Agustín. "Genesis del patronato laico de don Benito Juárez." *Christus* (Mexico City), 499 (June 1977) 49-55.

———. "El pensamiento de Morelos. Una ideología liberadora." *Christus* (Mexico City), 477 and 478 (1975) 13–20.
CLAR *(Conferencia Latinoamericana de Religiosos)*. *Pueblo de Dios y comunidad liberadora. Perspectivas eclesiológicas desde las comunidades religiosas que caminan con el pueblo*. Bogotá: CLAR, 1977.
Clavel, Leonico. "El conflicto Iglesia-Estado en Paraguay." *Víspera* (Montevideo), 3/13–14 (Nov.-Dec. 1969) 13–18.
CNBB *(Conferência Nacional dos Bispos do Brasil,* extraordinary general assembly). "Documento: CNBB prepara Puebla. Itaicí, 18–25 abril 1978."
Comblin, José. "De la acción cristiana." *Víspera* (Montevideo), 7/33 (Dec. 1973) 19ff.
———. "La doctrina de la Seguridad nacional." *Mensaje* (Santiago, Chile), 247 (March-April 1976) 96–104.
———. "La Iglesia latinoamericana desde el Vaticano II. Diez años que hacen historia." *Mensaje* (Santiago, Chile), 253 (Oct. 1976) 486–94.
———. "Medellín: problemas de interpretación." *Pasos* (Santiago, Chile), 64 (Aug. 1973).
———. "Movimientos de ideologías en América Latina," in *Fe cristiana y cambio social en América Latina* (Instituto Fe y Secularidad). Salamanca: Sígueme, 1973, pp. 101–27.
———. "Notas sobre el documento básico para la II Conferencia general del CELAM." *Cuadernos de Marcha*, 17 (Sept. 1968) 47–57.
———. •"La nueva práctica de la Iglesia en el sistema de la Seguridad nacional. Exposición de sus principios teóricos," in Encuentro Latinoamericano, *Liberación y Cautiverio*, pp. 155–76.
———. *Le pouvoir militaire en Amérique latine; L'idéologie de la Sécurité nationale*. Paris: J. P. Delarge, 1977.
———. *Théologie de la pratique révolutionnaire*. Paris: Ed. Universitaires, 1974.
———. "Versión latinoamericana de Seguridad nacional." *America Latina* (CEFRAL, Paris), 33 (May-June 1976).
Communauté "Pacem in Terris." •"L'Eglise catholique du Chili et les perspectives démocratiques." *Foi et Développement* (Paris), 41 (Nov. 1976).
Congresso Internacional Ecuménico de Teología. *A Igreja que surge da base (Eclesiología das comunidades cristãs de base)*. São Paulo: Paulinas, 1982. (For the same conference, see Torres, Sergio, and Eagleson, John eds. *The Challenge of Basic Christian Communities*. Maryknoll, N.Y.: Orbis, 1981.)
Consejo Mundial de Iglesias. *Hacia una Iglesia solidaria con los pobres*. Geneva, 1980.
Contacto (editorial). "Militarismo, Pueblo y Evangelio." *Contacto* (Mexico City), 13/6 (Dec. 1975) 5–15.
Cosmao, Vincent. •*Nouvel ordre mondial. Les chrétiens provoqués par le développement*. Paris: Châlet, 1978.
———. "En réalisant 'Populorum Progressio' 10 ans après." *Foi et Développement* (Paris), 45 (March 1977).
———. "Le salut d'après la Théologie de la Libération." *Foi et Développement*, 49 (July-Aug. 1977).
———•*Los cristianos y la revolución. Un debate abierto en América Latina*. Santiago, 1973.
Cristianos por el Socialismo (Secretariado Encuentro). •*Cristianos por el Socialismo. Primer encuentro latinoamericano. Texto de la edición internacional*. Santiago:

Editorial Mundo Nuevo, 1972. (For the same conference, see John Eagleson ed. *Christians and Socialism: Documentation of the Christians for Socialism Movement in Latin America*. Maryknoll, N.Y.: Orbis, 1975.)

Croatto, J. Severino. "La dimensión política del Cristo liberador." *Cristianismo y Sociedad*, 46 (1975) 5-23.

Danel J., Fernando. "América Latina en la nueva estructura capitalista internacional. Un diagnóstico con vistas a la III reunión general de los obispos latinoamericanos." *Christus* (Mexico City), 43/506 (Jan. 1978) 32-47.

———. •"Crísis y reconstitución del capitalismo internacional: las nuevas condiciones de la división internacional del trabajo," in Tamez and Trinidad, *Capitalismo*, pp. 63-90.

"Declaración sobre el documento preparatorio de la III Conferencia en Puebla." *Páginas* (Lima), Feb. 1978.

Dri, Ruben R. "Sobre la Iglesia popular." *Servir*, 13/69-70 (1977) 255-78.

Duclerq, Michel. •"L'Eglise face aux dictatures militaires en Amérique latine." *Foi et Développement* (Paris), 44 (Feb. 1977).

Dussel, Enrique. *Caminhos de libertação latinoamericana*, II. São Paulo: Paulinas, 1985.

———. "Coyuntura de la praxis cristiana en América latina." *Christus* (Mexico City), 42/504 (Nov. 1977) 10-24 and 64.

———. •*El episcopado hispanoamericano, Institución misionera en defensa del índio, 1504-1620*. Cuernavaca: Sondeos, 32-38 (1969-71).

———. *Filosofía de la liberación*. Mexico City: Edicol, 1977. (English translation: *Philosophy of Liberation*. Maryknoll, N.Y.: Orbis, 1985.)

———. "Fray Bartolomé de Las Casas, profeta crítico del imperialismo europeo." *Contacto* (Mexico City), 2/5 (1974) 27-33.

———. •"Hipótesis para elaborar un marco teórico de la historia del pensamiento latinoamericano (el estatuto ideológico del discurso populista)." *Christus* (Mexico City), 42/497 (April 1977) 12-26.

———. •*Historia de la Iglesia en América Latina. Coloniaje y liberación, 1492-1972*. Barcelona: Nova Terra, 2nd ed., 1972. (English translation: *A History of the Church in Latin America; Colonialism to Liberation (1492-1979)*. Grand Rapids: Eerdmans, 1981.)

———. *De Medellín a Puebla: uma década de sangue e esperança*. São Paulo: Paulinas, 1981.

———. "Relaciones de Iglesia y Estado en las formaciones sociales periféricas." *Christus* (Mexico City), 41/493 (Dec. 1976) 35-40.

———. "Sobre la historia de la teología en América latina," in Encuentro Latinoamericano de Teología, *Liberación y cautiverio*, pp. 19-68.

Echegaray, Hugo. *Derecho del pobre, derecho de Dios. Reflexión Biblicoteológica*. Mexico City, 1977.

Encuentro Latinoamericano de Teología. •*Liberación y cautiverio. Debates en torno al método de la teología en América Latina*. Mexico City: 1976.

Estevão, José C., and Ramalho, José R. "Iglesia y Estado en el Brasil." *Cristianismo y Sociedad*, 16/55 (1978 31-38.

Fernandes, F., Poulantzas, N. et al. •*Las clases sociales en América Latina. Problemas de conceptualización*. Mexico City: Siglo XXI, 2nd ed., 1975.

Fierro, Alfredo, and Mate, Reyes. *Cristianos por el Socialismo. Documentación*. Estella, Spain: Verbo Divino, 1975.

Fontaine, Pablo, "La Iglesia chilena en los ultimos 20 años." *Mensaje* (Chile), 202-3 (1971) 422-32.
Fragoso, Antônio. *Evangile et révolution sociale*. Paris: Cerf, 1969.
Frank, André Gunder. •*Capitalism and Underdevelopment in Latin America: Historical Studies of Chile and Brazil*. New York: Monthly Review Press, 1967.
———. •*Le développement du sous-développement. L'Amérique latine*. Paris: Maspero, 1977.
———. •*Lumpenburguesía; Lumpendesarrollo*. Mexico City: 1971. (English translation: *Lumpenbourgeoisie: Lumpendevelopment—Dependence, Class, and Politics in Latin America*. New York: Monthly Review Press, 1972.)
———. *Reflections on the World Economic Crisis*. New York: Monthly Review Press, 1981.
Frei Betto. *CEBs rumo a nova sociedade: 5º Encontro Intereclesial das CEBS* (Canindé, July 1983). São Paulo: Paulinas, 1983.
———. *O fermento na massa*: *4º Encontro Intereclesial das CEBs* (Itaicí, April 1981). Petrópolis: Vozes, 1981.
Freire, Paulo. "La misión educativa de las Iglesias en América Latina." *Pasos* (Santiago), 9 (July 10, 1972).
Galeano, Eduardo. •*Las venas abiertas de América latina*. Montevideo, 2nd ed., 1972. (English translation: *The Open Veins of Latin America: Five Centuries of the Pillage of a Continent*. New York: Monthly Review Press, 1973.)
Galilea, Segundo. *Entre Medellín y la III Conferencia*. Mexico City, 1977.
———. "Los Estados, la Iglesia, y el pueblo." *Servir*, 13/69-70 (1977) 347-50.
Garcia G., Jesús. "Changement social et religion. Un point de vue mexicain." *Foi et Développement* (Paris), 23 (Jan. 1975).
———. "Del desarrollo a la liberación." *Contacto*, 8/2 (June 1971) 19-44.
Gera, L., Büntig, A., and Catena, O. *Teología, pastoral y dependencia*. Buenos Aires: Guadalupe, 1974.
Gera, L. and Rodríguez M., Guillermo. •"Apuntes para una interpretación de la Iglesia argentina." *Víspera* (Montevideo), 4/15 (Feb. 1970) 59-88.
Germani, Gino, Tella, Torcuato di, and Ianni, Octavio. •*Populismo y contradicciones de clase en Latinoamérica*. Mexico City: Era, 1973.
Gheerbrant, Alain. •*The Rebel Church in Latin America*. Baltimore: Penguin, 1974.
Gibellini, Rosino, ed. *Frontiers of Theology in Latin America*. Maryknoll, N.Y.: Orbis, 1979.
Giménez, Gilberto. "De la 'doctrina social de la Iglesia' a la ética de la liberación." *Panorama de la teología latinoamericana* (SELADOC). Salamanca: Sígueme, 1975, pp. 45-62.
Girardi, Giulio. "Los cristianos y el socialismo: de Medellín a Santiago." *Pasos*, 2 (May 22, 1972).
Gómez, Fernando. "Como vemos nosotros la situación de la Iglesia frente al actual regimen." *SEUL*, 43 (Oct. 1973) 5-9.
Gómez de Souza, Luis Alberto. "Los condicionamientos socio-políticos actuales de la teología en América Latina." Encuentro Latinoamericano de Teología, *Liberacíon y Cautiverio*.
Gonzalez, G. Fernan E. *Partidos políticos y poder eclesiástico. Reseña histórica: 1810-1930*. Bogotá, 1977.
González M., Tristán. "Los derechos humanos y la represión en América latina." *Cristianismo y Sociedad*, 40-41 (1974) 93-109.

Gorostiaga, Xabier. •"Cuadros sinópticos sobre la coyuntura económica-política, como marco estructural de la evolución de la Iglesia latinoamericana," in Tamez and Trinidad, *Capitalismo,* pp. 175-95.

——. "Notas sobre metadologia para un diagnóstico económico del capitalismo latinoamericano," in Tamez and Trinidad, *Capitalismo,* pp. 39-62.

Guerrero, Francisco Javier. "Historia del proceso mexicano." *Estudios Indígenas* (Mexico City), 6/1 (Sept. 1976) 3-83.

Gurgel, José Alfredo. *Segurança e democracia.* Rio de Janeiro: José Olympio, 1975.

Gutiérrez, Gustavo. •"La fuerza histórica de los pobres," in CEP, *Signos de Lucha y Esperanza,* pp. 15-42 (= *Power of the Poor,* chap. 4).

——. *La fuerza histórica de los pobres.* Lima: CEP, 1979. (English translation: *The Power of the Poor in History.* Maryknoll, N.Y.: Orbis, 1983.)

——. •*Lineas pastorales de la Iglesia en América latina.* Lima: CEP, 1970.

——. "Mouvements de libération et théologie." *Concilium* (Paris), 93 (1974) 121-30.

——. •"Sobre el Documento de Consulta par a Puebla." *Páginas,* 16-17 (June 1978) 1-24 (= *Power of the Poor,* chap 5).

——. *Teología de la Liberación.* Lima: CEP, 1971. (English translation: *A Theology of Liberation.* Maryknoll, N.Y.: Orbis, 1973.)

——. •*Teología desde el reverso de la historia.* Lima: CEP, 1977 (= *Power of the Poor,* chap. 7).

——, Cussianovich, A., et al. *Profecía y evangelización. Bartolomé de Las Casas—Medellín.* Lima: CEP, 1978.

——, and Shaull, R. •*Liberation and Change.* Atlanta: John Knox Press, 1977.

Guzman, G., et al. *La violencia en Colombia. Estudio de un proceso social.* Bogotá: Universidad Nacional, 1962, 2 vols.

Halperin, Tulio. •*Historia contemporánea de América Latina.* Madrid: Alianza, 1969.

Hermet, Guy. •"Les fonctions politiques des organisations religieuses dans les régimes à pluralisme limite." *Revue Française de Sciences Politiques* (Paris), 23/3 (June 1973) 439-71.

Hernández-Pico, Juan. "Fe y política (enfoques)." *Contacto,* 11/1 (Feb. 1974) 12-35.

Hinkelammert, Franz. •*Las armas Ideológicas de la muerte.* San José, DEI, Costa Rica: 2nd 1981. (English translation: *The Ideological Weapons of Death.* Maryknoll, N.Y.: Orbis, 1986.)

——. •"El Dios mortal: lucifer y la bestia. La legitimación de la dominación en la tradición cristiana," in Tamez and Trinidad, *Capitalismo,* pp. 199-213.

——. •*Ideología de sometimiento. La Iglesia Católica chilena frente al golpe: 1973-1974.* Costa Rica: Educa, 1977.

Hoornaert, Eduardo. •*Formação do catolicismo brasileiro 1550-1800: Ensaio de interpretação a partir dos oprimidos.* Petrópolis: Vozes, 1974.

——. •"As relações entre Igreja e Estado na Bahia colonial." *Revista Eclesiástica Brasileira,* 32 (1972) 274-308.

Houtart, François. *La Iglesia latinoamericana en la hora del Concilio.* Fribourg/ Bogotá: Feres, 1963.

——. *Religião e modos de produção pre-capitalistas.* São Paulo: Paulinas, 1982.

——, and Rousseau, André. *L'Eglise face aux luttes révolutionnaires.* Brussels/Paris, 1972.

——, and Rousseau, André. *L'Eglise et les mouvements révolutionnaires. Vietnam— Amérique latine—Colonies portugaises.* Brussels/Paris, 1972.

Huck, Eugene R., and Mosely, Edward H., eds. *Militarists, Merchants, and Missiona-*

ries. *United States Expansion in Middle America.* University of Alabama Press 1972.

Ianni, Octavio. •*La formación del estado populista en América Latina.* Mexico City: Era, 1975.

———. *Imperialismo y cultura de la violencia en América Latina.* Mexico City: Siglo XXI, 1974.

IDEP *(Instituto de Estudios Políticos).* •*Cristianos por el Socialismo. ¿Consecuencia cristiana o alienación política?* Santiago, 1972.

IEPALA. *Las relaciones entre cristianismo y revolución.* Madrid: IEPALA, 1982.

•*Iglesia Latinoamericana. ¿Protesta o Profecía?* Avellanada, Argentina: Búsqueda, 1969.

Iglesia Metodista en America Latina. *Evangelización y revolución en América latina* (Documentos prévios, trabajos y conclusiones de la consulta continental de evangelización, realizada en Cochabamba, Bolivia 1966). Montevideo: Iglesia Metodista, 1969.

Iglesia de Nicaragua—Tiempo de crísis: tiempo de discernimiento y de gracia. Lima: Documentación MIEC-JECI, Doc. 25.

INDAL *(Information Documentaire d'Amérique Latine).* •*La Iglesia latinoamericana y el socialismo.* INDAL (Belgium), dossier no. 8 (July 1973).

Instituto Fe y Secularidad. *Fe cristiana y cambio social en América Latina. Encuentro de El Escorial.* Salamanca: Sígueme, 1973.

ISAL *(Iglesia y Sociedad en América Latina). América Latina: movilización popular y fe cristina.* Montevideo: ISAL, 1971.

ISER *(Instituto Superior de Estudos da Religião).* "Igreja e Estado no Brasil: a Igreja católica." *Cadernos do ISER* (Rio de Janeiro), 7 (1977).

Jiménez, Julio. "Sobre Iglesia y política en la historia chilena." *Teología y Vida* (Santiago), 12 (1971) 218-54.

Kadt, Emanuel de. •*Catholic Radicals in Brazil.* London: Oxford University Press, 1970.

———. •"JUC and AP: the Rise of Catholic Radicalism in Brazil," in Landsberger, *The Church and Social Change,* pp. 191-219.

Klare, Michael T. *War without End.* New York: Knopf, 1972.

Krumwiede, J. *La transformación del papel político de la Iglesia católica en América Latina.* Geneva: Ed. Ildis, 1971.

Lalive d'Espanay, Christian. *El refugio de las masas. Estudio sociológico del protestantismo chileno.* Santiago, 1968.

———. *Religion, dynamique sociale et dépendance. Les mouvements protestants en Argentine et au Chili.* Paris, 1975.

Landsberger, Henry A., ed. •*The Church and Social Change in Latin America.* University of Notre Dame Press, 1970.

Lassègue, Juan B. *La larga marcha de Las Casas. Selección y presentación de textos.* Lima: CEP, 1974.

Lewin, Bolesao. *La rebelión de Tupac Amaru y los orígenes de la independencia de Hispanoamérica.* Buenos Aires, 3rd ed., 1967.

Libânio, João Batista. *A volta grande a disciplina: Reflexão teológico-pastoral sobre a atual conjuntura da Igreja.* São Paulo: Loyola, 1981.

López, O. Enrique. *Los católicos y la revolución latinoamericana.* Havana: Ed. de Ciéncias Sociales, 1970.

———. "Manipulación imperialista de la fe religiosa. La CIA entra en la Iglesia pero no para rezaro." *Contacto,* 10/4 (Aug. 1973) 63-70.

Maduro, Otto. "Notas para una discusión sobre las relaciones entre hechos religiosos y lucha de classes." *SCCS* (Bogotá), 5/11 (Nov. 1975).

Maier, Hans. *Revolution and Church in the Early History of Christian Democracy, 1789-1901.* University of Notre Dame Press, 1969.

Maldonado, Oscar. "La révolution cubaine et le catholicisme." *Spiritus* (Paris), 66 (1977) 79-95.

Mandel, Ernest. •"Classes sociales et crise politique en Amérique latine." *Critiques de l'économie politique* (Paris), 16-17 (April-Sept. 1974) 6-42.

MARCHA (Uruguay). "Igleisa latinoamericana. Crísis y renovación." *Cuadernos de Marcha* (Montevideo), 24 (April 1969).

Mariátegui, José Carlos. •*El alma matinal y otras estaciones del hombre de hoy*. Peru: Amauta, 4th ed., 1940.

———. •*Peruanicemos al Perú*. Peru: Amauta, 1970.

———. •*Siete ensayos de interpretación de la realidad peruana*. Peru: Amauta, 18th ed., 1970. (English translation: *Seven Interpretative Essays on Peruvian Reality*. Austin: University of Texas Press, 1971.)

Marini, Ruy Mauro. •*Dialéctica de la dependencia*. Mexico City: 2nd ed., 1974.

———. •*Subdesarrollo y revolución*. Mexico City: 6th ed., 1975.

Mayol, A., et al. *Los católicos postconciliares en la Argentina: 1963-1969*. Argentina: Ed. Galerna, 1970.

Meecham, Loyd J. •*Church and State in Latin America*. Chapel Hill: University of North Carolina Press, 1966.

Mendes, Cândido. *Justice—Faim de l'Eglise*. Paris: Desclée, 1977.

———. Mementos dos vivos. A esquerda católica no Brasil. Rio de Janeiro: Ed. Tempo Brasileiro, 1966.

Mercader, Manuel M. *Cristianismo y revolución en América Latina*. Mexico City, 1974.

Mesters, Carlos. •"Una Iglesia que nace del Pueblo." *MIEC-JECI Servicio de Documentación* (July-Aug. 1975), doc. 17-18.

Methol, Alberto. •"Las épocas. La Iglesia en la historia latinoamericana." *Víspera* (Montevideo), 2/6 (1968) 68-86.

Meyer, Jean A. *Apocalypse et révolution au Mexique. La guerre des cristeros (1926-1929)*. Paris: Payot, 1975.

———. •*La cristiada. I: La guerra de los cristeros. II: El conflicto entre la Iglesia y el Estado en México. III: Los Cristeros: sociedad e ideología*. Mexico City: Siglo XXI, 1973.

———. *La christiade. L'Eglise, l'Etat et le Peuple dans la révolution mexicaine (1926-1929)*. Paris: Payot, 1975. (English translation: *The Cristero Rebellion: The Mexican People Between Church and State—1926-1929*. New York: Cambridge University Press, 1976.)

———. •"Meterse en política: ideología de la jerarquiá mexicana durante el conflicto de 1926-1929." *Christus* (Mexico City), 42/499 (June 1977) 44-48.

———. •"Las organizaciones religiosas como fuerzas políticas de substitución." *Christus* (Mexico City), 41/493 (Dec. 1976) 30-34.

Micheo, Alberto. •"Proceso histórico de la Iglesia venezolana." *Cristianismo Hoy* (Venezuela), 1977.

MIEC-JECI. •"Iglesia y Estado. Documentos de obispos brasileños." *MIEC-JECI* (Lima), 13-14 (June 1977) 1-79.

Míguez-Bonino, José. *Christians and Marxists. The Mutual Challenge to Revolution*. Grand Rapids: Eerdmans, 1976.

Monde Diplomatique. "En Amérique latine, les chrétiens entre la dictature et la révolution." *Le Monde Diplomatique* (Paris), May 1976, pp. 15-20.
Mondragon, Rafael. "La novisima teología latinoamericana." *Contacto*, 13/6 (Dec. 1976) 14-24.
Mora, S. Clovis. "Los cristianos y la revolución en Bolivia." *Pasos*, 24 (Oct. 23, 1972).
Motessi, Osvaldo Luis. "Haciendo teología en el contexto latinoamericano." *CELADEC-Docet*, G5 (Oct. 1977).
MSPTM *(Movimiento Sacerdotes para el Tercer Mundo)*. *Que pensamos*. Mendoza, Argentina, 1970.
Munoz, Ronaldo. *Evangelho e libertação*. São Paulo: Paulinas, 1981.
———. *La Iglesia en el pueblo: Hacia una ecelsiología latinoamericana*. Lima: CEP, 1983.
———. •*Nueva conciencia de la Iglesia en América Latina*. Salamanca: Sígueme, 1974.
Mutchler, David E. •*The Church as a Political Factor in Latin America*. New York: Praeger, 1971.
Negre R., Pedro. "Los análisis de clase y clase media." *Pasos*, 5 (June 12, 1972).
———. "El cristiano y el cambio políitico." *Dialogo Social* (Panama), 74 (Dec. 1975) 36-37.
———. "Los cristianos, la liberación y sus opciones pastorales." *Cristianismo y Sociedad*, 42 (1974) 32-42.
Nobma, Albert. *Du Mexique à la Terre de Feu, une Église en colère*. Paris/Brussels/Montreal: Bordas, 1973.
Oliveros M. Roberto. •*Liberación y teología. Génesis y crecimiento de una reflexión (1966-1976)*. Lima: CEP, 1977.
Padim, Cândido, et al. "La doctrina de la Seguridad nacional a la luz de la doctrina de la Iglesia." *DIAL*, 302 (May 6, 1976); *SEDOC*, special issue, 431 (Sept. 1968) 432-44.
Pagura, Federico J. "Los obispos latinoamericanos. ¿Traidores, complices o profetas?" *Pasos*, 45 (April 9, 1973).
Parada, Hernan. "Hace 5 Años . . . en Medellín. Marco histórico de un 'gran momento.' " *Pasos*, 59 (July 16, 1973).
Pike, Frederick, ed. •*The Conflict Between Church and State in Latin America*. New York: Knopf, 1967.
———. *Hispanismo 1898-1936: Spanish Conservatives and Liberals and their Relation with Spanish America*. University of Notre Dame Press, 1971.
Piñol, José M. *Iglesia y liberación en América Latina. Diálogos con la vanguardia católica latinoamericana*. Madrid: Marova, 1972.
Pixley, Jorge V. "La sistematización en la teología latinoamericana." *Pasos*, 3 (May 29, 1972).
Portelli, Hugues. •"La fonction idéologique de l'Eglise d'après A. Gramsci." *Projet* (Paris), 99 (Nov. 1975) 1075-85.
———. •*Gramsci et la question religieuse*. Paris: Anthropos, 1974.
Poulat, Emile. *La crísis modernista. Historia, dogma y crítica*. Madrid: Taurus, 1974.
———. •*Eglise contre bourgeoisie. Introduction au devenir du catholicisme actuel*. Tournai/Paris: Casterman, 1977.
Prien, Hans Jürgen. •*Die Geschichte des Christentums in Lateinamerika*. Göttingen: Vandenhoeck, 1978.
Proaño, Leónidas. *Pour une Eglise libératrice*. Paris: Cerf, 1973.
———. "Obispos ecuatorianos: poniendo los ojos en Puebla." *Noticias Aliadas*, 22 (June 1978) 7-8.

Queiroz, María Isaura P. de. *Historia y etnología de los movimientos mesiánicos.* Mexico City: Siglo XXI, 1969.
Rabenoro, Aubert. "Avenir des communautés juives en Amérique latine." *Les Cahiers des Amériques latines,* 13-14 (1976) 247-54.
———. "Minoría religiosa y cambio social." *Estudios Ecuménicos* (Mexico City), Jan. 1975, pp. 3-12.
———. "Protestantisme et mobilité sociale au Chili," in *L'Autre et l'Ailleurs. Hommages à Roger Bastide.* Paris: Berger-Levrault, 1976, pp. 306-13.
Rama, Carlos M. •*Historia del movimiento obrero y social latinoamericano contemporáneo.* Montevideo: Ed. Palestra, 1967.
———. •*Mouvements ouvriers et socialistes. Chronologie et bibliographie: l'Amérique latine 1492-1986.* Paris: Ed. Ouvrières, 1959.
Las relaciones entre Cristianismo y revolución. Madrid: IEPALA, 1982.
Richard, Pablo. "Amérique latine: Une Eglise qui naît des luttes du peuple." *Evangile Aujourd'hui* (Paris), 99 (July 1978) 31-52.
———. *Cristianos por el Socialismo. Historia y Documentación.* Salamanca: Sígueme, 1976.
———. "La démocratie chrétienne en Amérique latine (1938-1976)." *Lumière et Vie,* 26/132 (1977) 74-90.
———. "L'Evangile entre la modernité et la libération." *Parole et Société,* 86/1 (1978) 21-34.
———. *A Igreja latino-americana entre o temor e a esperança.* São Paulo: Paulinas, 1982.
———. *El Neo-conservadurismo progresista latinoamericano. Concilium,* 161 (Jan. 1981) 96-103.
———. "La théologie de la libération dans la situation politique actuelle en Amérique latine." *Foi et Développement,* 42 (Dec. 1976).
———, and Irarrázaval, Diego. *Religião e política na América Central.* São Paulo: Paulinas, 1983.
———, and Meléndez, Guillermo. *La Iglesia de los pobres en América Central: Un análisis socio-político y teológico de la Iglesia centroamericana (1960-1982).* San José, Costa Rica: DEI, 1982.
Rodriíguez, José H. "O clero e a independência." *Revista Eclesiástica Brasileira,* 32 (1972) 309-26.
Roja, Victoria. "La Iglesia y la junta militar. Tres etapas y tres sectores a un año del golpe." *SEUL,* 52 (Aug.-Sept. 1974) 5-22.
Rolim, Francisco C. "Pentecostalismo. Gênese, estrutura e funções" (doctoral thesis). Rio de Janeiro, 1976.
Romero, Oscar Arnulfo, et al. *La Iglesia de los pobres y Organizaciones Populares.* San Salvador: UCA Editores, 1979.
Roncagliolo, Rafael. "Iglesia y crísis en América Latina." *Cuadernos del Tercer Mundo* (Mexico City), 2 (June 13, 1967) 36-44.
Ruiz, Samuel. "Los cristianos y la justicia en América Latina." *Pasos,* 60 (July 23, 1973).
Sacchi, Hugo M. •*El movimiento obrero en América Latina.* Buenos Aires, 1972.
Sanders, Thomas G. •"Catholicism and Development: The Catholic Left in Brazil," in Silvert, *Churches and States.*
Sandoval, Isaac. *Las crísis políticas latinoamericanas y el militarismo.* Mexico City: Siglo XXI, 1976.

Santa Ana, Julio de. *El desafío de los pobres a la Iglesia*. San José, Costa Rica: Educa, 1977.

——. *Protestantismo, cultura y sociedad. Problemas y perspectivas de la fe evangélica en América Latina*. Buenos Aires, 1970.

Schooyans, Michael. •*Destin du Brésil. La technocratie militaire et son idéologie*. Gembloux, Belgium: Duculot, 1973.

Secretariado Social Interdiocesano (El Salvador). *Persecución de la Iglesia en El Salvador*. San Salvador, 1977.

Secretariado Social Mexicano. *Desarrollo, justicia, liberación. Ocho documentos doctrinales*. Mexico City: SSM, 1972.

Segundo, Juan Luis. *Acción pastoral latinoamericana—sus motivos ocultos*. Buenos Aires, 1972. (English translation: *The Hidden Motives of Pastoral Action*. Maryknoll, N.Y.: Orbis, 1977.)

——. *Liberación de la teología*. Buenos Aires and Mexico City 1975. (English translation: *The Liberation of Theology.* Maryknoll, N.Y.: Orbis, 1976.)

——. *De la sociedad a la teología*. Buenos Aires, 1970.

Silva, Golberry do Couto e. •*Geopolítica do Brasil*. Rio de Janeiro: José Olympio, 1967.

Silva G., Samuel. •"Una ideología concreta: el desarrollo de la ideología de los grupos cristiano-marxistas en América Latina." *Contacto* (Mexico City), 10/6 (Dec. 1973) 27–51.

Silva, Sergio. "El model Ideológico de la Democracia Cristiana chilena (1962–1969) comparado con el de la Doctrina social de la Iglesia chilena (1962–1963) y latinoamericana (en Mar Del Plata, 1966)." *Pasos*, 63 (Aug. 8, 1973).

Silvert, Kalman, ed. *Churches and States*. New York: Universities Field Staff International, 1967.

Sobrino, Jon. *Ressurreição da verdadeira Igreja*. São Paulo, 1982. (English translation: *The True Church and the Poor*. Maryknoll, N.Y.: Orbis, 1984.)

Soler, Ricaurte. •*Clase y Nación en hispanoamérica*. San José, Costa Rica: Educa, 1977.

Sotelo, Ignacio. *Sociología de América Latina. Estructuras y problemas*. Madrid, 1975.

Souza, Luis Alberto. •"Los condicionamientos socio-políticos actuales de la teología en América Latina," in Encuentro Latinoamericano de Teología, *Liberación*, pp. 64–101.

Stavenhagen, Rodolfo. "Siete tesis equivocadas sobre América Latina." *SEUL* (April 1971) 10–20. (English translation: "Seven Fallacies about Latin America," in Petras, James and Zeitlin, Maurice, eds. *Latin America: Reform or Revolution?* New York: Fawcett World Library, 1968.)

Tamez, E. and Trindiad, S. eds. *Capitalismo y anti-vida. La Opresión de las mayorías y la domesticación de los dioses*. (Ponencias del encuentro latinoamericano de científicos sociales y teólogos, Costa Rica, 1978.) San José, Costa Rica: Educa, 1978, 2 vols.

Tayacán-CEHILA. *Historia de la Iglesia de los pobres en Nicaragua (versión popular)*. Managua, 1983.

Tormo, Leandro, and Gonzalbo, A. Pilar. *Historia de la Iglesia en América Latina. III: La Iglesia en la crísis de la independencia*. Bogotá: Feres, 1981.

Torres R. Edelberto. *Proceso y estructuras de una sociedad dependiente*. Santiago, 1969.

Torres, Héctor. *Roger Vekemans colaborador de la CIA presente en Colombia*. Bogotá, 1978.

Torres, Sergio, and Eagleson, John, eds. *Theology in the Americas.* Maryknoll, N.Y.: Orbis, 1976.

Turner, Frederick C. •*Catholicism and Political Development in Latin America.* Chapel Hill: University of North Carolina Press, 1971.

UCA *(Universidad Centramericana). La fe de un pueblo. Historia de una comunidad cristiana en El Salvador (1970-1980).* San Salvador: UCA Editores, 1983.

Uran R., Carlos H. *Participación Política de la Iglesia en el proceso histórico de Colombia.* Servicio Documentación MIEC-JECI (Lima), 1973.

Valcarcel, D. *La rebelión de Tupac Amaru.* Mexico City/Buenos Aires, 2nd ed., 1965.

Vallier, Ivan. *Catholicism, Social Control, and Modernization in Latin America.* Englewood Cliffs, N.J.: Prentice-Hall, 1970.

Vanderhoff, Francisco. "La credibilidad del 'compromiso cristiano.' Consideraciones socio-teológicas." *Contacto*, 10/6 (Dec. 1973) 12–25.

———. "Ideología en la religiosidad popular." *Estudios Indígenas* (Mexico City), 6/2 (Dec. 1976) 3–14.

———, and Campos, Miguel Angel. "La Iglesia popular. Condiciones político-ideológicas para su surgimiento." *Contacto*, 12/6 (Dec. 1975) 46–56.

Vicaria de la Solidaridad. *Chile: La lucha por un pueblo de hermanos. Antecedentes para una historia del colonialismo y los derecho humanos.* Santiago: Vicaria de la Solidaridad, 1976.

Vidales, Raúl. •*La Iglesia latinoamericana y la política después de Medellín.* Bogotá: Departamento Pastoral CELAM and IPLA, 1972.

———. •"Iglesia popular y proyecto de liberación popular." *Christus* (Mexico City), 42/503 (Oct. 1977) 35–39.

———, and Kudo, Tokihiro. *Práctica religiosa y proyecto histórico. Hipótesis para un estudio de la religiosidad popular en América Latina.* Lima: CEP, 1975.

Villela, Hugo. •"Iglesia y democracia en América Latina. Algunas consideraciones a partir de la situación chilena," in Tamez and Trinidad, *Capitalismo,* pp. 137–157.

Vitale, Luís. •*Interpretación marxista de la historia de Chile. II: La colonia y la revolución de 1810.* Santiago, 1969.

Vuskovic, Pedro. "Luca socialista y conciencia cristiana," in *Una sola lucha.* Paris: CIAL, 1978, pp. 123–32.

Whitaker, Arthur, ed. *Latin America and the Enlightenment: Essays.* New York, 1971.

Willems, Emilio. *Followers of the New Faith.* Nashville: Vanderbilt University Press, 1967.

———. "Religious Mass Movements and Social Change in Brazil," in Baklanoff, Eric, *New Perspectives on Brazil.* Nashville: Vanderbilt University Press, 1966.

Witker Velásquez, Alejandro. *Los trabajos y los días de Recabarren.* Cuba: Casa de las Américas, 1977.

Yrarrazaval, Diego, "Las clases populares evangelizan. ¿Como?" *Servir*, 12/63 (1976) 319–40.

———. •"Religión del pueblo y teología de la liberación: Hipótesis." *Pasos*, 61 (July 30, 1973).

Zorzin, Luis E. "L'Eglise catholique en Argentine. Analyse d'un Argentin." *Foi et Développement* (Paris), 32 (Dec. 1975).

FUNDERBURG LIBRARY
MANCHESTER COLLEGE

WITHDRAWN
from
Funderburg Library